THEORIES OF RHETORIC

AN ANTHOLOGY

FIRST EDITION

THEORIES OF RHETORIC

AN ANTHOLOGY

Edited by Mary E. Triece

cognella® | ACADEMIC PUBLISHING

Bassim Hamadeh, CEO and Publisher

Jennifer Codner, Senior Field Acquisitions Editor

Michelle Piehl, Senior Project Editor

Alia Bales, Production Editor

Jackie Bignotti, Production Artist

Stephanie Kohl, Licensing Coordinator

Natalie Piccotti, Director of Marketing

Kassie Graves, Vice President of Editorial

Jamie Giganti, Director of Academic Publishing

ISBN: 978-1-5165-3992-5 (pbk) / 978-1-5165-3993-2 (br)

CONTENTS

INTRODUCTION

Over the past two thousand years, scholars have debated the definition and roles of rhetoric in society. There are many textbooks that cover theories of rhetoric from what we might call a traditional perspective. These books discuss the key thinkers whose writings have influenced understandings of public communication for centuries. Some of these notable theorists include Plato, Aristotle, Cicero, Quintilian, Giambattista Vico, Kenneth Burke, and Chaïm Perelman.

Theories of rhetoric developed by these and many other scholars have evolved over the centuries as society has changed. The advent and growth of technology, increased mobility, and the success of various democratic struggles have all shaped understandings of how rhetoric takes place and what role it plays in society. *The purpose of this anthology is to enhance our understandings of rhetoric and rhetorical theories by offering a critical/cultural lens through which to view the history and definition of rhetoric and how it functions in society.* This proposed view for understanding rhetorical theories shines light on the effect of gender, race, and power on understandings of rhetoric. A critical/cultural approach to rhetorical theory holds three related assumptions:

1   Theories are not neutral constructs;

2   Theories take shape within and are influenced by the political, economic, and cultural contexts in which they arise, therefore;

3   Our understandings of rhetorical theories should be grounded in historical contexts and understood as shaped by the particular power dynamics and disparities of a given time period.

More than twenty years ago, the rhetorical theorist Richard A. Cherwitz (1990) urged scholars and students of rhetoric to recognize how one's choice of a rhetorical theory "will have consequences and implications for one's understanding and evaluation of the world.... How the art of rhetoric is conceived, what theoretical assumptions are made about its operation and scope, and what is posited as rhetoric's relationships to the other essential dimensions and components of human activity will affect our understandings and evaluations" (p. 3). This anthology takes on the task of uncovering and understanding the "consequences and implications" of theory building by introducing students to theories of rhetoric that have been obscured or ignored throughout history but that are requisite for developing a fuller understanding of rhetoric's historicity and its relationship to power.

Let's begin by defining rhetoric and theory from a traditional approach. "Unit 1" will explore an alternative way of understanding rhetoric and theory that opens the door to viewing theories on public speech, deliberation, and debate as historically grounded and politically imbued.

The Traditional Approach to Theories of Rhetoric

Broadly speaking, rhetoric is defined as public speech intended to effect some change in thought or behavior. The ancient Greek philosopher Aristotle, considered the grandfather of the discipline, associated rhetoric with persuasion, explaining the concept as the "faculty of observing in any given case the available means of persuasion" (p. 3). Contemporary scholars broaden the understanding of rhetoric to envelop all forms of symbolic behavior (not just speech or oratory) and to include efforts to describe and invite understanding (not just persuade). The influential twentieth century rhetorical theorist and critic Kenneth Burke (1950) defined rhetoric as the "use of words by human agents to form attitudes or to induce actions in other human agents" (p. 41). A similar definition is provided by the rhetorical theorist and critic Gerard Hauser (2002), who explains rhetoric as the focus on "how humans use symbols, especially language, to reach agreement that permits coordinated effort of some sort" (pp. 2, 3). Sonja K. Foss suggests a broader definition of rhetoric as the "human use of symbols to communicate" (p. 3). These contemporary definitions—rhetoric as the practice of employing symbols—open the door to studies of poetry, drama, music, architecture, and literature for the ways these act symbolically to influence understandings, thoughts, and behaviors about ourselves, others, and society.

Numerous definitions of rhetoric have been suggested over the past two thousand years, and while they differ in various ways, we can identify common elements that have endured.

First, rhetoric is public communication, designed for an audience, and crafted as a response to a given situation in a specific context characterized by constraints (Bitzer 1968). What distinguishes rhetoric from, say, interpersonal communication, is its *public-ness*. A public is a group of individuals (e.g., a community, a nation) that is together affected by a particular idea or action (e.g., toxic dumping, health care) and that involves a degree of controversy or uncertainty. Rhetoric consists of those efforts to address, intervene in, shape, or influence those public issues perceived as requiring attention on the part of publics. The rhetorical scholar Martha Cooper (1989) explains that public discussion (i.e., rhetoric) is important to the formation of public opinion. *Note the assumption underlying this aspect of the definition; namely, that individuals have access to, and equal standing within, the public sphere. We will further explore this point in units II and III.*

Second, rhetoric is intentional and motivated. Rhetoric exists for some reason beyond itself, that is to say, rhetoric is instrumental. The twentieth-century rhetorical theorist Douglas Ehninger

(1972) defined rhetoric as the study of "all of the ways in which men [sic] may influence each other's thinking and behavior through the strategic use of symbols" (p. 3). More recently, James Herrick (2013) explains the motives underlying rhetoric "include making converts to a point of view, seeking cooperation to accomplish a task, building a consensus that enables group action, finding a compromise that breaks a stalemate, forging an agreement that makes peaceful co-existence possible ..." (p. 11). The twentieth-century theorists James L. Golden, Goodwin F. Berquist, and William E. Coleman (1989) explain that "since rhetoric is concerned with probability and not scientific certainty, the communicator by definition possesses a certain measure of freedom to determine the structure of his [sic] message ... the concept of 'choice' becomes apparent" (p. 297). *Note the assumption underlying this aspect of the definition; namely, that individuals act freely and have agency. We will return to this point in subsequent units.*

Third, rhetoric assists decision making in cases where certainty and perfect knowledge are not available. Rhetorical scholars over the centuries have debated rhetoric's relationship to philosophy and knowledge. Plato—and thinkers who came after him, such as Descartes and Peter Ramus—separated rhetoric from philosophy, assigning to rhetoric a secondary function as a tool that could be utilized to explain knowledge once it had been attained. The assumption in this view is that perfect knowledge is attainable, and rhetoric is employed to convey that knowledge once it is in hand.

Theorists of the twentieth to early twenty-first century have increasingly emphasized the challenges and complications inherent in the process of coming to know. In debates over the prevailing political/economic/cultural issues of the day (e.g., matters of poverty, war, technology, medicine, and the environment), we recognize that our understandings of these problems change over time as we attain more—but not perfect or static—knowledge. That is, we make decisions based on limited, imperfect information available to us at the time. Another way of explaining this is to say rhetoric plays a role in how we come to know and understand our world. Scholars continue to debate *to what degree* rhetoric is epistemic (i.e., facilitates the process of coming to know), with some holding to the idea that some aspects of the world can be known with a degree of certainty. Other theorists from the Sophists to present-day thinkers influenced by poststructuralism/postmodernism embrace the idea that nothing is knowable, that reality and knowledge are elusive and malleable. On this view, what counts as reality is rhetorically constructed. Whether one holds to the view that reality is partially or fully knowable, rhetorical theorists largely agree that rhetoric assists us—to a greater or lesser extent—in the pursuit of knowledge and in making claims about what counts as knowledge. *Missing from discussions of this dimension of rhetoric is an account of the ways gender, race, and power are implicated in how we come to know. We will explore this issue in units IV and V.*

A fourth element common to most theories of rhetoric is the idea that the art of rhetoric relies, at least in part, on appeals to reason and the ethical standing of the speaker. In *Rhetoric*, written in the fifth century BCE, Aristotle elaborated on the importance of utilizing appeals to logos, or reason, which he deemed more important for speakers than appeals to ethos and pathos (Bizzell and Herzberg 2001, p. 31). The contemporary theorist Karl Wallace (1971) defined rhetoric as the act of supplying good reasons, which he suggested held an ethical dimension. He suggested "good reasons" consisted of "statements, consistent with each other, in support of an *ought* proposition or of a value judgement" (p. 360, italics in original). *To foreground the element of reason and appeal to ethical standing carries assumptions about the nature of rhetor and the prevailing values in a given historical moment, a point that will be taken up in the units that follow.*

In sum, even as rhetorical theories have changed over the centuries, most of the definitions share these aspects:

1   Rhetoric is public;

2   Rhetoric is instrumental;

3   Rhetoric plays a role in how we come to know and what counts as knowledge; and

4   Rhetoric consists, in part, of appeals to reason and ethical standing.

In units I through V, we will be encouraged to rethink this traditional definition in light of the economic, political, and cultural contexts of the specific time. "Unit 1" introduces the *critical/cultural approach* to theories of rhetoric. Units II through V are arranged chronologically, with each unit introduction providing background on life during the respective time period, including elements of the context that shaped issues of public expression and civic engagement. Unit readings give us new ways to understand the study of rhetoric by exploring this wide-reaching area of study from a contextualized and historicized perspective.

References

Aristotle. 1984. *The Rhetoric and Poetics of Aristotle.* Translated by W. Rhys Roberts and Ingram Bywater. Random House.

Bitzer, L. 1968. "The Rhetorical Situation." *Philosophy & Rhetoric, 1*, 1–14.

Bizzell, P., and B. Herzberg. 2001. *The Rhetorical Tradition: Readings from Classical Times to the Present.* 2nd ed. Boston: Bedford/St. Martin's.

Burke, K. 1950. *A Rhetoric of Motives.* Berkeley: University of California Press.

Cherwitz, R. 1990. *Rhetoric and Philosophy.* Hillsdale, NJ: Lawrence Erlbaum Associates.

Cooper, M. 1989. *Analyzing Public Discourse.* Prospect Heights, IL: Waveland Press.

Ehninger, D. 1972. *Contemporary Rhetoric: A Reader's Coursebook.* Glenview, IL: Scott, Foresman.

Foss, S. K. 2009. *Rhetorical Criticism: Exploration and Practice.* Long Grove, IL: Waveland Press.

Golden, J. L., Berquist, G. F., and W. E. Coleman. 1989. *The Rhetoric of Western Thought.* 4th ed. Dubuque, IA: Kendall Hunt.

Hauser, G. A. 2002. *Introduction to Rhetorical Theory.* 2nd ed. Prospect Heights, IL: Waveland Press.

Herrick, J. 2013. *The History and Theory of Rhetoric: An Introduction.* New York: Routledge.

Wallace, K. 1971. "The Substance of Rhetoric: Good Reasons." In R. L. Johannesen (ed.), *Contemporary Theories of Rhetoric: Selected Readings.* New York: Harper and Row.

UNIT 1

TOWARD A CRITICAL/ CULTURAL UNDERSTANDING OF THEORIES OF RHETORIC

Consider:

1   What is your understanding of the term "rhetoric?"

2   Where do we see rhetoric used and for what purposes?

3   How do twenty-first century technologies shape/influence rhetoric and how it is practiced?

4   Identify a few well-known public speakers. What made their communication compelling?

On the surface, it seems straightforward to understand rhetoric as public, instrumental communication, consisting of appeals to reason and ethics and playing a role in acquiring knowledge. But if we examine these theories through a critical/ cultural lens, we see how they are not, in fact, neutral; but rather, carry with them assumptions and consequences concerning power and equality.

Let's return to the traditional definitions of rhetoric outlined in the "Introduction," but now let's consider them refracted through a lens that historicizes and contextualizes. Theories of rhetoric offered over the past two thousand years contain within them assumptions grounded in specific histories marked above all by gender, race, and other disparities. For instance, in ancient Greece only "adult males descended on both sides of their families from citizens were granted citizenship" (Berlin 1992, p. 58). Excluded from citizenship was the large population of slaves along with nonnatives and women. Gender norms in ancient Greece and Rome (i.e., the cultural expectations for how women should behave, what roles they should play, etc.) prevailed for much of the past two thousand-plus years and have worked to deny women and marginalized "others" access to public spaces and the basic rights of citizenship. For example, women were expected to be submissive to husbands and fathers. Also, women were believed to be naturally emotional and incapable of reasoning. Even as recent as the nineteenth century in the United States, legal doctrine known as coverture deemed married women the property of husbands and denied women the right to their own wages and inheritances and also custody of their children. And from the seventeenth century through 1865, slavery was the law of the land and slave codes controlled the lives of both free and enslaved black people.

These cultural norms and laws, and the economic and political restrictions that resulted, precluded citizenship to many and thus denied these individuals the ability to speak and act freely in public spaces. Traditional definitions of rhetoric assume a native, male, propertied speaker who has access to the public sphere.

Recall the definition of rhetoric established previously:

- Rhetoric consists of public messages.

- Rhetoric is intentioned and motivated.

- Rhetoric plays a role in how we come to know.

- Rhetoric appeals to reason and ethical standing.

A careful understanding of history shows us:

- Women and other marginalized/colonized groups (e.g., slaves of the seventeenth and eighteenth centuries, indigenous groups, African Americans in contemporary society) have been historically denied access to the public sphere.

- Women (as the property of husbands/fathers) and colonized groups have been denied agency and self-determination.

- How we come to know is intertwined with our social position as shaped by sex, race, class, etc.

- Women and peoples of non-European descent have historically been associated with emotion as opposed to reason.

In some senses, the very act of public speaking was an oxymoron for women (Campbell 1973) and marginalized others. To the extent the embodiment of the rhetor (public speaker) was white, male, and elite, the practice of public speaking precluded women, non-Europeans, the poor, et al.

A critical/cultural approach to the study of rhetorical theory provides a way to examine traditional rhetorical theories as constructs grounded in and shaped by history, and it opens a door to new ways of understanding rhetoric that account for the ways gender, race, and other power differentials shape how we come to know, how we express our views, and attempt to shape public issues in public settings. This approach has two benefits. First, we are able to *broaden* our understanding of what counts as rhetoric and rhetorical theory by including the voices of marginalized actors (e.g., women, slaves, undocumented people). Second, we *deepen* our understanding of rhetoric and rhetorical theory by shining a light upon—and challenging—the theoretical assumptions that have enabled marginalization and silencing to go unnoticed/unexamined/unchallenged. The readings in this book are intended to augment traditional thought on rhetoric and to encourage us to think critically about issues concerning public voice, access to the public sphere, and the right to speak publically. In the following units, we will be encouraged to view rhetorical theories as historically grounded, politically imbued, and constructed in gendered and racialized ways.

The reading in "Unit 1", Revisionary Histories of Rhetoric provides a framework for understanding rhetoric as historically situated. As students of rhetoric, we will take up James Berlin's call to understand rhetoric and rhetorical theories "within their unique economic, social, political, and cultural conditions" (p. 116). Our goal is not to dismiss nor do away with classical theories of rhetoric; but rather, to carefully interrogate these theories for the ways they were shaped by the conditions of their time and to situate them in dialogue with other, lesser known or obscured theories of rhetoric (e.g., the contributions of Aspasia of Miletus, Christine de Pizan, and Anna Comnena). Berlin's article encourages us to understand theories as they have evolved over time; as they have accommodated for cultural and political shifts; adjusted to or in support of economic hierarchies/disparities/changes; and have either reinforced silences and muted voices or, alternatively, pushed back in efforts to resist various forms of marginalization.

References

Berlin, J. 1992. "Aristotle's *Rhetoric* in Context: Interpreting Historically." In S. P. Witte, N. Nakadate, R. D. Cherry (eds.), *A Rhetoric of Doing: Essays on Written Discourse in Honor of James L. Kinneavy*, 55–64. Carbondale, IL: Southern Illinois University Press.

Campbell, K. K. 1973. "The Rhetoric of Women's Liberation: An Oxymoron." *Quarterly Journal of Speech, 59*, 74–86.

Revisionary Histories of Rhetoric

Politics, Power, and Plurality

James A. Berlin

Our "official" histories of rhetoric—the formulations of George Kennedy (1980a) and Edward P. J. Corbett (1990) and Brian Vickers (1990) and Wilbur Samuel Howell (1971), for example—depict rhetoric's historical trajectory as a march of ideas, ideas characterized as unified, coherent, and rational. Rhetoric has a life of its own in the aerie realm of the intellectual firmament, transcending the play of economics and politics and power. From this lofty perch it serves as a mighty helpmate to those who would serve truth and virtue and a demystifying foe against illusion and self-interest. The tradition of rhetoric is one, and its authentic exponents are united in a common language and purpose. Plato speaks to Aristotle and Aristotle to Cicero and Cicero to Quintilian and Quintilian to Augustine and Augustine to himself until Aristotle and Cicero and Quintilian are again given their due respect in the Renaissance, when the word of words, "rhetoric," is again taken forward. This traditionalist account, furthermore, is accepted with appropriate modifications even by those who disagree about the foundation and objective of this transparent conversation. Whether the one, true, holy, catholic, and apostolic rhetoric is situated in the golden age of the past or anticipated in the golden age of the future, there is no disagreement about its monolithic character, even though the two constituencies—the traditionalists and the progressives—disagree about the elements that make up the monolith and their trajectories. The role of women, subordinate classes, and other subaltern groups in these narratives does, however, remain consistent: they are conspicuous by absence.

For Kennedy, Corbett, and Vickers, the eternal rhetoric is located at the source of the dialogue, among the ancients who set the fundamental terms of the discussion in motion. (Vickers has even recovered for us the Sophists and their anticipation of contemporary developments in rhetoric, although not without reservations about the consequences [1990, 121–28].) Subsequent events in the narrative of rhetoric thus build on this solid foundation, or, alternately, they cultivate seeds first planted at the origins. Disruptions in this trajectory, of repeating the past while discovering the already prefigured new in it, are historical aberrations, temporary displacements. These are to be explained away as the products of failed cultures—the most frequently named being that of the Middle Ages and the nineteenth century.

Thus, in Corbett's scheme Aristotle is the foundation of all future rhetorics: "With his philosophic treatise, Aristotle became the fountain-head of all later rhetorical theory" (1990, 543). Unfortunately, during the Middle Ages, rhetoric became a "scholastic exercise" rather than a "practical art" so that during this time "the art of rhetoric stood still, if it actually did not retrogress" (548–49). And although the authentic tradition is eventually restored, it again undergoes so precipitous a decline in England in the nineteenth century that Corbett must conclude: "The history of English rhetoric might well terminate with the end of the eighteenth century" (569). Still, as he explains in the conclusion to his history, "the long and honorable tradition that classical rhetoric has enjoyed" may have "risen and fallen periodically in public prominence," but "it always stages a comeback" (578). George Kennedy admits that rhetorical theories and practices other than the classical merit study (1980a), yet he cannot resist portraying departures from this tradition in a narrative of degeneration, describing the movement of the eighteenth century away from classical rhetoric as "The Decline of Neoclassical Rhetoric" (240). He also announces with approval a return to rhetoric's classical sources in the twentieth century, explaining that at Cornell and Chicago, in Kenneth Burke and Chaim Perelman, "the classical tradition in rhetoric seems to have entered a new phase in its long and distinguished history" (241). And in the concluding chapter of his study, a section in which he stages a dialogue pitting the ancients against the moderns, Kennedy finally comes down firmly on the side of "the old eloquence" (245), this time "Plato's ideal rhetoric," which, his spokesperson explains, "has never really been worked out in all its implications" (244). Finally, Vickers (1990) confidently announces that rhetoric has undergone "two great breakdowns," one in the Middle Ages, the other in the nineteenth century. Both have been short-lived, however, as the first is followed by "rebuilding and rediscovery in the Renaissance" and the second creates the occasion today for "the beginnings of a second renaissance in rhetoric" (215).

In contrast, Howell (1971) argues that the historical conversation of rhetoric has been a mistaken, formalized, and repetitive parlor game, with each voice reproducing the errors of its predecessor, the ancient sources of rhetoric finally setting in motion error and repression. Rhetoric, however, is too powerful for its false servants, those who set up foolish idols in its place, so that at last the genuine progressive unfolding of the one, true, holy, etc. rhetoric is inaugurated. For Howell, Locke is the bringer of great tidings, through induction able to transcend at a single bound the falsehood of the Aristotelian syllogism, freeing us from the hollow forms of the classics: "The history of an intellectual revolution would not normally have a hero, but it is tempting in the present instance to pronounce this dictum inapplicable and to confer the title of hero upon John Locke....So far as its dominant thrust may be said to be embodied in the works of one man, the movement under examination here is hardly anything more than the expression of Locke's influence in this or that of its many ramifications" (7). Howell's history, like its antagonistic traditionalist counterparts, sees the action as the conflict between the good guys and the bad guys (but not women, since there are none in these scripts), the good guys finally arriving to save the day.

For both the traditionalists and the progressives, rhetoric has, despite its corrupt opponents, been restored to its holy mission, to serve truth, justice, and the rhetorical way.

When I encounter these reverential readings of the history of rhetoric, my first impulse, I must confess, is to resist, to portray the heroes as villains and the villains as heroes. For example, some Sophists were indeed fast-buck artists, selling their knowledge to the highest bidder, but many were also opponents of Greek slavery, misogyny, and a "democratic" *polis* that enfranchised only male descendants of native-born Athenians. As Eric Havelock (1957) has argued, some Sophists supported a radical democracy in economic and social as well as political arrangements. In contrast, Plato—the darling of the conservatives—was an unremitting enemy of democracy in any form, allowing rhetoric into the republic only to enable the philosopher-monarchs to manage the lower orders. (To give him his due, he did allow women into his ruling elite.) After all, since the soldiers and workers could not discover the dictates of reason and pursue them disinterestedly, they would have to be manipulated through psychological appeals to desire what their betters knew to be best for them (see Kauffman 1982). Aristotle, the great defender of reason and the democratic polis, was convinced that some of us are born slaves and that all women are inherently inferior and incapable of citizenship. Dying one of the richest three hundred men in Athens, his politics favored an educated and wealthy elite, and his rhetoric teaches this elite to dominate and control their inferiors (see Berlin 1992). Cicero was a dirty politician among dirty politicians, supporting in his intellectual and political work one of the cruelest, most violently repressive governments ever to exist (for a summary of these charges, see Dorey 1964). Progressives who would take comfort in my vilification of the ancients, however, ought to recall that Locke, himself always wise to the ways of financial investment, encouraged an epistemology whose main use has been to dominate nature and human beings in the service of economic gain for the few, meanwhile denying reality to any experience that cannot be commodified and exchanged in the open market.

But I realize my response is unjust, serving as a simple reversal of the binary oppositions on which the histories I have mentioned are formulated, oppositions repeated in more extreme forms today in our general discussions of rhetoric. Thus, the enemies of rhetoric argue that it is inherently corrupt (usually because they want to conceal or naturalize their own rhetoric) while we defenders of rhetoric too often take the opposite tack, insisting that it is inherently good. The problem with this dichotomy is that it is ahistorical. It argues that rhetoric is a practice that can somehow transcend the historical conditions of its own time, speaking in its essential purity (or, alternately, corruption) to all ages. It forgets that the formulation of a rhetoric is a product of the economic, social, and political conditions of a specific historical moment. The mission of the revisionary historian of rhetoric I have in mind is to resist the notion of rhetoric as a unified, coherent, and univocal collection of texts stretching over time, texts that support either truth and virtue on the one hand, or error and vice on the other. The revisionary historian must instead locate the variety of rhetorics that exist at any particular moment and examine their interaction with each other and with the conditions of their production. This will require seeking out the suppressed rhetorics of women, workers, and other marginalized and silenced groups. In this study, some rhetorics will prove noble and good, but some will inevitably prove quite the contrary.

This synchronic investigation will often lead to a diachronic one. There is no question that throughout history earlier rhetorics were studied with a view to discovering their contemporary relevance. Rhetorics often do carry on an intertextual correspondence with the rhetorics of other times and places. These relations are of course important considerations. Those who construct rhetorics, on the other hand—however much they may keep before them the example of one or another rhetorical tradition—are first and foremost concerned with addressing the play of power in their own day. Plato, Aristotle, Cicero, Augustine, Margaret Fell, Locke, and Mary Wollstonecraft were all concerned with the uses of language in the economic, social, and political institutions of their own times. When Cicero appropriates Aristotle, he does so in a way that serves his political purposes in the Roman senate, not the Athenian assembly (Douglas 1964). Indeed, his very reading of Aristotle is conducted through the terministic screens of his own historical conditions; just as when we today attempt to recover Aristotle, we focus on those features that most reinforce our desires for our own society—his privileging of the rational appeals and his apparent endorsement of democracy, for example—while conveniently overlooking what we find less admirable—his class and gender bias and his advocacy of the wealthy.

The examination of historical rhetorics, then, must be historicized. This means finding their differences from us as well as their similarities. Revisionary readings, however, must acknowledge that locating these differences is only possible through situating rhetorics within their unique economic, social, political, and cultural conditions. Rhetorics never answer only to themselves: they reflect and, of equal importance, refract the conditions of their creation and functioning. Rhetorics provide a set of rules about the dispositions of discourse at a particular moment. They codify who can and cannot speak (the wealthy but not the poor, men but not women, the certified expert but not the ordinary citizen); what can and cannot be said (the wealthy must be protected from the poor, the expert always knows best); who can and cannot listen and act (men only, the propertied classes only, the certified experts only); and the very nature of the language to be used (the register of the ruling class, the parlance of technocracy, the narratives of patriarchy). Rhetorics do not make these decisions on their own. They are constructed at the junctures of discourse and power, at the points at which economic, social, and political battles are waged in public discourse. To paraphrase Marx, it is within rhetorics that humans become aware of ideological battles and fight them out (Marx 1970, 21).

This is why there are always at a given moment a plurality of rhetorics, even during the most repressive times. This is hard for us to see because our traditional histories have insisted upon creating a monolithic tradition. Thus, until recently, even the Sophists were banished from the engulfing folds of the one true tradition, a result of the judgments made on them by the canonical

Plato and Aristotle. The Sophists indeed belong outside of the tradition descending from these two powerful figures, but not because Plato and Aristotle are truly rhetorical and the Sophists are not. Certain Sophists represented a set of discursive practices that stood for another economic and political order, an order that their more established and popular rivals found dangerously subversive. As Havelock (1957) has taken pains to demonstrate, these Sophists argued for democratic and political arrangements that denied slavery and the inherent inferiority of women. Fortunately for us, this sophistic rhetoric achieved enough currency in its own day to require resistance by its opponents. Thus, although we know it almost exclusively through the denials of it by its adversaries, at least its existence was thereby made a part of the historical record. The revisionary historian of rhetoric must realize that there are also numerous rhetorics of the past that never attained enough currency in their own day to offer a serious challenge to the powerful. It is her business, then, to attempt to recover these rhetorics—for example, the rhetorics of slaves and women in Athens and Rome and the United States, or the rhetorics of the working class when a Neo-Ciceronian bourgeois and elitist rhetoric was shaping the formation of our constitution. This involves looking for lost and neglected documents attesting to these formulations. Since the texts of these marginalized rhetorics were often not formally recorded or were destroyed by their oppressors, finding the past will often mean examining the fragments of documents in which a rhetoric is demonstrated or discussed, in which the adversarial position is articulated. Nancy Streuver (1970) and John Poulakos (1984) and Richard Enos (1976) and others have done this for the Sophists, Eugene Genovese (1972) has carried out this project for African-American slaves of the last century, and E. P. Thompson (1963) has demonstrated it in writing about the working class in England. Today, many are attempting to locate the suppressed rhetorics of women—Karlyn Kohrs Campbell (1989) and Susan Jarratt (1990) and Sue Ellen Holbrook (1991), for example.

This revisionary/subversive position does not, as I said earlier, preclude a diachronic treatment of rhetoric. There is no question, for example, that Aristotle and Cicero and Locke can be made to speak to our conditions today. We must realize, however, that they are first addressing the situations of their own cultures, cultures that in many ways, and probably most, constitute our other. We must realize that inscribed in these historical texts are the power relations of their day, complete with all of their cruelties and injustices. Victor Vitanza has reminded us of the cognitive and psychic shackles these rhetorics impose (1987a; 1987b). I would remind us that they enforce ideological conditions as well—for example, brutalizing relations of race, class, and gender—that are difficult to resist, often because they are so much like our own. I do not wish to deny that readers finally construct texts rather than simply surrender to them. I wonder, however, if we can construct texts so unmistakably concerned with power in a way that resists their inequities, particularly when we canonize them as exceptional and exemplary, doing so because we find in them our own failures validated. We are also situated in politics and power, and our awareness of this inevitability must be self-consciously included in our investigation. We must own up to our own political agendas.

There is a final reason for writing histories (the plural intended) along the lines drawn here—lines that are crooked and subversive of narratives of peace, order, and harmony. Our search for alterity, for rhetorics other than the familiar, can reveal to us alternative possibilities in conceiving discursive practices and their power formations. Thus, the departure of an age from a dominant rhetorical tradition is a strong argument for its receiving special attention—as Michael Leff (1983) and Marjorie Woods (1990) have shown us in treating the Middle Ages, as Susan Jarratt (1985) has demonstrated in discussing the nineteenth century. We must look for the dangerous other, the subversive silences of earlier ages and our own.

But does my proposal involve a categorical refusal of other kinds of history, as some have suggested? Could I ever in my wildest flights of Leftist frenzy wish the histories of Kennedy and Corbett and Vickers and Howell be banished from consideration? I would have to answer an emphatic no to both questions. As I have reiterated throughout this essay, I see rhetorical history in pluralistic terms. Corbett's history did not foreclose Kennedy's nor did Kennedy's foreclose Vickers's. Despite their sharing a dominant narrative plan, they each make a unique contribution. Each, however, is incomplete, as is obvious from the fact that Kennedy's treatment followed Corbett's and Vickers's followed Kennedy's and Corbett's revision then followed all three. None considered that its predecessor had exhausted the field. As I said earlier, these three excellent studies demonstrate the contention that rhetorics arise in response to their predecessors, and their authors do an admirable job of articulating this conversation, showing the influences and cross-influences. These studies have been valuable if only because they have placed much of the materials of rhetoric on record, or at least the materials favored by the professional middle class, the group represented most recently by the likes of E. D. Hirsch and Allan Bloom and William Bennett. They also display an intelligent and insightful reading of the materials of rhetoric, offering a rich array of observations. And the same could be said for Howell's different kind of history.

The problem is not their strengths, however: it is their weaknesses—not what they do so well, but what they do not do at all. The final impression one is left with in examining Kennedy and Vickers is that their method is unproblematically exemplary: all that is genuinely important in pursuing the history of rhetoric has been here presented, and the reader need look no further. (Corbett acknowledged the incomplete nature of his history.) I wish that each had been more self-conscious about his methods, explaining them and acknowledging their limitations. Admittedly, this would have been difficult for Kennedy writing when he did. The same, however, cannot be said for Vickers. Nonetheless, I will agree that all the histories I have criticized in this essay are worthy and necessary reading for anyone interested in the history of rhetoric. Readers must, however, be made aware of their incompleteness, their gaps and fissures, in both omitting other rhetorics and other ways of reading the rhetorics included, and in failing to foreground their own methods. I suspect that given the recent concern for historiographic method, it will be more difficult for anyone to make a similar mistake in the future. (But obviously it will not be impossible since the faith in the "definitive" history, despite its very denial of historicity, not to mention rhetoricity, remains strong in certain conservative quarters.)

I would also like to comment on another criticism of the position I am forwarding. As I have already indicated, my proposed historiographic method does not prohibit other methods: all it asks is that these others foreground their intentions with all their implications. If, for example, a historian decides that politics is not a part of rhetoric despite all the evidence to the contrary, then she ought to say so, explaining her reasons for taking her position. In other words, my comments are especially intended to discourage unreflective accounts—not simply accounts that disagree with my own. I am also offering, of course, what I take to be a more productive approach. (I will be the first to acknowledge that what I am proposing is difficult since it requires an interdisciplinary method, looking at rhetorics in relation to culture in its most expansive formulation, but that is not really at issue here.) I would at the same time emphasize my openness to other historical accounts, accounts that inevitably provide me with materials for my own formulation. But of course I reserve the right to continue to criticize what I take to be their errors and inadequacies.

I also feel constrained to make one other peace offering. I have been told at conferences (but never, to my knowledge, in print) that my recommendations would preclude the normal appropriations of historical rhetorics that are a continuing part of theory building, as Kenneth Burke has done with Aristotle. My objection is not to such uses—a necessary strategy of writing rhetorics—but to its unreflective operation. As Burke calls upon certain key concepts in Aristotle in A *Rhetoric of Motives*, for example, he not only does so selectively, but he also makes no extravagant claims about the historical authority of his reading. A typical case occurs early on when Burke calls on Aristotle's contention that rhetoric "proves opposites" in support of his own more expansive assertion that identification and division appearing together make for "the characteristic invitation to rhetoric" (1969b, 25). In the section in which this appears, Burke undertakes this gesture with the appropriate recognition of the differences between the political conditions of the past and the present; he even includes specific reference to differences in "the purely technical means of communication," meaning here the contemporary use of journalism. The differences finally are more important than the similarities, even though Aristotle does prove useful in making the point. Mining the rich storehouse of historical rhetorics for their contemporary applications in this way will continue and ought to continue. It should not be undertaken, however, without striving to understand the full political and cultural implications of the appropriation: differences are here as important as identities.

Finally, I would like to say a last word about the complex relation between the past and present in writing the contextualized history I am recommending. As I have suggested repeatedly, objectivity is out of the question. All historians are interested, writing their narratives from a particular ideological position. It is impossible to become a *tabula rasa* innocently recording the raw data of the historical record. For one thing, the raw data is simply too overwhelming to be dealt with without selection, and some ideological principle will always guide the selection. As I have argued (1987a; 1987b) both the data selected and formulations about the significance of this data are interpretive gestures. My position here is that the historian must acknowledge the principles— primarily ideological in nature—that are to govern this interpretation. The historian studying the nineteenth century, for example, is working from her position in the twentieth century, and it is impossible to transcend her historically formed consciousness in order to enter innocently into that of another historical moment. Instead, she must strive to understand as much as is possible her own situatedness, primarily by realizing her decisions in writing history will be based on her own loyalties in economic, social, political, and cultural considerations.

Writing history involves judgments about which scenes and actors and events are important and which are not. These judgments engage the historian in a critique of historical records, a criticism of their relative value and importance. This in turn is a product of the historian's own ideological predilections, her own vision of preferred economic, social, and political arrangements. The historian who sees no reason to search for the rhetorical texts of those out of power at a particular moment because these are not important in the unfolding of historical events has made an ideological decision, not a choice of fact. The contention here is that history is the record of great and conspicuous events and great and conspicuous people—the winners of history, however ill-gotten their gains. All else is mere backdrop, mere stage and setting for this more significant action. These interpretive decisions, furthermore, are based on a utopian gesture, a vision of the world as it ought to be. My conception of the significance of past events will be based on my conception of the perfect society, and it will be from this vantage point that I will select data and offer an interpretation of those data. Thus, historians will sometimes agree about the significant texts—as do Corbett and Kennedy, for example—without agreeing on the interpretation of them: Corbett valorizing Aristotle while Kennedy enthrones Plato. And the difference will be in their conceptions of the world as it ought to be, as well as in their conceptions of what it actually is. In the case of this example, I would disagree with both, looking to certain Sophists as the most fruitful demonstration of rhetoric in ancient Greece because they offer the best precedent for a modern democracy.

I would also argue that this historiographic method encourages a dialectical reading of past and present that will encourage a variety of conflicting readings, even among those who share ideological loyalties. A commonplace of historical studies is that the past is studied in order that we may not repeat its mistakes, encountering in it lessons of value for the present. While this formulation cannot be rejected out of hand, it is often employed in the service of a historical conception that sees the past and present as identical. For instance, those who see in Cicero's Deoratore a discussion of argument that "serves as a good index to the subsequent history of rhetoric" (Sloan) somehow overlook the obvious differences between the violently antidemocratic Rome of Cicero and the contemporary commitment to democracy found in most Western states (however much the commitment remains unfulfilled). As I have said repeatedly, the historiographic method I am suggesting foregrounds difference over identity. This difference, furthermore, is useful not simply because it offers new conceptions of the past not yet entertained. I am also convinced it offers new interpretations of the present.

To see the past as different is often to render the present disparate and strange, offering the defamiliarization of tacitly maintained truisms about our own time. Once again, I will insist that the past is not always better than the present, as classicists will argue, nor is it always worse, as progressives maintain. Often it is both at once. Aristotle reveals the inevitably probabilistic nature of political decision making and the centrality of the *polis* in the decision-making process, while simultaneously preferring the wisdom of the wealthy and educated over the judgment of the ordinary citizen. In his complex divergence from us, then, Aristotle can underscore our own distrust of communal decision making, as well as our denial of contingency in favor of scientific certitude even in areas where such certitude is simply not possible. He can also remind us of our failures in democratic representation that so much resemble his—in our methods of financing political campaigns or in the subtle devices we have devised to discourage citizens from voting. I am arguing finally for a dialectic between past and present. Our conceptions of the present guide us in looking at the past, but in looking for our other we discover disruptions in our conceptions so that past and present are simultaneously reconceived. Thus, my position is not doctrinaire—not a privileging of economic universals over cultural universals, or vice versa, for example—but a search for interpretations that cast the past and the present in new conceptual formulations. And this dialectical process is never finally ended, since the relation of past and present will continually change through time, each generation needing to reformulate its historical understanding.

In the closing section of this essay I want to offer a more detailed description of the historiographic method I am proposing. I want especially to address the challenge to history writing posed by the postmodern disruption in our confidence in grand historical narratives, a challenge that has been constantly kept in mind in what has already been said. (I have also discussed this issue along somewhat different but related lines in Berlin 1990.) Jean-Francois Lyotard (1984b) has been the central figure in denying the possibility of metanarratives of history, of accounts that exhaustively elucidate the significance of the entirety of human conditions in the past or present. He has disputed the totalizing discourses of such schemes as Hegelianism and Marxism or the faith in scientific progress and the invisible hand of economic law. All are declared language games that are inherently partial and interested, intended to endorse particular relations of power and to privilege certain groups in historical struggles. Against this totalizing gesture, Lyotard argues for a plurality of particular narratives, limited and localized explanations that attempt to address features of experience that grand narratives exclude. This requires (as I have underscored in this essay) looking for what has been left out in ordinary accounts, searching for the events at the unspoken margins of a culture. This moves attention to such categories as class, race, gender, and ethnicity in the unfolding of historical events. This is often history from the bottom up, telling the stories of the people and events normally excluded from totalizing discourses.

Against this plea for the complete and entire rejection of comprehensive historical accounts, however, I would argue for the necessity of provisional, contingent narratives in explaining the past and present. While history may be without an inherent plan or progression, it is the product of the complex interactions of people, social institutions, ideologies, technological conditions, and modes of production. To relinquish the comprehensive attempt to make sense of history is to risk being victimized by it. Meanwhile, those who have the most to gain from totalistic historical explanations that validate present economic and political arrangements, the most recent victors of historical battles, will continue to sponsor histories from their point of view, framing master narratives that authorize their continual power and privilege. The attempt to make sense of history will always be undertaken by dominant groups, at the very least to account for the justness of their access to power. These histories of course deny the ideological commitments of their master narratives, usually in the name of an innocent empiricism, and insist that the facts of the matter, not any ruling narrative codes, are making the case. As we have seen, the mediating role of language in all human activities challenges this formulation. After all, past events that contributed to the formation of social and political arrangements are simply too numerous to be presented in their entirety. Some principle of organization and selection must always be invoked, and it is in these choices that the ruling narrative is to be located.

The postmodern turn demands that the role of such narratives be acknowledged, while preventing the move to forward any as essential or universal: all are provisional and contingent, always subject to revision and possible rejection. Cornell West has recently offered a similar proposal and in distinctly rhetorical terms, looking upon provisional and contingent notions of the total as a necessary heuristic and synecdochal way of proceeding: "Without 'totality,' our politics become emaciated, our politics become nothing but existential rebellion. Some heuristic (rather than ontological) notion of totality is in fact necessary if we are to talk about mediations, interrelations, interdependence, about totalizing forces in the world. In other words, a measure of synecdochal thinking must be preserved, thinking that would still invoke relations of parts to the whole It is true, on the other hand, that we can no longer hang on to crude and orthodox 'totalities' such as the idea of superstructure and base" (Stephanson 1988, 270). Despite their conditionality, these provisional narratives are always preferable to the atomistic responses that, in the words of Stanley Aronowitz and Henry Giroux, "run the risk of being trapped in particularistic theories that cannot explain how the various diverse relations that constitute larger social, political, and global systems interrelate or mutually determine and constrain each other." Contingent narratives then become heuristics that open up "mediations, interrelations, and interdependencies that give shape and power to larger political and social systems" (1991, 70).

To use Fredric Jameson's formulation, such narratives provide cognitive maps that at the simplest level are indispensable to daily experience, providing "that mental map of the social and global totality we all carry around in our heads in variously garbled forms" (1991, 415). For projects as complex as the estimation of history, complex cognitive maps that serve as provisional heuristic devices for responding to the vast array of data are indispensable. Indeed, in a remarkable departure from Marxist traditions, Jameson even concurs with Cornell West in placing the concept of the base/superstructure relationship in this category, identifying it as "a starting point and a problem, an imperative to make connections, as undogmatic as a heuristic recommendation simultaneously to group culture (and theory) in and for itself, but also in relation to its outside, its content, its context, and its space of intervention and effectivity" (1991, 409). The directing narratives to be invoked in writing history here recommended similarly offer this capacity to provide connections while never determining in advance exactly what they will be. The narrative and the facts it discovers engage in a dialectical interaction in which the two terms of the encounter are always open *to* revision, the narrative revealing and deciphering data while the data revise the narrative.

Teresa Ebert has recently offered an instructive conception of this use of a provisional totality within a postmodern frame. Her model is feminist and resistant, what she calls "resistant postmodernism" in contrast to the indefinite play of difference found in "ludic postmodernism": "There are two radically different notions of politics in postmodernism. Ludic politics is a textual practice that seeks open access to the free play of signification in order to disassemble the dominant cultural policy (totality), which tries to restrict and stabilize meaning. Whereas resistance postmodernism, I contend, insists on a materialist political practice that works for equal access for all to social resources and for an end *to* the exploitative exercise of power" (1991, 887). While Ebert is thoroughly appreciative of the critique offered by feminist ludic postmodernists, she finds it wanting in its politics. It is not enough for postmodernism to examine difference and the excluded other in an effort *to* reverse or displace hierarchical binaries, however valuable this may have been at an earlier historical moment: "Instead it needs to inquire into the power relations requiring such suppression" (1991, 889). Ebert poses a scheme for regarding the central role of signifying practices in the formation of subject and society that makes for a coherent commentary on the position I have offered in this essay. For her, language, the sign, is "an ideological process in which we consider a signifier in relation to a matrix of historically possible signifieds. The signifier becomes temporarily connected to a specific signified—that is, it attains its 'meaning'—through social struggle in which the prevailing ideology and social contradictions insist on a particular signified" (897). Language is thus the arena of struggle for determining the meaning of key signifiers, signifiers that then operate in the formation and maintenance of economic and political conditions, as well as in the very construction of the consciousness of the subjects of history. The important addendum is that resistance is always possible since the contradictions between signified and signifier—for example, the promises of supply-side economic policies and the actual living conditions of what is now being characterized as "the bottom ninety percent" of the population—continually provoke opposition to hegemonic ideologies.

Ebert also offers a reading of difference that leads to a conception of the inevitability of provisional and contingent notions of a constantly changing totality: "But a postmodern materialist feminism based on a resistant postmodernism, I contend, does not avoid the issues of totality or abandon the struggle concept of patriarchy; instead, it rewrites them. Totality needs to be reunderstood as a system of relations, but such a system is not a homogeneous unity as the Hegelian expressive totality proposes: *It is an overdetermined structure of difference.* A system—particularly the system of patriarchy—is thus always self-divided, different from itself and multiple; it is traversed by 'differences within,' by difference." Difference here becomes the conflict of social and material conditions conceived as a totality of shifting relations of the economic, political, and cultural: "If totalities are structures of differences and thus multiple, unstable, changeable arenas of contradictions and social struggle, then they are open to contestation and transformation. But such transformations are themselves contingent on analyzing the ways in which the operation of power and organization of differences in a specific system are overdetermined by other systems of difference, because systems of difference are also situated in a social formation— which is itself a structure of differences made up of other systems of differences, including the social, economic, political, cultural, and ideological" (1991, 899).

All of this means that any category of investigation—whether gender, class, race, ethnicity, or age—must be considered in its complex relations to other mutually influencing categories within a complex and shifting totality of differences. For example, at the most obvious level gender relations in the United States during this century can be characterized as consistently inequitable in the distribution of political power between men and women. This inequity, however, has manifested itself differently among different classes and races, and even these differences have varied greatly from decade to decade as economic and social conditions have changed. This shifting totality requires that any investigation of human behavior must be historically specific in its methods and materials, never resting secure in any ahistorical, universal mode of thought.

The historiographic method recommended here, then, demands honesty of the historian, a candid acknowledgement of her ideological stance, her conception of perfect economic, social, and political arrangements, her vision of utopia. The historian is never simply writing an account of the past. She is also writing an account of the present and, of equal importance, a hope and vision of the future. In telling us what happened, the historian is telling us what ought to happen now and tomorrow. These are matters too important to be left to the silently implicit, to be obscured in the insistence on history as facts and only facts. Acknowledging the postmodernist critique of all totalistic thinking, furthermore, the historian realizes the provisionality of any conception of the good life and the good society. She must always reserve the right to revise and refigure her position. The historian then owes it to us and to herself to tell us where she stands so that we can know whether we want to stand with her.

References

Aronowitz, Stanley, and Henry A. Giroux. 1991. *Postmodern Education: Politics, Culture, and Social Criticism.* Minneapolis: University of Minnesota Press.

Berlin, James A. 1987a. "Revisionary History: The Dialectical Method." *PRE/TEXT* 8.1–2: 47–61.

Berlin, James A. 1987b. *Rhetoric and Reality: Writing Instruction in American Colleges, 1900–1985.* Carbondale: Southern Illinois University Press.

Berlin, James A. 1990. "Postmodernism, Politics, and Histories of Rhetoric." *PRE/TEXT* 11.3–4: 169–187.

Berlin, James A. 1992. "Aristotle's Rhetoric in Context: Reading Historically." In *A Rhetoric of Doing: Essays on Written Discourse in Honor of Hames L. Kinneavy.*, edited by Stephen P. Witte, Neil Nakadate and Roger D. Cherry. Carbondale: Southern Illinois University Press.

Burke, Kenneth. 1969b. *A Rhetoric of Motives.* Berkeley: University of California Press.

Campbell, Karlyn Kohrs. 1989. *Man Cannot Speak for Her.* 2 vols. Westport, Conn.: Greenwood Press.

Corbett, Edward P. J. 1990. *Classical Rhetoric for the Modern Student.* N.Y.: Oxford University Press.

Dorey, T. A. 1964. "Honesty in Roman Politics." In *Cicero*, edited by T. A. Dorey, 27–45. London: Routledge and Kegan Paul.

Douglas, A. E. 1964. "Cicero the Philosopher." In *Cicero,* edited by T. A. Dorey, 135–170. London: Routledge and Kegan Paul.

Ebert, Teresa L. 1991. "The 'Difference' of Postmodern Feminism." *College English* 53:8: 886–904.

Enos, Richard Leo. 1976. "The Epistemology of Gorgias' Rhetoric: A Re-Examination." *Central States Speech Journal* 25: 4-10.

Genovese, Eugene. 1972. *Roll, Jordan, Roll: The World Slaves Made.* N.Y.: Pantheon Books.

Havelock, Eric. 1957. *The Liberal Temper in Greek Politics.* Cambridge: Harvard University Press.

Holbrook, Sue Ellen. 1991. "Women's Work: The Feminizing of Composition." *Rhetoric Review* 9: 201–229.

Howell, Wilbur Samuel. 1971. *Eighteenth-Century British Logic and Rhetoric.* Princeton: Princeton University Press.

Jameson, Fredric. 1991. *Postmodernism or, The Cultural Logic of Late Capitalism.* Durham: Duke University Press.

Jarratt, Susan C. 1990. "Speaking to the Past: Feminist Historiography in Rhetoric." PRE/TEXT 11.3–4:189–209.

Jarratt, Susan C. 1985. "A Victorian Sophistic: The Rhetoric of Knowledge in Darwin, Newman and Pater." Doctoral dissertation, University of Texas at Austin.

Kauffman, Charles. 1982. "The Axiological Foundations of Plato's Theory of Rhetoric." *Central States Speech Journal* 33: 353–66

Kennedy, George A. 1980a. *Classical Rhetoric and Its Christian and Secular Tradition from Ancient to Modern Times.* Chapel Hill: The University of North Carolina Press.

Leff, Michael. 1983. "The Topics of Argumentative Invention in Latin Rhetorical Theory from Cicero to Beothius." *Rhetorica* 1.1: 32–44.

Lyotard, Jean-Francois. 1984b. *The Postmodern Condition.* Minneapolis: University of Minnesota Press.

Marx, Karl. 1970. *A Contribution to the Critique of Political Economy.* N.Y.: International Publishers.

Poulakos, John. 1984. "Rhetoric, the Sophists, and the Possible." *Communication Monographs* 51: 215–26.

Sloan, Thomas O. 1989. "Reinventing *inventio.*" *College English* 51: 161–473.

Stephanson, Anders. 1988. "Interview with Cornell West." In *Universal Abandon? Politics of Postmodernism,* edited by Andrew Ross, 269,286. Minneapolis: University of Minnesota Press.

Streuver, Nancy S. 1970. *The Language of History in the Renaissance.* Princeton: Princeton University Press.

Thompson, E. P. 1963. *The Making of the English Working Class.* N.Y.: Vintage.

Vickers, Brian. 1990. *In Defense of Rhetoric.* Oxford: The Clarendon Press.

Vitanza, Victor J. 1987a. "Critical Sub/Versions of the History of Philosophical Rhetoric." *Rhetoric Review* 6.1: 41–66.

Vitanza, Victor J. 1987b. "'Notes' Towards Historiographies of Rhetorics; or, Rhetorics of the Histories of Rhetorics: Traditional, Revisionary, and Sub/Versive." *PRE/TEXT* 8.1–2: 63–125.

Woods, Marjorie Curry. 1990. "The Teaching of Writing in Medieval Europe." In *A Short History of Writing Instruction: From Ancient Greece to Twentieth-Century America,77-94.* Davis, Calif.: Hermagorus Press.

CONCLUSION

Comprehension Questions

1. What are the key elements of definitions of rhetoric provided over the past two thousand years?

2. What does Berlin suggest as an antidote to traditional exclusionary narratives of rhetorical history?

Critical Thinking Questions

1. Why is it important to "think outside the box" when it comes to learning about the development of rhetoric and rhetorical theory?

2. What do we, as students and practitioners of rhetoric, have to gain from rethinking the realm of rhetoric?

Unit Summary

"Unit 1" suggested taking a critical/cultural view of rhetoric that both broadens and deepens our understandings of rhetoric. A critical/cultural approach prompts us to explore the ways the theories and practice of rhetoric are shaped and delimited by the economic, political, and cultural contexts of the time period.

"Unit 2" will take us back in time nearly five thousand years to explore the origins of rhetorical theory. We will don the hat of the critical/cultural scholar as we situate these early theories on public speech within the surroundings of life in ancient Greece and Rome.

UNIT 2

RECOVERING LOST VOICES

Who Is Missing from Traditional Accounts of Rhetoric in the Classical Era?

Consider:

1. Identify a famous writer, speaker, or poet from the ancient world. How did this person get their ideas out there?

2. Now identify a famous female or person of color who was a writer, speaker, or poet from the ancient world. Was this question more challenging than the first one? If so, why?

3. What are the ancient world's equivalents of Instagram, Snapchat, and Twitter? During the times of ancient Greece and Rome, who got to communicate and why?

4. Now consider primary modes of public communication in the twenty-first century. What has changed and what has remained the same concerning outlets for public expression? Who gets to communicate and through what means? Why is this significant?

The "Introduction" and reading in "Unit 1" reminded us that theories of rhetoric—from the fifth century BCE to the present—are not neutral descriptions/understandings of public speaking and debate. Rather, theory making was/is shaped by the structures, systems, traditions, values, and beliefs of specific historical contexts. "Unit 2" will help us tease out how the theories of ancient Greek and

Roman scholars—considered the "grandfathers" of the discipline—were shaped by prevailing views on government, home life, and social relationships of the period.

In many, if not most accounts of the history of rhetoric, Socrates, Plato, Aristotle, and Cicero figure in as the originators of thought on speech, dialogue, and public influence. The traditional lineage goes something like this: Socrates taught Plato, Aristotle was a student in Plato's Academy, and the Roman politician, Cicero, was greatly influenced by the writings of Aristotle. These men and many other influential thinkers during the time period, referred to as the classical era (fifth century BCE–430 CE), provide us with key concepts and theories on public speaking that remain relevant today.

"Unit 2" will bring to life other figures who had a hand in the development of rhetorical theory, individuals whose contributions have been marginalized or silenced within the widely accepted history of rhetoric. "Unit 2" is an effort to both *recover* voices and *rethink* how we conceptualize the discipline of rhetoric. To accomplish this, we will begin with a brief history lesson that takes us back to a period existing three thousand years prior to the classical era and then to ancient Greece and Rome during the fifth through first centuries BCE (before Common era).

The Original 'Grandfather' of Public Speaking

Aristotle and his colleagues were not the first to theorize the relationship between public speaking and governance. Around 3100 BCE in Egypt, the African philosopher Ptah-Hotep wrote *The Instruction of Ptah-Hotep and the Instruction of Ke'gemni: The Oldest Book in the World*, which provides readers a theory on rhetoric that both parallels and diverges from traditional Greco-Roman notions of public speaking. The writings of Ptah-Hotep point to the African origins of rhetoric and encourage us to rethink basic assumptions of rhetoric—for instance, assumptions concerning the primacy of logos and persuasion (Blake 2009).

Written in ancient Egypt, Ptah-Hotep's book is a set of instructions to his son on how to become an effective public speaker and leader. Ptah-Hotep's lessons are firmly rooted in the African Maatian principles of moral integrity and social responsibility. The basic principles of Maat are: respect for hierarchy; adherence to the truth; obedience/righteousness; humility; rightness and justice; harmony, balance, and order. From this list, we can draw a number of parallels to the tenets of effective public speaking elaborated by Plato and Aristotle, who were writing and teaching three thousand years after Ptah-Hotep.

Like Plato, who reflected on the connection between truth and justice, Ptah-Hotep emphasized a key Maatian principle of truth, saying, "Great is Truth, appointing a straight path.... Let that which thou speakest implant true things and just in the life of thy children. Such training pays off eventually, because when people listen to them, they will say 'Surely, that man hath spoken to good purpose'" (quoted in Blake 2009, p. 54). Additionally, two Maatian principles—i.e., humility, rightness/justice—underscore the importance of ethos in public speaking. Ptah-Hotep urged his readers to avoid excess and extravagance in speech and to be guided by what is right and just. These guidelines align with and stand as the precursor to the Roman scholar Quintilian's notion of rhetoric as the "good man speaking well" (Blake 2009, p. 32).

Other Maatian principles outlined in Ptah-Hotep's book point to ways traditional African rhetorical theory diverged from Greco-Roman thought of the fifth to first centuries BCE. These differences encourage us to broaden our understandings of basic tenets of rhetoric that have been widely assumed as normative. Ptah-Hotep based his writings on the core African principles of harmony and balance. Accordingly, obedience is deemed essential for maintaining harmony and balance. In contrast, Aristotle and his contemporaries stressed processes of persuasion, particularly through appeals to reason (logos), credibility (ethos), and emotion (pathos), by which listeners would consider all sides of an issue and make an informed decision. The Maatian principle of obedience in many ways precludes persuasion as it suggests adherence to authority; however, in the context of Maatian principles, authority figures had to earn their leadership status based on "responsible behavior" toward the community and a commitment to justice (Blake 2009, p. 27).

This brief overview of Ptah-Hotep's book, *The Instruction of Ptah-Hotep and the Instruction of Ke'gemni: The Oldest Book in the World*, suggests the origins of rhetoric predate the writings of Greco-Roman scholars often thought to have laid the foundation for rhetorical theory. Recovering the writing of Ptah-Hotep does more than simply add another voice to the canon. It should prompt us to examine the political and ideological dimensions of rhetorical theory and what we presume as taken-for-granted assumptions of effective public speaking. The traditional Western idea of Africa as the "dark continent"—or as uncultured, ignorant, or otherwise inferior to the West—has contributed to erasure of the contributions of nonwhite, non-Western thinkers and obscured the ways ancient Egyptian society developed a theory of public speaking and citizenship.

The Status of Women in Ancient Greece and Rome

In addition to challenging the notion of the Greco-Roman "origins" of rhetoric, we can deepen our understanding of the development of rhetorical theory by examining the social and political context of Greece and Rome in the classical era. "Unit 1" reminded us of the importance of situating theory in its historical context. Toward this end, we should ask: What was life like for the average Athenian/Roman during the times of Aristotle and Cicero?

Although ancient Greece and Rome were considered democracies, they did not function in the way we in the twenty-first century would typically understand a democracy. In Athens, the largest city-state in Greece, only native Athenian men had political rights and freedom of movement in public spaces. Girls and women were situated under the guardianship (kyrios) of fathers or husbands. Athenian women were considered citizens but not "politikai," meaning they could not vote, could not defend themselves in a court of law, and had no say in economic or political decision making (Connors 1992, p. 68). Most girls were not educated outside the home, although they may have received a limited education in the home, learning the basics of domestic duties and perhaps literacy from their mothers. Athenian women were largely sequestered from public spaces, made to remain in an area of the home called the "gynacaeum" (Blundell 1995; Connors 1992). They rarely even left the home to shop in the marketplace; that task was often left to household slaves or to husbands (Blundell 1995, p. 135). Glenn (1997) points out that the seclusion of women "signaled cultural efforts to keep women in the possession of men" (p. 54). Athenian women were viewed as "nonrational beings" whose primary purpose was to bear children of unquestionable paternity (Connors 1992, p. 68). Aristotle's observation sums up the prevailing, albeit not the only, Athenian view of women: "between the sexes, the male is by nature superior and the female inferior, the male ruler and the female subject" (*Politics* 1.2.12). Socrates is thought to have a more enlightened view of women, believing it was not inherent inferiority but lack of opportunity and education that kept women in a low social status (Cantarella 1987, p. 53).

Non-Athenian women were either "hetairai," slaves, or "metics." Hetairai translates roughly to companion or mistress. These nonnative Athenian women were allowed to associate with men at social gatherings where wives were not permitted. Female slaves carried on household duties such as cooking, cleaning, and shopping. Metics were resident nonnative Athenians, often the wives of non-Athenian men who lived and worked in Athens. What is notable about hetairai, slaves, and metics was their relative freedom of mobility and association not granted to native Athenian women. Since these women were not valued for the capacity to carry on a pure Athenian lineage through childbirth, they were not held to the same strictures as Athenian women. Metics may have worked outside the home, slaves could mingle and shop in the marketplace, and hetairai could socialize with men. In sum, most Athenian women of citizen status remained confined to the home; some attained literacy, and a very few noncitizen women in Athens—among them, the influential Aspasia of Miletus—associated with notable male philosophers of the day.

The legal status of Roman women during the fifth to first centuries BCE was not much more favorable than their Athenian sisters. Legal discrimination against women in Rome was justified by what was believed to be their "natural inferiority," their "congenital weakness," and "limited intellectual faculties" (Glenn 1997, p. 62). Cicero's view of women's abilities was akin to his predecessor, Aristotle. Cicero wrote, "How great will be the misfortune of that city, in which women will assume the public duties of men" (quoted in Hallett 1984, p. 8). Cicero's observations notwithstanding, Roman women were allowed to defend themselves in a court of law if there was no male relative to speak on their behalf. Roman mothers were expected to know the discipline of rhetoric so as to be able to educate their sons. And during the period of the late republic and early empire, it was not uncommon to see "respectable women" in public spaces (Cape 1997, p. 113). Thus, Roman women could exercise a role as "writers and public speakers" albeit not "in their own right" but "in relation to their capacity to educate the next generation" (Cape 1997, p. 116).

Also notable, the Roman idea of rhetoric enveloped the area of conversation, "sermo," which provided an opening for women to learn and practice rhetoric in ways deemed appropriate for their sex. Sermo, according to the Roman rhetorician Cicero, was the counterpart to argument. Sermo consisted of private conversations with friends or in social situations and centered on domestic or state affairs, professions, or learning. Sermo was characterized by politeness and courtesy. The domestic and private nature of sermo situates this type of speech within the private sphere of the home—considered women's sphere—and thus suggests a way Roman women could exercise voice, even if only primarily within the context of private conversation (Cape 1997).

The prevailing views of women and girls in ancient Athens and Rome served to justify their exclusion from public decision making and debate. Indeed, the discipline of rhetoric was "shaped by male rituals, male contests, male ideals, and masculine agendas" (Connors 1992, p. 65). Rhetoric, then as now, was conceived as a sort of verbal combat, a contest of two sides—pro and con—each of which attempts to show his opponent as the weaker through argument, refutation, and rebuttal. Connors suggests that "rhetorical theory" taught "verbal gladiators how to create persuasive arguments, how to develop and win cases, ... how to make themselves look clever and their enemies look stupid—how to stake out turf and verbally hold it against opponents in public contest" (p. 73). In short, rhetoric was a quintessentially manly and masculinized affair. As we learned in "Unit 1," the very act of public speaking presumed manhood. This agonistic rendering of rhetoric was antithetical to the Maatian principle of harmony and balance, and also served to exclude women and girls from exercising voice and agency in public settings.

Women Who Spoke Publicly in Ancient Greece and Rome

Given the legal and social strictures that kept women and girls by and large bound to the home and in the possession of fathers and husbands, it is remarkable that women engaged in public speaking; yet, history reveals to us a number who did influence the discipline of rhetoric. Aspasia traveled to Athens from her home in Miletus, an area in Asia Minor, and became connected to a well-known circle of philosophers including Pericles and Plato. Although we do not have her writings to draw upon, we know of Aspasia and her contributions from the writings of Plato, Xenophon, Cicero, Plutarch, and Athenaeus. Aspasia is often portrayed in art and literature as a "hetairai" or mistress who socialized with Athenian men. She was much more than that. She was a teacher to Pericles and Socrates and is believed to have heavily influenced—and in some cases written—the speeches of Pericles, including his well-known Funeral Oration (Carlson 1994; Glenn 1997, pp. 36–44). From his writings, we see that "Socrates deeply respected Aspasia's thinking and admired her rhetorical prowess" (Glenn 1997, p. 40). Aspasia opened a school for girls from reputable families and her home became a hot spot for popular philosophers—e.g., Socrates, Plato, Sophocles, and Pericles—to socialize and discuss issues of the day (Glenn 1994). Another woman known to have influenced rhetorical thought in ancient Greece was Diotima of Mantinea. Diotima shaped the views of philosophers in the topics of love and desire. In his work, *Symposium*, Plato suggested Diotima as the authoritative voice on a philosophy of love (Glenn 1997, p. 45).

In Rome, Hortensia was a significant figure who asserted a case before Roman leaders to repeal a tax imposed on married women's property. Hortensia's primary argument was that women should not have to pay newly imposed war taxes if they were not allowed a say in governance. Hortensia's speech drew on specific examples, reflected sound reasoning, and embodied the Roman dictates of decorum (Cape 1997, pp. 124, 125). She was joined by hundreds of other women who gathered to hear her deliver her speech. Her oratory effort was successful in persuading the triumvirs to reduce the number of women who had to pay taxes, despite making the male leaders "angry that women should dare to hold a public meeting" (Connors 1992, p. 72).

A few other Roman women argued court cases with varying success. Maesia Sentinas successfully defended herself in a court trial and was praised for arguing her case "like a man" (Cape 1997, p. 122). In contrast, Gaia Afrania was accused of "unwonted barking in the forum" and depicted as an "example of feminine maliciousness" (Cape 1997, p. 121). The anxiety surrounding women's public-speaking efforts is revealing; the concerns expressed by men underscore the assumptions of a gendered idea of public speech.

We also have evidence of Roman women's writing in the form of letters written by the influential Roman matron Cornelia to her sons, who were active political leaders in the second century BCE. Cornelia's letters—the focus of one of the readings in "Unit 2"—illustrate the Roman concept, sermo. Cornelia's writing is respectful, not overly emotional, and garnered the respect of fellow Roman men such as Quintilian who said of Cornelia, she "had contributed greatly to the eloquence" of her sons (quoted in Hallett 2002, p. 16).

Preview of Unit Readings

The first "Unit 2" reading, "Cracking the Code of Silence," takes a unique approach to uncovering the voices and experiences of marginalized groups in ancient Athens by interrogating the silences or gaps in legal cases surrounding women and slaves. The author Steven Johnstone reminds us that legal cases omitted or "suppressed" the interests and viewpoints of women and slaves, and that these gaps can potentially tell us a great deal about women's experiences in Athens. Johnstone takes us through an exploration of a number of ancient Athenian legal cases to try to uncover how women and slaves experienced relationships and were constrained by legal hierarchies.

Judith Hallett's article, "Women Writing in Rome and Cornelia, Mother of the Gracchi," explores in greater detail the letter writing of the well-known Roman matron Cornelia, who was briefly discussed in the "Unit 2" introduction. Cicero and Quintilian praised Cornelia's letters as exemplary efforts to instill in her sons the qualities of the ideal orator. Hallett notes Cornelia's letters embody a motivational political style that suggests the emotional and educational ties between mothers and their sons during this period.

References

Aristotle. 1977. *Politics*. Translated by H. Rackham. Cambridge, MA: Loeb-Harvard University Press.

Blake, Cecil. 2009. *The African Origins of Rhetoric*. New York: Routledge.

Blundell, Sue. 1995. *Women in Ancient Greece*. London: British Museum Press.

Cantarella, Eva. 1987. *Pandora's Daughters: The Role and Status of Women in Greek and Roman Antiquity*. Baltimore: Johns Hopkins University Press.

Cape, Robert W., Jr. 1997. "Roman Women in the History of Rhetoric and Oratory." In Molly Meijer Wertheimer (ed.), *Listening to Their Voices: The Rhetorical Activities of History Women*, 112–132. Columbia, SC: University of South Carolina Press.

Carlson, Cheree. 1994. "Aspasia of Miletus: How One Woman Disappeared from the History of Rhetoric." *Women's Studies in Communication, 17*, 26–44.

Connors, Robert. 1992. "The Exclusion of Women from Classical Rhetoric." In Stephen P. Witte, Neil Nakadate, and Roger D. Cherry (eds.), *A Rhetoric of Doing: Essays on Written Discourse in Honor of James L. Kinneavy*, 65–78. Carbondale, IL: Southern Illinois University Press.

Glenn, Cheryl. 1994. "Sex, Lies, and Manuscript: Refiguring Aspasia in the History of Rhetoric." *College Composition and Communication, 45*, 180–199.

——. 1997. *Rhetoric Retold: Regendering the Tradition from Antiquity Through the Renaissance*. Carbondale, IL: Southern Illinois University Press.

Hallett, Judith P. 1984. *Fathers and Daughters in Roman Society*. Princeton, NJ: Princeton University Press.

CRACKING THE CODE OF SILENCE

Athenian Legal Oratory and the Histories of Slaves and Women

by Steven Johnstone

B oth men insisted that the other's desire for the woman ignited the conflict. The accuser claimed that the defendant, a longstanding enemy who had been captivated by the charms of the accuser's mistress, had barged into his house, seized the woman, and tried to kill him with a piece of pottery. The defendant admitted there had been a melee, but contended that he had been invited to a drinking party at the accuser's house—slaves, flute girls, and wine had been promised—to celebrate their reconciliation. The accuser, the defendant continued, was the first to attack him in a drunken, jealous fit over the woman, who was not a free mistress but a slave whom they jointly owned (Lysias 4).

Our knowledge of this dispute comes from a speech delivered in a fourth- century BCE law court that seems to open a window onto the social world of slaves and wom-en in classical Athens. The evidence it offers, however, presents serious difficulties for historians. As with most Athenian legal orations, only one litigant's speech has survived. With only the defendant's plea (in fact, only part of it) and no independent information, it is impossible to evaluate the factual claims of either side; indeed, even the accuser's arguments must be inferred from what the defendant said. Faced with such factual quandaries, historians have noted that though speakers may have lied to Athenian juries, they are unlikely to have invented implausible lies. Although we cannot know what actually happened in this case, we may assume (so this reasoning goes) that the defendant's speech represents the type of things that were likely to occur. Thus, we may understand this conflict in the context of amorous and honorific

Steven Johnstone, "Cracking the Code of Silence: Athenian Legal Oratory and the Histories of Slaves and Women," *Women and Slaves in Greco-Roman Culture: Differential Equations, ed. Sandra R. Joshel and Sheila Murnaghan*, pp. 221-235, 256-276. Copyright © 1998 by Taylor & Francis Group. Reprinted with permission.

rivalries between aristocrats: each of these men, whose honor was bound up with his sexual achievements, was quick to react to a competitor.

Compelling as such an interpretation is, however, it fails to ask an obvious question: What about the woman? What were her interests in this conflict? At one point the defendant admitted (in an offhand remark) that the woman cared much more for the accuser than for him and had actually done him wrong in league with his opponent (Lysias 4.17). What was her complaint against this man? Was it related to his claim that she was not free, as the accuser said, but a slave? Had she, in fact, incited the conflict? Is it possible that this case originated less in aristocratic male rivalry than in a woman's assertion of her own interests? Despite this tantalizing hint, the possibilities of providing answers look dim. The defendant's narrative, focused as it is on his conflict with the other man, provides little evidence for uncovering the woman's interests in the dispute. Against the reality of litigation between men, it seems as if the woman's subjectivity must remain entirely speculative. Indeed, the substantial body of legal speeches extant from classical Athens consistently represents conflict between citizen men; slaves and women figure largely incidentally. If there is any hope of getting beyond this silence of the sources, some methodological ingenuity is necessary.

Subjects and Silence

Despite their great treasure of details about slaves and women, in one fundamental way Athenian legal speeches remain silent about them. They are silent because marginalized people did not appear as agents in their own right, but only in relationship to the free men who were the subjects of the law's stories. The narrative conventions of a legal story consistently suppressed full accounts of the agency, experience, interests, and subjectivity of women and slaves. The danger of these sources, then, is that all they do say about these groups will obscure their fundamental omissions, and that we will unwittingly adopt their narrative constraints as our own in writing history. The silences themselves must be interrogated.

The silences of the sources present obstacles to writing the history of marginalized people, of course, but such silences are much more than just inconvenient accidents that cloak these people's experiences. Rather, they were essential features of ancient modes of representation which actively constituted and produced those experiences. As Joan Scott notes, "It is not individuals who have experiences but subjects who are constituted through experience" (Scott 1991, 779). There is no "authentic" subject outside history. An essential part of recovering slaves and women as historical subjects is problematizing the subject: that is, recognizing the degree to which subject positions are constituted through unique historical forces (cf. Hunter 1992). This is true not only for slaves and women, moreover, but for masters and men as well—an insight which provides a basis for a critical evaluation of the sources for writing history, sources which do not merely reflect social structures (although they certainly do that), but which also were part of the complex process of reproducing them (cf. Johnstone 1994). Silences, then, are not (or not only) the result of hierarchy and oppression, but also one of the means through which these were reproduced. Although to us these silences occlude marginalized subjects, they were also one of the ways these subjects were created.

People make their own history, as Marx almost said, but not under conditions of their own choosing. The project of problematizing subjects does not mean annihilating them, but analyzing them. Although an extreme poststructuralism would see subjects as pure effects, as only illusions, some of the best work has sought to temper this tendency: writing in the wake of Michel Foucault, for example, Judith Butler (1990) uses French psychoanalytic feminism to reanimate a sense of agency in Foucault's theories, and John Law (1994) argues that since attempts at imposing order (Foucault's "discourses") cannot be as totalizing as Foucault sometimes suggests, there is always room for individual action. The inhabitants of Athens who were not male citizens did exercise agency, even if in limited ways (Maurizio, forthcoming). Thus, the analysis of subjects should see them as both effects and agents—in historically specific ways. A full account of marginalized subjects (or, indeed, of hegemonic ones) should reveal not only what they experienced, but also how they were constituted as experiencing subjects. It should show how subject categories—female and male, slave and master—were created and reproduced. A history of slaves or women, then, should explicitly consider the gaps in the evidence because these gaps did not merely reflect social hierarchies—as systemic, structuring elisions they actively constituted them.

Situating these silences within a theory of the creation and reproduction of subjectivities, then, may provide a way to advance our understanding of marginalized groups. Scholarship on slaves and women has usually employed one of two strategies. The first has attempted to recover the "voices" of marginalized groups, whether that means their experiences, their subjectivities, their agency, or texts they themselves wrote; the second has sought to study the ideology, representations, or discourses concerning marginalized groups (cf. Scott 1988). Both approaches have yielded substantial insights, but both can be extended by more fully confronting and interrogating the gaps in the evidence. The first method, in constructing a traditional historical narrative with a new subject, has not always acknowledged its precarious evidentiary foundations. Pomeroy's groundbreaking book on women in antiquity, for example, briefly acknowledges in the introduction the problems the evidence presents (1975, x–xi), but its body is a seamless narrative unbroken by epistemological considerations. The second method focuses on a subject for which there is much more secure evidence. In the case of Athenian women, then, the study of gender—of the socially perceived differences between the sexes—sidesteps questions which traditional literary texts cannot answer well. Tragedy, for example, does not reveal much about how most Athenian women actually lived, much less what they thought, but it does provide rich representations of gender. The considerable insights of this approach, however, do not necessarily shed light on the historical reality of the lives of actual women (cf. Smith-Rosenberg 1986, 31–2). Confronting the gaps in the evidence not as epistemological problems but as facts to be understood and incorporated into historical accounts provides one way to build on these two approaches and to link ideology with lived experience.

Law and Narratives

As one of the best sources of Athenian social history, legal speeches provide an opportunity to examine these silences and their operation. Instead of ignoring or even inadvertently reproducing their omissions, I want to examine these speeches in light of the anthropological theory of disputes which recognizes that legal representations are not reality, but one of many competing ways of constructing experience. A dispute is, broadly, a conflict between people (Comaroff and Roberts 1981; Mather and Yngvesson 1980–1; Yngvesson and Mather 1983). One of the great advantages of thinking of disputes rather than legal cases is the recognition that conflict can take many forms, only one of which is legal. The particular shape of a conflict is an outcome of the parties' struggles to impose competing meanings on the dispute. Thus the meaning or shape of the dispute is part of what is at stake in a conflict. The transformation from one shape to another (say, from a domestic quarrel to a legal case) is strategic. It is not inherent in the conflict, but the outcome of a party's interested claim. Such transformations, however, are also structural and systemic. The ability of parties to impose a definition is in part an outcome of structural factors (class, gender, status, etc.). The degree to which a particular definition has been accepted as authoritative in turn determines the resources available at any given moment to different parties.

From the perspective of dispute theory, no shape, even the most authoritative, is the "correct" one—indeed every shape represents the interested perspective of particular parties. One person hitting another could be seen as a criminal assault, an excusable peccadillo, an instance of domestic discipline, a manifestation of a psychological problem; all definitions are contestable, and dispute theory, rather than assuming that one is authoritative, seeks to understand how each of these definitions might be imposed. Dispute theory also conforms to what John Law calls a "modest sociology" by beginning with as few assumptions as possible (Law 1994, 13–14). For example, rather than unreflectively assuming a difference between litigants and third parties (witnesses, interested relatives, etc.), it sees this very distinction as the effect of a particularly legal way of narrating the dispute. The law, as a narrative mode, creates and differentiates disputants. Disputes, then, are not legal cases. The important point is not that only a small fraction of all disputes ever go to law,[1] but that the law imposes a particular shape on a dispute. It systematically transforms it.

The shape that Athenian legal stories took derived from the context in which litigants told them. The Athenian judicial system differed radically from our own.[2] Litigants who faced Athenian juries did so with minimal professional help. There were no legal experts, no lawyers, in Athens. Litigants found and cited whatever laws they thought relevant and the jury alone interpreted them. Litigants usually addressed the jury themselves, sometimes supported by friends or relatives who appeared as witnesses, added a brief plea, or showed solidarity by sitting with them. Now and then, if a party to a suit claimed to be unusually disadvantaged in speaking for himself (old age and youthful inexperience were the most common reasons), a close friend or relative might speak for him. Though there were no lawyers, some litigants paid an expert in legal rhetoric to compose their speech; such professionals wrote most of the hundred or so speeches that survive. There were no police and no public prosecutors; cases were investigated, initiated, and conducted by private citizens.[3] Each litigant had only a limited amount of time in which to speak, and trials never lasted more than a day. There was no judge; although a magistrate presided at the trial, his role was negligible. Without legal experts, the jurors were the heart of the system. All citizens over thirty could serve as jurors. Each jury consisted of hundreds of randomly selected jurors (usually 201 or 501, sometimes more, very rarely up to 6,000), the majority of whom determined the verdict. They voted immediately after the litigants' presentations without deliberation.

The legal capacity of slaves and women was extremely circumscribed. Neither ever spoke before a jury. Slaves could neither sue nor be sued except insofar as they were the instrument of their owner who would have conducted the case himself (Todd 1993, 186–7, 192–4). Women were occasionally defendants and inheritance cases were often initiated on their behalf, but in every case their male guardians spoke for them. Even suits where a male represented a woman or slave seem to have been rare: of the extant speeches, except for inheritance cases, only two involve female defendants and none concern slaves. Neither slaves nor women could appear as witnesses.

The law abridged the voices of women and slaves not just by preventing them from speaking, but, through the conventions governing stories told in courts, by refiguring disputes as legal cases (Johnstone, forthcoming). The law worked through simplification. Its conventions required that the dispute be between only two parties, a prosecutor and a defendant; however many parties might have a stake in a dispute, a legal story attempted to impose a dyadic structure on the conflict. Because in almost all cases only adult male citizens could act as litigants, these stories also defined the dispute as fundamentally between male citizens; the interests of other parties—of women and of slaves—were eclipsed. A legal narrative (for prosecutors, at least) also had to focus on a specific act which allegedly violated the law; although many disputes involved ongoing relationships of hostility or a general dissatisfaction, a legal story had to tell of a single, illegal act. Thus legal narratives required a story which might differ from that told by a party who was not a litigant and even by what the litigant himself might say in a nonlegal context. There is often a tension between specifically legal and lay modes of narration (Conley and O' Barr 1990, 12–19, 172; Merry 1990, ...), and Athenian litigants often told a story fuller than the law required. This is important because details which were irrelevant from the perspective of the law often provide the clues for understanding the degree to which litigation imposed a particular meaning on a complex set of events. The boundaries of the law's stories thus imposed silences on slaves and women not by suppressing all information about them, but rather by making it impossible in court to narrate from their perspectives.

Although litigants commonly represented cases as arising from conflict between citizen men, there are strong reasons for believing this was often not the case. Scholars have recognized that it would be naive to read the orations as presenting truthfully historical accounts. Instead, because litigants had to appeal to the audience of jurors, they have suggested that events (even if untrue) must have been plausible to be persuasive (E. Cohen 1992, 36–40; Millett 1991, 2). Thus, they infer, even if we cannot be certain of what happened in this particular case, we can know the kinds of things that commonly happened. But care is required: a story may seem plausible not because it corresponds to the way things normally happen, but because it follows the way stories are usually told (Dershowitz 1996; cf. Ober 1989). It would be wrong to assume, therefore, that most conflict in Athens was between citizen men, or that only this type of conflict spawned litigation, even though most speeches represent it this way. Nevertheless, much of the best recent work (for example Hunter 1994; Cohen 1995) implicitly retains the perspective of the evidence: though it situates litigation within a broader social context ("social control" for Hunter, "elite competition" or "feuding" for Cohen) it still sees this context as the litigants represented it. It therefore suggests that conflict in Athens was fundamentally between men, and that it was only this conflict between male citizens that generated litigation. Dispute theory suggests, on the contrary, that for a dispute to be litigated it had only to be plausibly transformed, and represented as a conflict between men.

Omissions and Theories

Euphiletus' defense (Lysias 1) on a charge of murdering Eratosthenes illustrates how a legal narrative represented conflict in a particular, selective way and how it both suppressed and gave shape to women's subjectivity. Euphiletus told the jury that he and his young wife were living a happy married life, made even more intimate and trusting by the birth of a child. But then one day an old woman lurking near his house accosted Euphiletus. Sent by a woman, a lover whom a certain Eratosthenes had discarded, she warned him to watch out for this man: "He's seduced not only your wife, but many others as well. He's a real professional" (Lysias 1.16). Euphiletus told the jurors he was stunned by this news, so he interrogated his housemaid, a slave whom, the old woman had identified as his wife's accomplice. When she disclaimed knowledge, he threatened torture. When she persisted in her denial, he mentioned the name Eratosthenes and claimed he knew everything. The servant broke down, begged Euphiletus not to harm her, and revealed a continuing liaison between Eratosthenes and Euphiletus' wife. Euphiletus demanded she help him catch Eratosthenes in the act. Days passed. Then, one night, the servant awoke Euphiletus to tell him that Eratosthenes was in the house, in his wife's room. Euphiletus went out, rounded up some friends who lived nearby, returned home, and burst into the room. Naked, Eratosthenes jumped up. Euphiletus knocked him to the ground, pinned his arms behind his back. Eratosthenes implored Euphiletus, he begged him to let him pay compensation, but Euphiletus told him he had broken the law. "Thus," Euphiletus euphemistically told the jury, "that man got what the laws prescribe for people who do such things" (Lysias 1.27). (Euphiletus here referred to the law which excused a husband who impulsively killed a man caught in the act of adultery with his wife. The law certainly did not require such a response.)

The traditional analysis of this case conforms closely to Euphiletus' narrative: a conflict between two men over adultery ultimately spawned a lawsuit. More generally, David Cohen has argued that adultery figured in contests of honor between men, that the male adulterer gained honor at the cuckolded husband's expense (D. Cohen 1990). Although there is much to recommend Cohen's understanding, by adopting the law's perspective, it has made adultery a transaction between men through a woman. Cohen, it is true, admits that wives must have had reasons for taking lovers (D. Cohen 1990, 164), but it is necessary to go further: Within the Athenian courts at least, it was impossible to tell the story of adultery as a conflict between a husband and a wife. The very decision to litigate crystallized the dispute, focusing it on two men. The reasons Cohen suggests for wives taking lovers—loneliness, dissatisfaction—were not merely structural features of women's lives in Athenian society; they are also ways of describing wives' disputes with their husbands. Thus adultery may have been not only the cause of a dispute between two men, from another perspective—unspeakable in legal terms—it may have been the result of a dispute between a wife and a husband.

The legal narrative failed to relate the stories that other parties to this dispute might have told, but in this case enough traces of them remain to begin to see how they might have represented the dispute differently. From these suppressed perspectives, the conflict was less about a contest of male honor as trouble between women and men. Euphiletus first learned of Eratosthenes' activities through a messenger sent by one of his previous lovers who was evidently jealous that he was neglecting her. From one perspective, then, the whole affair was the outcome of the discord between Eratosthenes and his earlier lover, which, however, could be told in a legal venue only as a footnote to the subsequent conflict between citizen men. Moreover, Euphiletus himself admitted to trouble with his wife: he revealed that she was angry because she believed he had been forcing their maid to have sex with him (Lysias 1.12). If the absence of a denial indicates Euphiletus' culpability on this point (Carey 1989, 70), it is reasonable to understand his wife's involvement with a paramour as a stage in an ongoing dispute between wife and husband. But such a conflict could not itself take legal form. Because the conditions of legal discourse mandated that citizen men privilege each other as the primary, even exclusive, disputants, other possible narratives, other possible understandings of the events, were elided. The problem with the evidence, then, is not merely that women could not speak for themselves, but that even male speakers could not fully represent a woman's interests. Figuring adultery as primarily about men and their honor repeats this systematic silence of the sources.

This speech shows, too, that legal narratives allowed a certain room for women's subjectivity, but that it was always reinterpreted in terms of men's interests, especially as these were bundled in the idea of the household or *oikos*. During his defense, Euphiletus quoted the law which allowed a husband to kill an adulterer caught in the act and the law that set monetary damages for rape. Considering these two laws together he concluded:

> In this way, gentlemen, [the lawgiver] thought that those who use force merit a lesser penalty than those who use persuasion: He sentenced the latter to death, but made the damages for the former double [than if they had raped a slave]. He did this because he thought that those who accomplish their ends by force are hated by those who are overpowered, but that those who use persuasion corrupt the souls of their victims. The consequence is that the wives of others are more attached to their seducers than to their husbands, that the whole *oikos* is in their control, and that it is unclear whether the husbands or the adulterers are the fathers of the children.

> (Lysias 1. 32–3)

Thus the law recognized that a woman's interests mattered, but not in the same way that they may have mattered to her: her interests were admitted only in terms of the *oikos*—in her relationships to the husband, the property, and the children. Even her amorous interests were interpreted in light of these, so that her consent to extra-marital sex was significant (it determined the difference between adultery and rape), but it was significant only because of its implications for the *oikos*, not because of its effect on her (whether she suffered violence or not). The law recognized the woman's desire not as an aspect of her experience, but only for its implications for the relationship between her husband and her lover.

As mothers, wives, and daughters of citizen men, women were recognized as having an interest in the preservation or disposition of the property of the household. Although women could not own property in the same way men could (though they may have informally controlled it (Hunter 1994)), they were recognized as depending on it. Generally, therefore, citizen women appear prominently in legal speeches in two contexts. First, in inheritance and guardianship cases women played a prominent role (for example Demosthenes 27–9; Lysias 32). Second, in instances where the defendant faced a possible dire penalty—especially death or confiscation of property—he sometimes invoked the citizen women who depended on him as objects of pity should the punishment be inflicted (Demosthenes 19.283; 25.84; 27.65; 53.29). It is easy to imagine, of course, that most women did take an interest in their households, husbands, and children, but in the law's stories, these were the only interests women had. Thus the oikos was an ideological construct which, far from representing the "sphere" of women, was employed in legal narratives to attribute to women subject positions which reinforced male dominance—precisely by constructing a realm where women's agency could support or oppose only male interests.

The law bolstered this representation of women's interests as defined by the *oikos* by providing the resources to express men's anxiety about it. The most notoriously vague Athenian law nullified wills made by a man who was "deranged on account of insanity, old age, drugs, or illness, or because of the influence of a woman, or forced by necessity or by being held captive" (Demosthenes 46.14; Rhodes 1981, 443–4). Speakers could thus attack the validity of a will alleging the nefarious influence of a woman (for example, Isaeus 6.21, 48; cf. Isaeus 2.19–20, Hyperides 3.17–18). While such claims depended upon highly negative depictions of women (which equated their influence with insanity), like the positive portrayals of good women, they limited female subjectivity to the way it effected a man's interests. Male litigants might represent the expression of women's interests as good or bad, but in either case they were largely circumscribed by the *oikos*.

Slaves and Women

Slaves appear in Athenian legal orations in three notable contexts. First, disputants often dared their opponents to torture a slave as a way of formalizing the settlement of a dispute.[4] Certainly slaves must have considered that this impinged on their interests, but this symbolic, sadistic displacement of hostility onto their bodies was possible because they were legally depicted as largely devoid of humanity and therefore of interests. Indeed, the common claim that "truth" spontaneously issued from slaves under torture posits the slave not as a subject but as a body with a reflex (for example Isaeus 8.12). Second, slaves appear frequently in litigation on mercantile matters. But since male slaves often worked as free men's representatives in trade, especially in running banks, they were represented as having no interests of their own. Third, speakers mentioned slaves in the context of the household. In many of these cases, there is enough information to suspect that slaves may have been disputants with interests of their own. In Ariston's suit against Conon for assault, for example, he traced the hostility that led to their brawl back two years to when he was serving in the army on the frontiers and Conon's drunken sons used to attack his slaves and urinate on them (Demosthenes 54.4).

Generally, however, despite hints that slaves may have taken an active part in disputes (for example, Demosthenes 55.31–4 or Lysias 4.17, referred to at the beginning of this paper), the speeches fail to represent them with even the limited subjectivity allowed to women. In Euphiletus' narrative, for example, the slave who brokered the trysts between Euphiletus' wife and Eratosthenes (conveying secret messages, distracting Euphiletus in a jam) and who subsequently collaborated in Euphiletus' plan to ensnare the lovers, was represented as entirely without loyalty, affection, or interests—except for her fear of being tortured by Euphiletus (Lysias 1.19). Similarly, the young slave Euphiletus' wife accused her husband of molesting was depicted merely as an object. Indeed, Euphiletus made it clear that his wife raised the subject not out of a concern for the girl, but for its effects on her own relationship with her husband. This incident in a slave's life entered the legal narrative, then, only because it had been appropriated by the wife for her own interests, which the legal narrative took account of because of their impact on the *oikos*.

With slaves, too, silence was constitutive: the law reproduced the distinctions between slaves and free people. By this I do not mean the true but unremarkable claim that the law formally distinguished the two categories, but rather that although the law was capable of recognizing a citizen woman's interests in certain cases and in limited ways, it was altogether impossible for it to acknowledge those of a slave. The law's representation of slaves was interested and selective. It is sometimes said that, because they were property, slaves were considered part of the household, but not part of the family (MacDowell 1989; Pomeroy 1994, 65). This reflects more the limits of legal narration than reality. Indeed, it is hard to imagine that slaves had no interests simply because they were sometimes considered property. Nor, in fact, did free individuals always consider slaves property: there are indications that free individuals could form deep affectionate bonds with slaves, bonds of trust, even of love (for example, Lysias 3; Demosthenes 36.8; 47.59ff.). But, although the confiscation of a man's property would certainly affect his slaves (in some ways more than his immediate family), no litigant ever asked the jurors to pity the fate of his servants. It was not that slaves had no interests because they were property, but that they were constituted as property in part because legal stories could not be told which attributed interests to them.

The law does, however, provide glimpses into slaves' involvement in disputes in one kind of situation: when a slave or ex-slave (usually a woman) became the lover of a citizen. The frequency of such references probably has less to do with how often it actually occurred than with certain structural features which allowed for a legal narration, features illustrated by Callistratus' prosecution of his wife's brother Olympiodorus (Demosthenes 48). When a mutual relative died, these two conspired to keep his fortune to themselves. Other relatives demanded adjudication. When the court awarded Olympiodorus the entire estate, he kept it for himself, so Callistratus sued him demanding half in accord with their previous agreement. The legal case thus gave a specific shape to the dispute: Callistratus had been wronged by his brother-in-law when he refused to honor their agreement to split the loot. Yet the legal narrative contains hints that the dispute was much broader than this: during his speech, Callistratus defamed Olympiodorus for living with an ex-slave whose freedom he had bought. "Olympiodorus here, men of the jury, never married an Athenian woman in conformity with your laws, nor has he ever had children. Instead, he bought the freedom of a mistress and keeps her at home. She's the one who insults us all and makes Olympiodorus more and more insane" (Demosthenes 48.53). Callistratus' sudden reference to Olympiodorus' mistress—whom he then blames for the whole trouble—suggests a dispute wider and more complex than a merely legal narrative would reveal. In keeping with the law's conventions for negatively representing the effects of a women's assertion of her interests, Callistratus characterized the mistress's influence as insanity. But there was more. Callistratus then began speaking of his own wife (Olympiodorus' sister) and daughter—who were apparently involved in the dispute more than the legal case alone revealed:

Aren't they being wronged, aren't they suffering terribly when they see this rich man's mistress in gold jewelry and fancy clothes going around in luxury and acting with hubris with our money—meanwhile my wife and daughter are worse off in every way—aren't they being wronged even more than I am? Isn't he obviously crazy and out of his mind in devising such things for himself? So that he cannot allege, men of the jury, that I am saying these things out of slander because of this suit, I will read to you a deposition from his relatives and mine.

(Demosthenes 48.55)

There was clearly more at issue here than the simplified story the law would tell. Even in Callistratus' account, from the perspective of his wife and daughter, the dispute hinged on Olympiodorus' lover, a former slave whose elevated status inspired considerable jealousy. But the law allowed expression of the women's interests in this case only insofar as they could be represented as concerning the oikos, Callistratus' property.

Agency and Anxiety

The prominent appearance in this account of Olympiodorus' unnamed lover reflects an important structural conjunction between the categories of slaves and women: she seems to have changed her status from being a slave to being a woman. Elizabeth Spelman (1988) has suggested that for Aristotle gender was a privilege of the free: the difference between females and males did not matter among slaves, whom he treated without discriminating by sex. Similarly, in Athenian legal oratory, though slaves took part in many events, both sexes alike were regularly represented without even the circumscribed subjectivity of women.[5] In this case, Olympiodorus' lover had acquired the ability to have her interests expressed indirectly, even if negatively—an ability free women had, but slaves did not. This woman's status changed not merely because Olympiodorus had legally freed her; her legal freedom, in fact, was in part an *effect* of becoming his lover. Scholars have argued that acts of sex for the Greeks were invariably hierarchical, that they established relationships of power (Halperin 1990, following Foucault 1985). In doing so, they have usually focused on the ways in which sex elevated the male at the expense of the woman, slave, or boy. But since power can both constrain and enable—since subjects are both effects and agents—what we see in the case of Olympiodorus' lover is the ability of one oppressed person to strategically deploy its enabling capacity. Far from being only limited or stigmatized by being treated "like a woman" in this sexual relationship, this female slave actually *became* a woman.

Though the law imposed a particular, interested, and contestable shape on conflict, the authority of this assertion carried consequences even for those with different perspectives. The subject positions of slaves and women did not exist beyond the law, but were profoundly affected by it, as is shown by a story Apollodorus told when he prosecuted Neaera on a charge of passing herself off as the wife of a citizen (Demosthenes 59.30–40, 45–8). When Neaera, who began her life as a slave in a brothel, felt abused by her lover Phrynion, who had earlier helped her buy her freedom, she fled Athens taking some of their household goods. Wanting to return to Athens but fearful of Phrynion, she enrolled her subsequent lover Stephanus as her patron and went back to live with him. There, when Phrynion tried to seize her, Stephanus asserted her freedom ("in accordance with the law," as the narrative states) and bond was posted with a magistrate pending adjudication. Phrynion brought charges against Stephanus both for wrongly claiming Neaera was free and for holding property stolen from him. Here friends intervened and persuaded each man to submit their quarrel to a group of three arbitrators, one chosen by each man and a neutral third. These reconciled the men, affirmed Neaera's freedom, returned the goods to Phrynion, allowed Neaera to keep her own, and stipulated that Neaera should be shared between them.

The invocation of the law fundamentally transformed the shape of this dispute. It allowed for only two disputants, it insisted each be a legally competent male, and it focused on specific acts defined by the law (a formal assertion of freedom and the theft of property). Even in the settlement, the aim of the arbitrators (chosen because of their relationships to the men) was to reconcile Stephanus and Phrynion—they were, after all, the legal adversaries. Neaera's future became just another condition stipulated by their reconciliation. The language of the law formulated the dispute (and its resolution) as a dyadic conflict between citizen men about a wrong one did to the other.

The inability of a legal narrative to represent Neaera as a subject stands as an obstacle to recovering her experiences as a slave and as a woman; more than this, though, it partially constituted those experiences. Neaera does not seem to have been an impotent pawn of the men around her. Indeed, she enrolled Stephanus as her protector precisely to more effectively stand up to Phrynion. In seeking the leverage of the law against Phrynion, however, Neaera had to displace her interests because a legal narrative could express them only insofar as they were subsumed by a citizen male's. To invoke the law she had to effect this displacement herself. Neaera did not merely require a patron to champion her interests; more importantly, she had to sublimate those interests into someone else's, she had to mediate her relationship with her own interests through a citizen male. Stephanus was not her representative or advocate in a direct sense: he did not bring a suit against Phrynion on her behalf for legal wrongs she had suffered. Rather, Stephanus' formal legal intervention—actively sought by Neaera—decisively transformed the dispute: he now spoke for himself in his dispute with Phrynion which was partially (but only partially) about Neaera. His interests subsumed hers. The silence of Athenian legal speeches was part of what caused women like Neaera to live alienated from their own interests.

The ability of either slaves or women, even within the relationships that constrained them, to exercise agency could provoke considerable anxiety. Near the close of his prosecution of Neaera on the charge of passing herself off as married to a citizen (Stephanus), Apollodorus asked the jurors to imagine what they would say to their wives, daughters, or mothers after the trial if they acquitted Neaera. If that happened, Apollodorus warned, the laws will be annulled; the habits of whores will reign supreme. So you should look out for the women of citizen status as well so that the daughters of poor citizens don't end up unmarried. As it is now, if nature has allowed a girl anything like an average appearance, even if she is poor, the law contributes a sufficient dowry. But if you drag the law through the mud and make it invalid by acquitting this woman, the daughters of citizens who cannot be married because of poverty will certainly be drawn into the business of prostitution and prostitutes will assume the status of free women if they get the right … to share in the religious rites, the sacred ceremonies, and the honors in the city.

(Demosthenes 59.112–13)

Apollodorus suggested that the anxiety about slaves becoming citizens was keenly felt by citizen women, especially those near the bottom whose difference from slaves was least apparent. Yet Apollodorus' imaginary feminine consciousness looks suspiciously like male subjectivity in drag: it concerns itself with public standing, honor, and competition with others. Even his concern for marriage and the *oikos* was not for the bonds of affection this might foster, nor for the economic subsistence it could provide (indeed, Apollodorus envisions an alternative means of support for these unmarried, poor women), but rather for the status it bestowed (cf. Vilatte 1986). In fact, Apollodorus himself imagined a very different reaction by some women: while the most decent would react to Neaera's acquittal with anger, he claimed, those women who lacked discretion would take it as permission to do as they pleased without regard to the laws or their male guardians (Demosthenes 59.111). Neither of Apollodorus' imaginary feminine consciousnesses provides strong evidence that women did—or did not—think like this. In fact, free women's reactions must have varied. In some cases, women and slaves became allies in their conflicts with men (Lysias 1 or Antiphon 1); in others, hostility flared between slaves and women when their interests conflicted, perhaps especially when female slaves gained the status of women through their relationship with free men (Demosthenes 48). But though it may be unclear to what extent Athenian women took part in a culture of public, competitive honor like men or, on the contrary, how far they found their virtues within the *oikos* (Foxhall 1996 and Versnel 1987, both relying on comparative anthropological studies, come to diametrical conclusions), it is clear that neither slaves nor women could pursue their interests in the same ways as men. The silence of the sources in fact constituted part of the structural conditions within which such people acted.

Conclusion

Histories of disputes must allow for a plurality of perspectives, including those of slaves and women, without privileging any as authoritative. Neaera's perspective on her conflict with Phrynion, for example, was no more authentic than the legal formulation; the legal case between Phrynion and Stephanus was not merely a shadow of the "real" dispute between Neaera and her former lover. In fact, the dispute was about different things to different people—a complexity the legal narrative entirely failed to capture. The law gave a particular shape to conflict, a shape which consistently excluded the direct representation of slaves or women as subjects.[6] The law also asserted the authority of its own representations, an authority augmented by the failure of any evidence but the legal orations to survive. Historical accounts of women and slaves must work against both of these features of legal narratives, yet these accounts must also recognize that these characteristics of the law carried important consequences for the lives of slaves and women. The silence of the sources was not merely an unfortunate effect of free men's power; it was also one of its foundations. Yet is was within the structure of the power relations constituted by these silences that women and slaves recognized and pursued their interests, that they became subjects.

Notes

1 The study of these other ways of pursuing disputes is the subject of a literature on "social control": Ellickson 1991; Black 1984. Hunter 1994 considers this form of social control in classical Athens.

2 In trying to give a brief summary of the Athenian legal system, I have had to flatten considerably its procedural complexity. MacDowell 1978, [...].

3 There was a significant distinction among cases based on who had the right to prosecute: in one kind of case, a *dike*, only an aggrieved party himself could sue; in another, a *graphe*, any citizen had the right to initiate proceedings. Scholars often name these suits "private" and "public" respectively. The distinction does not correspond to the division between civil and criminal cases in American law.

4 The practice of challenging someone to torture a slave has usually been understood as a way of introducing the testimony of the slave to the court (for example, Todd 1990, Gagarin 1996). Against this view I argue elsewhere (Johnstone, forthcoming) that although litigants found a rhetorical advantage in having dared their opponent to torture a slave, such dares were used primarily outside the law as a

way of conducting a dispute. The torture of a slave in response to an opponent's challenge was a way of formalizing the settlement of a conflict. It was, moreover, quite different from simply torturing one of your own slaves to extract information (as, for example, Euphiletus threatened to do).

5   In the many discussions of the torture of slaves, for example, no distinction was made between the bodies of males and of females (for example, Lycurgus 1.29–32).

6   It may be that men who brought cases arising from disputes involving women and slaves represented them as "really" about conflicts with other men in part because it was not honorable to litigate with someone of lower status. It seems to have been perfectly acceptable to say that a suit against a female ex-slave was really about her male guardian (Demosthenes 59.1), but in no extant speech did a litigant claim his suit was ultimately aimed at a slave or a woman.

Acknowledgments

The criticisms and suggestions of the volume editors were invaluable in improving this essay. I would also like to thank my friends who read it and responded with helpful comments: Mark Edwards, Mike Jameson, Lisa Maurizio, Ian Morris, and especially Adam Geary.

References

Black, Donald, 1984, "Social Control as a Dependent Variable," in *Toward a General Theory of Social Control*, vol. 1, Donald Black, ed., Orlando, Fla.

Butler, Judith, 1990, *Gender Trouble: Feminism and the Subversion of Identity*, New York.

Carey, C., ed., 1989, *Lysias: Selected Speeches*, Cambridge.

Cohen, David, 1990, "The Social Context of Adultery at Athens," in NOMOS: Essays in Athenian Law, Politics, and Society, Paul Cartledge, Paul Millett, and Stephen Todd, eds, Cambridge.

_____ 1995, *Law, Violence, and Community in Classical Athens*, Cambridge.

Cohen, Edward, 1992, *Athenian Economy and Society: A Banking Perspective*, Princeton, NJ.

Comaroff, John L. and Simon Roberts, 1981, *Rules and Processes*, Chicago.

Conley, John M. and William M. O' Barr, 1990, *Rules versus Relationships: The Ethnography of Legal Discourse*, Chicago.

Dershowitz, Alan M., 1996 "Life Is Not a Dramatic Narrative" in *Law's Stories: Narrative and Rhetoric in the Law*, Peter Brooks and Paul Gewirtz, eds, New Haven, Conn.

Ellickson, Robert C., 1991, *Order Without Law: How Neighbors Settle Disputes*, Cambridge, Mass.

Foucault, Michel, 1985, *The Use of Pleasure*, New York.

Foxhall, Lin, 1996, "The Law and the Lady: Women and Legal Proceedings in Classical Athens," in *Greek Law in Its Political Setting: Justifications not Justice*, L. Foxhall and A.D.E. Lewis, eds., Oxford.

Gagarin, Michael, 1996, "The Torture of Slaves in Athenian Law," *Classical Philology* 91: 1–18.

Halperin, David, 1990, *One Hundred Years of Homosexuality*, New York and London.

Hunter, Virginia J., 1992, "Constructing the Body of the Citizen: Corporal Punishment in Classical Athens," *Echos du Monde Classique* 11: 271–91.

_____ 1994, *Policing Athens*, Princeton, NJ.

Johnstone, Steven, 1994, "Virtuous Toil, Vicious Work: Xenophon on Aristocratic Style," *Classical Philology* 89: 219–40.

_____ (forthcoming), Disputes and Democracy: The Consequences of Litigation in Ancient Athens, Austin, Tex.

Law, John, 1994, *Organizing Modernity*, Oxford.

MacDowell, Douglas, 1978, *The Law in Classical Athens*, Ithaca, NY.

_____ 1989, "The Oikos in Athenian Law," *Classical Quarterly* 39: 10–21.

Mather, Lynn and Barbara Yngvesson, 1980-81, "Language, Audience, and the Transformation of Disputes," *Law and Society Review* 15: 775-821.

Maurizio, Lisa, (forthcoming), "The Panathenaic Procession: Participatory Democracy on Display?" in *Democracy, Empire, and the Arts*, Kurt Raaflaub and Deborah Boedecker, eds, Cambridge, Mass.

Merry, Sally Engle, 1990, *Getting Justice and Getting Even: Legal Consciousness among WorkingClass Americans*, Chicago.

Millett, Paul, 1991, *Lending and Borrowing in Ancient Athens*, Cambridge.

Ober, Josiah, 1989, *Mass and Elite in Democratic Athens*, Princeton, NJ.

Pomeroy, Sarah B., 1975, *Goddesses, Whores, Wives, and Slaves*, New York.

_____ 1994, *Xenophon: Oeconomicus*, Oxford.

Rhodes, P.J., 1981, *A Commentary on the Aristotelian "Athenaion Politeia,"* Oxford.

Scott, Joan W., 1988, *Gender and the Politics of History*, New York.

_____ 1991, "The Evidence of Experience," *Critical Inquiry* 17: 773–97.

Smith-Rosenberg, Carroll, 1986, "Writing History: Language, Class, and Gender," in *Feminist Studies/Critical Studies*, Teresa de Lauretis, ed., Bloomington, Ind.

Spelman, Elizabeth V., 1988, *The Inessential Woman: Problems of Exclusion in Feminist Thought*, Boston, Mass.

Todd, S. C., 1990, "The Purpose of Evidence in Athenian Courts," in *NOMOS: Essays in Athenian Law, Politics, and Society*, Paul Cartledge, Paul Millett and Stephen Todd, eds, Cambridge.

_____ 1993, *The Shape of Athenian Law*, Oxford.

Versnel, H. S., 1987, "Wife and Helpmate: Women of Ancient Athens in Anthropological Perspective," in *Sexual Asymmetry*, Josine Blok and Peter Mason, eds, Amsterdam.

Vilatte, Sylvie, 1986, "La femme, l'esclave, le cheval, et le chien: les emblemes du kalos kagathos Ischomaque," *Dialogues d'Histoire Ancienne* 12: 271–94.

Yngvesson, Barbara and Lynn Mather, 1983, "Courts, Moots, and the Disputing Process," in *Empirical Theories about Courts*, Keith O. Boyum and Lynn Mather, eds, New York.

Women Writing in Rome and Cornelia, Mother of the Gracchi

by Judith P. Hallett

From the first decades of the second century B.C.E. onward, Latin literary works represent women as creators of written texts. For example, at lines 20–75 of his *Pseudolus*, a comedy that can be dated by its production notice to 191 B.C.E., the playwright Plautus portrays a lovesick young man named Calidorus as smitten by the courtesan Phoenicium. He is especially distressed by a letter he has just received from her. In the excerpts from this letter that Calidorus and his ingenious slave—the title character Pseudolus—read aloud, she proclaims her passion for Calidorus and complains that she has been sold to another man. To be sure, Pseudolus makes sarcastic remarks about Phoenicium's handwriting, style, and sentiments. Still, she is characterized as employing a sophisticated literary vocabulary and several poetic figures of speech. Such details, albeit in the portrait of a fictional character, imply that Plautus (and presumably his audience) thought women, even those of nonelite backgrounds, capable of writing as men do.

Many later Roman authors of the classical era, which extends from the time in which Plautus wrote to the early second century C.E., refer to the writings of several historical women from the first centuries B.C.E. and C.E. Unfortunately, most of these Latin texts by women have not survived to modern times. One such woman, Clodia, enjoyed close ties with some of the most politically powerful men in mid-first century B.C.E. Rome. Her controversial brother, Publius Clodius Pulcher, served as tribune of the people in 58 B.C.E. and was a candidate for higher office when he was assassinated by his foes six years later. Her more conservative husband, Quintus Caecilius

Metellus Celer, served as consul in 60 B.C.E. after a military career that included commanding the province of Cisalpine Gaul in northern Italy.[1]

Scholars generally identify this Clodia as the lover of the poet Catullus (ca. 84–54 B.C.E.), a woman immortalized in his verses under the metrically equivalent name of "Lesbia." Catullus's choice of this particular pseudonym for his inamorata pays homage to the sixth-century B.C.E. Greek female poet Sappho of Lesbos. His high regard for Sappho took other forms as well: he translated some of her lyrics into Latin and adopted her distinctive meter in two of his poems. In calling Clodia "Lesbia," Catullus may also have implied that Clodia, like Sappho, not only wrote but also valued elegantly crafted poetry.[2]

Significantly, at *Pro caelio* 27.64, a lawcourt speech of 56 B.C.E. defending another young man with whom Clodia was romantically involved, the orator and statesman Cicero dismissively refers to Clodia by the Greek noun *poetria*, "female poet." Furthermore, several of Catullus's poems that represent "Lesbia" as speaking may be interpreted as alluding to her performances of poetry, some of it poetry that she wrote herself. Among these Catullan poems are two, 70 and 72, written in the elegiac meter. They portray her as voicing a memorable literary conceit: that she would prefer Catullus's affections even to those of the god Jupiter. In poem 51—which loosely translates lyrics by Sappho, retaining their original Sapphic meter—Catullus first speaks in his own person of "Lesbia" as "sweetly laughing"; later, he appears to assign "Lesbia" an entire, final, stanza in which she laughs at his idleness and self-preoccupation.

Clodia's own daughter, Caecilia Metella, would seem to have followed her mother's example. The poet Ovid represents her, at *Tristia* 2.437–38, as having written poetry, and at the same time as having been celebrated, pseudonymously, as "Perilla." In the early years of the first century C.E., Ovid also writes from exile on the Black Sea to another young female poet he calls Perilla, perhaps his own stepdaughter, at *Tristia* 3.7. Most noteworthy of these lost women writers is the younger Agrippina (15–59 C.E.), the sister of the emperor Gaius Caligula, wife of the emperor Claudius, and mother of the emperor Nero. Her memoirs are cited as an important historical source in the late first century C.E. by the elder Pliny at *Natural History* 7.46 and in the early second century C.E. by the historian Tacitus at *Annales* 4.53.3.

Nevertheless, a few writings in Latin by Roman women of the classical period have been preserved for posterity. The earliest dates from the second half of the second century B.C.E.: two fragments of a letter from a noblewoman named Cornelia to her son Gaius Sempronius Gracchus. This Cornelia was the daughter of Publius Cornelius Scipio Africanus, a military leader renowned for ending Rome's second Punic War against the North African city of Carthage when he defeated Hannibal at Zama in 202 B.C.E. But she is more often remembered as the mother of two politically radical sons, Gaius Sempronius Gracchus and his elder brother, Tiberius. Both of these men died at the hands of their enemies while serving as tribunes of the people, Tiberius in 133 B.C.E. and Gaius in 121.[3]

The letter urges Gaius not to seek the office of tribune, but to think of her sorrowful plight instead. It was likely to have been written ca. 124 B.C.E. Born ca. 195–190 B.C.E., Cornelia would have been in her late sixties or early seventies at the time she wrote it. According to Plutarch's biography of Gaius Gracchus, Cornelia for many years after Gaius died lived in her villa near the Bay of Naples, invariably "recalling the accomplishments and sufferings of her dead sons for her guests without any display of emotion."

According to Plutarch's *Life of Tiberius Gracchus,* Cornelia's husband Tiberius Sempronius Gracchus, consul in 177 B.C.E., had left her a widow in 153 B.C.E., shortly after she gave birth to the last of their twelve children. Plutarch also relates that after Cornelia was widowed, she rejected a marriage proposal from a Ptolemaic ruler of Egypt and devoted herself totally to rearing the three of her offspring who survived their childhood—Tiberius, Gaius, and a daughter, Sempro-nia.[4] Other Roman authors of later periods stress Cornelia's dedication to the upbringing of her children as well. In the *Dialogue on* Oratory, Tacitus has one of his characters maintain that the extensive role played by elite Roman mothers in their sons' education during the bygone republican era resulted in a superior breed of Roman political leader. Cornelia, mother of the Gracchi, is the first such woman Tacitus cites by way of illustration.

So, too, the first-century C.E. writer Valerius Maximus recalls an anecdote about Cornelia's emotional investment in her sons at *Memorable Deeds and Sayings* 4.4—namely, that when a woman staying at Cornelia's bayside villa insisted on displaying her own extremely beautiful jewelry, Cornelia detained her in conversation until Tiberius and Gaius returned from school, and then announced, "These are *my* jewels." Later in the same century the elder Pliny describes a celebrated statue of Cornelia at 34.31 of his *Natural History.* The inscription at its base—"Cornelia, daughter of Africanus, [mother] of the Gracchi"—survives to this day.[5] Pliny reports that in his own time the statue stood in the portico of Octavia, sister of the emperor Augustus, an edifice erected around 20 B.C.E. But Pliny also notes that the statue had originally been placed in the portico of Metellus, a structure built during Cornelia's own lifetime. Evidently Romans of later generations hailed Cornelia as a paragon of matronal and maternal excellence because her own contemporaries had inspired them to do so.

These two fragments of Cornelia's letter survive only in the manuscripts of the biographer and historian Cornelius Nepos. He is thought to have died in approximately 24 B.C.E., a full century after Cornelia would have written these words to her younger son. No other extant classical Roman source quotes from these fragments directly. Some scholars have found this fact disconcerting. Some also consider the unusual style of the letter, the self-absorption of its first-person speaker, the self-assertive stance adopted, the angry language employed, and the raw emotions expressed to be at strong variance with their own, modern notions of an admirable mother. As a result, there are those who would question Cornelia's authorship of this letter and even the female gender of the author.[6]

Yet both Cicero, in an essay of the mid-first century B.C.E., and the late first century C.E. oratorical authority Quintilian, at *Institutes* 1.1.6, provide evidence that letters of this sort were in public circulation after Cornelia's death, familiar to them and no doubt to others as well. At *Brutus* 211, Cicero portrays his friend Atticus as arguing for the powerful impact of fathers, teachers, and mothers on children's speech. To establish the beneficial influence of maternal speaking habits, he notes that he has read the letters of Cornelia and states that their style proves the Gracchi "to have been nurtured not so much in her bosom as in her speech." Quintilian invokes Cornelia for the same purpose, observing that "we have heard that their mother, Cornelia, had contributed greatly to the eloquence of the Gracchi, a woman whose extremely learned speech also has been handed down to future generations."

Echoes of Cornelia's letter also resonate in similarly indignant speeches assigned to mature women by Roman authors writing in the twenties and teens B.C.E. These echoes further suggest that Cornelia's letter is authentic, or at least that the letter was thought to be by Cornelia at around the time Nepos was writing. The earliest of these Latin texts that call Cornelia's letter to mind is the work of the historian Livy: in a speech delivered by the fictional Veturia—aged mother of the early republican leader Coriolanus—to dissuade her traitorous son from invading Rome in 488 B.C.E. It appears at chapter 40 of Livy's second book, which appears to have been completed around the time of Nepos's death.[7]

The other speeches are slightly later in date. Those of three other fictional figures—the Carthaginian queen Dido, the Latin queen Amata, and the mother of Euryalus—in books 4, 7, 9, and 12 of Vergil's epic *Aeneid* were written shortly before 19 B.C.E. The fictional speech that the love poet Propertius in his final elegy places in the mouth of a historical personage, Augustus's stepdaughter Cornelia, is generally dated to 16 B.C.E., the year of this woman's death.[8]

All of these texts resemble, and hence appear to echo, Cornelia's letter by utilizing—much as Cornelia does with Gaius—a series of rhetorical questions, two or more of them "anaphoric," that is, beginning with the same word. Several of these texts, like Cornelia's letter, emphasize the speaker's old age, characterizing it as wretched and sorrowful, and refer to old age with the word *senecta* (rather than with the more ordinary term *senectus*).[9] Several raise the prospect of the speaker's imminent death (indeed, Propertius's Cornelia is portrayed as already dead, and as speaking to her family from the grave). The speech that Livy gives to Veturia in particular recalls Cornelia's by using the conjunctions *nec ... nec* to negate a pair of comparative adjectives that govern personal pronouns in the dative case. Cornelia proclaims *id neque maius neque pulchrius cui quam atque mihi esse videtur*, "to no one does this seem either greater or more beautiful than it does to me" (with the alternative spelling *neque ... neque*); Livy's Veturia observes *nihil iam pati nec tibi turpius nec mihi miserius possum*, "I am able to endure nothing more shameful for you nor more miserable for myself."

Still, one peculiar feature of Cornelia's letter that it does not share with these later speeches assigned to women in Augustan literary works is its "genderless" style. There is no grammatical detail, such as an adjectival or pronomial form, in the first excerpt of Cornelia's letter that specifically identifies the author as a woman. Only two details in the second excerpt—the repeated use of the feminine adjective form *mortua*, "dead"—make Cornelia's sex clear. Indeed, at one point Cornelia uses the grammatically masculine phrase *deum parentem*, "parent-god, parent who has become a god" (rather than the feminine *deam*, "parent-goddess"), when speaking of herself.

Cornelia also behaves in what might be regarded as a "male-identified" or "transgendered" Roman fashion, too.[10] She one-ups Gaius in the "patriotism department" by deprecating his defense of vengeance against enemies. She appropriates the role of father-protector by portraying the future without her parental guidance as a time of unrelieved misery for her son. The paucity of feminine grammatical forms, obviously, lends support to those who deny the authenticity of this letter, viewing it as a male forgery. So do Cornelia's efforts to adopt masculine conduct in competing with, disparaging, and asserting her irreplaceability for her son. So, for that matter, do her outspoken criticisms of an adult male child, whose formal rights and authority far surpass her own in a patriarchal society such as that of republican Rome.

But among the similarities between Cornelia's letter and several of these speeches by women in later literary texts of the early Augustan period is what would appear to be a distinctively "female" approach to family matters of political import. Cornelia evinces, and several of the women whose words call hers to mind are portrayed as evincing, a similar style of "motivational" political speech in their communications with their sons. In determining what is best for the state as well as for their sons, they accord priority to family ties and family members— feelings over abstract political rights and principles. They define themselves through their connections with rather than their separation from others and ground their actions in an ethic based on relationships and responsibilities rather than one based on abstract rights.

In this way Cornelia and these female figures in Augustan literary texts call to mind observations about women's morally freighted decision making by the psychologist Carol Gilligan—albeit observations about how most women, in contrast to most men, tend to make moral judgments and decisions today.[11] The family-oriented, emotionally grounded nexus of political values to which Cornelia and these "maternal" females in Augustan literary texts subscribe certainly stands in sharp contrast to the value system of various Roman men who lived several centuries prior to Cornelia, men remembered for their conduct in their role as fathers. These are men renowned for upholding abstractly defined principles of civic conduct at the expense of family solidarity and for engaging in punitive behavior against family members who do not adhere to these same principles.

The individual family headed by a *paterfamilias*, father in his role as family head, comprised the basic structural unit of the ancient Roman state, *res publica* (referred to by the Romans themselves as their "fatherland," *patria*). Correspondingly, the Romans of the classical era viewed the right of *patria potestas*—the supreme power invested in a Roman father over offspring and other dependents—as the foundational basis for Rome's system of law and order. Several legends about the early republican period featured *patres* who, in their capacity as high officeholders, publicly exercised their *patria potestas* by exiling or even executing traitorous or merely insubordinate sons for offenses against the state. Whatever their historical accuracy, these legends furnished Romans of later times with an acceptable rationale for unfeeling paternal severity.[12]

One is the story of Rome's first consul, Lucius Junius Brutus, who—as Livy relates at 2.3–5 of his history—ordered his sons slain when they conspired to overthrow the republican form of government that their father had established in 509 B.C.E. Another such tale is that of Titus Manlius

Torquatus, consul in 340 B.C.E. At 8.7.15, Livy scripts for Torquatus a stern speech accounting for his decision to put his own adult son to death for military insubordination and thereby "set a painful but healthy example for the youth of the future." Livy portrays Torquatus as caught in a difficult situation, "having to forget either the Roman state or myself." Although Livy's Torquatus acknowledges that he is emotionally stirred by inborn affection for children, as well as by his son's display of manly excellence, he insists on having his son bound to the stake and hacked to death with an axe. He attributes greater importance to upholding, rigidly and inflexibly and by right, a single, abstractly defined principle of civic conduct—the necessity of adhering to military discipline—than to upholding the affective pull of family ties on him personally.

As a Roman woman, Cornelia—and, for that matter, the legendary Veturia—could not punish her son in the same way that Torquatus did his. She held no *patria potestas* and was ineligible to hold high political office. Nor was it in her interest for her son to leave Rome or even distance himself from their family. Women, even elite and privileged women like Cornelia, depended on their male kin for their social identity and personal validation far more than did a man like Torquatus. Thus, in instances where she and her son disagreed, she—like Veturia—was limited to motivational as opposed to punitive speech.

Admittedly, Cornelia's efforts in this letter at motivating Gaius to see things from her own point of view take the form of browbeating: angry, confrontational, demanding, egotistical, intimidating, and explicitly shame- (and implicitly guilt-) inducing rhetoric. She even compares the behavior of her son to that of a personal political enemy, *inimicus*. "Other than those who murdered Tiberius Gracchus," she says, "no *inimicus* has made my life as difficult as you have." Cornelia then proceeds to fault Gaius for failing to shoulder the responsibilities of his dead siblings, to minimize her anxieties in old age, and to make an adequate attempt at pleasing and obeying her. By associating her son's opposition to her own wishes with "destroying our country," she returns to the earlier theme of limiting revenge on personal enemies to activities that do not harm one's nation, suggesting that Gaius is not merely comparable to her enemies but also no better than his own.

So, too, Livy's Veturia engages in browbeating, referring to her son Coriolanus as an enemy (albeit *hostis*, an enemy of the state rather than a personal political foe, since he has in fact joined forces with the hostile Volscians). Like Cornelia, she confronts her son with a series of rhetorical questions to arouse his shame and guilt. Her guilt-inducing tactics additionally include blaming Rome's woes on herself because she gave birth to Coriolanus, and she comes across as angrier and more confrontational than Cornelia. But Coriolanus's more outrageous political conduct warrants as much—and Veturia, like Cornelia, proves successful in getting her son to do what she wants.

The first excerpt of Cornelia's letter implies that she has been asked by her son to endorse an abstractly defined mode of civic conduct: the principle of taking vengeance on personal enemies, *inimici*, in the political arena. And indeed Cornelia seems to voice agreement with Gaius in proclaiming this principle *pulchrum,a* beautiful thing. But at the same time she refuses to adhere to this principle rigidly and inflexibly. Instead, Cornelia asserts that such vengeance should not be pursued if it harms one's country. What is more, Cornelia does not view keeping the Roman state strong and harm-free as inimical to and incompatible with family loyalties or in conflict with the affective pull of family ties. Rather, a family-oriented, emotionally grounded ethos underlies her definition of appropriate moral, civic, and patriotic conduct.

For example, in voicing the expectation that Gaius would take the place of his dead siblings in the context of taking Gaius to task for mistreating her, Cornelia represents her son as derelict in his family duties and in turn seeks to exploit her son's own family feelings. She accuses their entire family of acting insanely, not just Gaius. Although she begs Gaius to postpone his campaign for tribune until she is dead and can no longer feel, she reminds him that he will eventually be praying to her as the god of his parent, and should feel shame at having abandoned ancestral deities when they were still alive.

Livy also portrays Veturia as linking what is politically consequential with what is best for a family and its feelings. Thus she emphasizes the emotional pain her son's conduct has caused her personally and underscores her son's emotional ties and obligations to both herself and his other family members. Strikingly, Livy has Veturia call attention to Coriolanus's wife and sons, whereas Cornelia says nothing about Gaius's wife and offspring.[13] Veturia goes further than Cornelia in another regard. In addition to citing her own role as Coriolanus's biological mother, she characterizes Rome itself as having given birth to and nurtured him (*te genuit atque aluit*). In so doing, Livy depicts Veturia as equating her son's native land with herself, recasting his *patria* as his "*matria.*"

A similar emphasis on obligations to and emotions roused by family members informs various speeches by Vergil and Propertius that echo Cornelia's letter. At *Aeneid* 7.359–72, Vergil portrays the Latin queen Amata as angrily addressing her husband Latinus in protest of his political decision to betroth their daughter Lavinia to the Trojan exile Aeneas rather than to her nephew Turnus. She demands that family ties and family feeling be given pride of place in forging political alliances. At 12.56–63 Vergil has Amata address Turnus himself. Employing language that Vergil also has the mother of the Trojan warrior Euryalus use when addressing her fallen son at 9.473 ff., she characterizes him as "a source of respite for my unfortunate old age" (*senectae / tu requies miserae*). She then urges him not to engage in single combat with Aeneas for Lavinia's hand. Significantly, at 7.357, Vergil describes Amata's indignant expression of family-first sentiments as speaking *solito matrum de more*, "in the manner customary for mothers." He thus implies that her fierce display of emotion, insistence on sensitivity to family members' feelings, and privileging of blood family ties over other political goals are typical features of maternal motivational speaking.

At 4.11.87–94, Propertius has his newly dead Cornelia issue two sets of orders to her two young sons (both of whom grew up to become consuls, one in 1 C.E. and the other in 6).[14] Cornelia's commands to them merely concern the way in which she would like them to treat their father's next wife or—if their father does not remarry—their father himself. And it merits notice that she defines her sons' major obligations to their father as emotional in nature. At 65–68 this Cornelia may mention her husband's and her brother's high public offices and demand that her daughter imitate her own monogamous and moral lifestyle. Nevertheless, she wants her male children to lift their father's spirits in her absence, not follow his political example.

Consequently, these Roman literary portrayals of motivational speeches by mature, maternal women—speeches expressing family-oriented, emotionally grounded political values that resemble Cornelia's letter in striking ways—do not merely argue for the authenticity of Cornelia's letter, or at least its perceived authenticity during the Augustan era. They also suggest that this kind of motivational speaking and these political values were closely associated with Roman women. And this is because such speaking and such values were initially associated with a much scrutinized and admired woman like Cornelia.

The word *initially* warrants emphasis. Cornelia's letter to Gaius, which articulates Roman political values that include a concern for families and their emotional needs, is a radical document. Its author's priorities differ greatly from those inculcated by Roman patriarchal tradition, which pitted political against familial and emotional concerns. We should also note that these family-first political priorities are not limited in their later influence to speeches assigned by Augustan authors to female characters. The Roman literary figures and historical personages who gave voice to these priorities in the generations after Cornelia include men as well. At 6.817 ff. of the *Aeneid*, for example, Vergil portrays Anchises, the father of Aeneas, as deploring the behavior of several political leaders who endured and caused suffering as a result of paying insufficient heed to family feeling. Among these men are the legendary son-slayers Brutus and Torquatus. Anchises also hails the men kindred to Cornelia—Gracchi who were her husband and sons, Scipiones who were her father and son-in-law—but merely as illustrious men destined to lead the Roman state. While Cornelia's letter may not be a canonical Latin literary text, or even a well-known one, the radical views it voices seem to have exerted a significant impact on the most highly esteemed work of classical Roman literature.

Notes

1 T. P. Wiseman, *Catullus and His World: A Reappraisal* (Cambridge: Cambridge University Press, 1985), pp. 35–53.

2 Wiseman, pp. 115 ff., 135, 138, and 152–55.

3 *Cornelius Nepos: A Selection, Including the Lives of Cato and Atticus*, trans. with introductions and commentary by Nicholas Horsfall (Oxford: Clarendon Press, 1989), pp. 125–26.

4 See also Horsfall, p. 125.

5 Horsfall, p. 42.

6 Horsfall, pp. 41–42, 104, 125–26.

7 R. M. Ogilvie, *A Commentary on Livy, Books 1–5* (Oxford: Clarendon Press, 1965), p. 2.

8 Horsfall, *A Companion to the Study of Virgil* (Leiden: E. J. Brill, 1995), pp. 20 ff.; *Propertius, Elegies Book* IV, ed. W. A. Camps (Cambridge: Cambridge University Press, 1965), p. 153.

9 P. G. W. Glare, ed., *Oxford Latin Dictionary* (Oxford: Oxford University Press, 1982).

10 For the concept of "transgendering," see Barbara McManus, *Classics and Feminism: Gendering the Classics* (New York: Twayne Press, 1997), pp. 91–118.

11 Carol Gilligan, *In a Different Voice: Psychological Theory and Women's Development* (Cambridge, Mass.: Harvard University Press, 1982), pp. 24–63.

12 See s.v. *"patria potestas" by* Barry Nicholas and Susan Treggiari in the *Oxford Classical Dictionary,* 3d ed., ed. Simon Hornblower and Antony Spawforth (Oxford: Oxford University Press, 1996), pp. 1122–23.

13 For Gaius's wife and son, see Plutarch, *Gaius Gracchus* 15, 17.5.

14 Judith P. Hallett, "Queens, *Princeps,* and Women of the Augustan Elite: Propertius' Cornelia-Elegy and the *Res Gestae Divi Augusti,"* in *The Age of Augustus,* ed. Rolf Winkes (Providence, R.I.: Acta Archaeologica, 1986).

Two Epistolary Fragments Attributed to Cornelia, Mother of the Gracchi

Verba ex epistula Corneliae Gracchorum matris ex libro Cornell Nepotis de Latinis Historicis excerpta.

1 Dices pulchrum esse inimicos ulcisci. Id neque maius neque pulchrius cuiquam atque mihi esse videtur, sed si liceat re publica salva ea persequi. Sed quatenus id fieri non potest, multo tempore multisque partibus inimici nostri non peribunt, atque uti nunc sunt erunt potius quam res publica profligetur atque pereat.

Eadem alio loco.

2 Verbis conceptis deierare ausim, praeterquam qui Tiberium Gracchum necarunt, neminem inimicum tantum molestiae tantumque laboris, quantum te ob has res, mihi tradidisse; quem oportebat omnium eorum quos antehac habui liberos partis tolerare atque curare ut quam minimum sollicitudinis in senecta haberem, utique quaecumque ageres, ea velles maxime mihi placere atque uti nefas haberes rerum maiorum adversum meam sententiam quicquam facere, praesertim mihi cui parva pars vitae superest. Ne id quidem tam breve spatium potest opitulari, quin et mihi adversere et rem publicam profliges? Denique quae pausa erit? ecquando desinet familia nostra insanire? ecquando modus ei

rei haberi poterit? ecquando desinemus et habentes et praebentes molestiis insistere? ecquando perpudescet miscenda atque perturbanda re publica? Sed si omnino id fieri non potest, ubi ego mortua ero, petito tribunatum; per me facito quod lubebit, cum ego non sentiam. Ubi mortua ero, parentabis mihi et invocabis deum parentem. In eo tempore non pudet te eorum deum preces expetere, quos vivos atque praesentes relictos atque desertos habueris? Ne ille sirit Iuppiter te ea perseverare, nec tibi tantam dementiam venire in animum. Et si perseveras, vereor ne in omnem vitam tantum laboris culpa tua recipias uti in nullo tempore tute tibi placere possis.

Translation by Judith P. Hallett

These words are excerpted from a letter of Cornelia, mother of the Gracchi, from the book of Cornelius Nepos on Latin Historians.

1 "You will say that it is a beautiful thing to take vengeance on enemies. To no one does this seem either greater or more beautiful than it does to me, but only if it is possible to pursue these aims without harming our country. But seeing as that cannot be done, our enemies will not perish for a long time and for many reasons, and they will be as they are now rather than have our country be destroyed and perish."

The same letter in a different passage.

2 "I would dare to take an oath swearing solemnly that, except for those who have murdered Tiberius Gracchus, no enemy has foisted so much difficulty and so much distress upon me as you have because of all these matters: you who should have shouldered the responsibilities of all of those children whom I had in the past. You should have shown concern that I might have the least anxiety possible in my old age; that, whatever you did, you would wish to please me most greatly; and that you would consider it sacrilege to do anything of rather serious significance contrary to my feelings, especially as I am someone with only a short portion of my life left. Cannot even that time span, as brief as it is, be of help in keeping you from opposing me and destroying our country? What end will there finally be? When will our family stop behaving insanely? When will we cease insisting on troubles, both suffering and causing them? When will we begin to feel shame about disrupting and disturbing our country? But if this simply cannot take place, seek the office of tribune when I am dead; as far as I am concerned, do what will please you when I shall not perceive what you are doing. When I have died, you will sacrifice to me as a parent and call upon the god of your parent. Does it not shame you

to seek prayers of those gods, whom, when they were alive and on hand, you considered abandoned and deserted, at that time? May Jupiter not for a single instant allow you to continue in these actions nor permit such madness to come into your mind. And if you persist, I fear that, by your own fault, you may incur such trouble for your entire life that at no time would you be able to make yourself happy."

BIBLIOGRAPHY

Primary Sources
Marshall, P. G., ed. *C. Nepotis vitae cum fragmentis.* Leipzig: Teubner, 1977.

Secondary Works
Camps, W. A., ed. *Propertius, Elegies Book IV.* Cambridge: Cambridge University Press, 1965.
Gilligan, Carol. *In a Different Voice: Psychological Theory and Women's Development.* Cambridge, Mass.: Harvard University Press, 1982.
Glare, P. G. W., ed. *The Oxford Latin Dictionary.* Oxford: Oxford University Press, 1982.
Hallett, Judith P. "Queens, *Princeps* and Women of the Augustan Elite: Propertius' Cornelia-Elegy and the *Res Gestae Divi Augusti*" In *The Age of Augustus: An Interdisciplinary Conference,* edited by Rolf Winkes. Providence and Louvain-La-Neuve: Acta Archaeologica, 1986.
Horsfall, Nicholas. *A Companion to the Study of Virgil.* Leiden: Brill Academic Publishers, 1995.
———. *Cornelius Nepos: A Selection Including the Lives of Cato and Atticus.* Translated with introductions and commentary by Nicholas Horsfall. Oxford: Clarendon Press, 1989.
McManus, Barbara F. *Classics and Feminism: Gendering the Classics.* New York: Twayne Press, 1997.
Nicholas, Barry, and Susan M. Treggiari. "*Patria potestas*" In *The Oxford Classical Dictionary,* edited by Simon Hornblower and Anthony Spawforth. Oxford: Oxford University Press, 1996.
Ogilvie, R. M. *A Commentary on Livy, Books 1–5.* Oxford: Oxford University Press, 1965.
Wiseman, T. P. *Catullus and His World: A Reappraisal.* Cambridge: Cambridge University Press, 1985.

CONCLUSION

Comprehension Questions

1   Who was Ptah-Hotep? What are the Maatian principles espoused in his writing?

2   How does Ptah-Hotep's conceptualization of public speaking differ from that developed by ancient Greek and Roman scholars? What are some similarities?

3   Describe life for women in ancient Greece and Rome.

4   Identify some female figures from ancient Greece and Rome who contributed to our understandings of rhetoric.

Critical Thinking Questions

1   Reflecting on the Johnstone article, what does it mean to interrogate the gaps and silences in ancient Greek legal oratory? How might this be useful to us as we attempt to theorize rhetoric "outside the box?"

2   How was the letter writing of the Roman matron Cornelia reflective of traditional female writing? How did it embody the attributes of male letter writers?

3   Why is it important to examine women's letter writing from earlier periods? What can be learned from examining women's letter writing?

Unit Summary

"Unit 2" took up the call to examine rhetorical theories from a critical/cultural lens by first taking us back to the African origins of rhetoric some three thousand years prior to the writings of ancient Greek and Roman scholars often pegged as the grandfathers of the discipline. We then explored the lives of Greek and Roman men and women to shed light on the ways traditional views of rhetoric are not, in fact, neutral, but presumptive of the elite male experience. The readings suggested ways to explore the lives and public-speaking efforts of women and slaves by looking at artifacts other than speeches, including the gaps in legal oratory and letter writing by women.

"Unit 3" continues our journey through the history of the development of rhetorical theory to the medieval period, roughly fifth century CE to the fifteenth century CE, and where we will further explore rhetoric as it was shaped by the historical context of the period.

UNIT 3

WRITING WOMEN IN

Rhetoric and the Medieval Era

Consider:

1   What comes to mind when you think of the medieval era?

2   Identify a famous figure from the medieval era (e.g., a writer, poet, political leader).

3   During the medieval era, the ability to read and write—although still not widespread during this period—became more common among the elite classes. How does literacy shape our understandings of communication? Of politics and governance?

The medieval era is the time that extends roughly from the fifth to the fifteenth century CE. "Unit 3" introduces us to life in the medieval era—also referred to as the Middle Ages—particularly as it was influenced by the spread of Christianity, literacy, and education. Each of these cultural trends shaped the development of rhetorical theory and, in some instances, opened doors for women who had been previously shut out from the public sphere of decision making and debate. This unit's introduction and readings show us how women drew upon and also augmented existing rhetorical styles and structures handed down from ancient Greek and Roman scholars. Their efforts point to ways that marginalized groups might practice rhetoric despite widespread cultural and economic sanctions against their speaking out.

The Influence of Christianity

A good deal of the work of the ancient Greco-Roman scholars of earlier centuries was lost during the medieval era. Proponents of Christianity were skeptical of what remained of the writings of the ancient scholars, who were deemed suspect due to their paganism. The prevailing Christian belief that speakers served as a mouthpiece of God and that persuasion was sparked by divine intervention undermined the classical emphasis on the canons of rhetoric. Explains Glenn (1997): the "Church Fathers pronounced pagan rhetoric to be ineffectual so far as Christian persuasion went, for successful evangelism depended on the grace of God" (p. 92). Still, Christians such as Augustine often utilized Greco-Roman rhetorical theory toward the ends of preaching, spreading, and defending Christian teachings. Early in this period, Augustine, who lived in North Africa, wrote *On Christian Doctrine* (397 CE, 427 CE) in which he drew from Plato and Cicero as he conveyed his ideas on Christian preaching.

Christian teachings shaped all facets of life including relationships between men and women. Much as Aristotle, whose beliefs on women were discussed in "Unit 2," Augustine and other well-known Christian leaders viewed women as inferior to men, as incapable of reason, and inherently weaker. Wrote St. Paul: "Let a woman learn in silence with all submissiveness. I permit no woman to teach or to have authority over men; she is to keep silent" (1 Tim. 2.11-15, quoted in Glenn 1997, p. 79).

As was the case in earlier centuries, women in the medieval era had few if any rights, although their lives varied considerably depending on whether they were a member of the aristocracy or the peasantry. Options for girls and young women were largely limited to marriage or the convent. As was the case in earlier periods, wives were deemed the legal property of husbands but this did not mean they lacked influence in families and marketplaces. When husbands were away on business or military expeditions, or when wives became widowed, women of the elite classes managed family estates, directed large staffs, and ran family businesses. Women of lesser means worked side by side with husbands tending and managing land or in the trades (Glenn 1997; Richardson 1997).

Literacy was not widespread during the medieval period, least of all among women and girls. Misogynist Christian teachings, much as the Aristotelian writings on the sexes centuries earlier, were influential on this point. Women were believed to be naturally emotive and irrational and thus incapable of intellectual activity and development. St. Thomas Aquinas, writing in the thirteenth century, situated women's primary purpose as procreation, that woman is "undisciplined by mind, an imperfection that justified her subjection to men" (Glenn 1997, p. 78). Convents provided a way for girls and women to obtain an education, limited though it may have been. Girls may have received tutoring at home or occasionally alongside boys in schools. But universities were closed to women.

Medieval Women and Visionary Writing

Despite formidable obstacles in the form of legal sanction, dubious science, and religious reprimand, the medieval era was not bereft of women who wrote books, poems, letters, and plays (Thiébaux 1994). Given the economic and legal structures, religious institutions and prevailing norms, expectations, etc., how did women establish their right to speak?

First, women who wrote during the medieval era devised unique ways to cultivate ethos. Recall from "Introduction to Unit 1" the contradiction—or impossible position, if you will—faced by women when it came to establishing ethos, the Aristotelian proof indicating the importance of speaker credibility. Women (and other marginalized groups, e.g., slaves) were deemed by nature to be "lesser men," emotional, irrational, and thus not credible as orators or decision makers. Women, then, had to devise creative ways to establish their authority to speak or write. One way women did this was through appeals to divine intervention. Many women, among them Hildegard of Bingen (1098–1179), Julian of Norwich (1343–1415), and Angela Merici (1474–1540) wrote as church mystics or visionaries who rhetorically positioned themselves as vessels for the word of God. These women situated themselves squarely within the widely accepted conservative tradition of the Christian church, but did so to justify their right to speak.

Hildegard was a German nun who founded a convent where she lived and wrote most of her life. Her writings cover a wide range of topics including weather patterns, the nature of the cosmos, and medicine. In her books and letters, Hildegard details visions she received from God. She assumed a humble position stating that she was writing "in the name of the 'living light', not her own" voice (Dronke 1984, p. 203). Rhetorically, Hildegard established authority to speak since to deny her voice would ostensibly be to deny the voice of God. Additionally, Hildegard referenced her own weakness, modesty, and status as a church outsider to further underscore her authority to criticize the power structures of the church.

Julian of Norwich was an English woman, most likely convent-educated, whose most well-known work was *Revelations of Divine Love Showed to a Devout Ankress by Name Julian of Norwich*. The rhetorical scholar Cheryl Glenn (1997) calls *Revelations* an example of "feminist liberatory theology" wherein Julian draws on the words of the Bible to justify women's place within the church (p. 99). Julian articulated a "theology of inclusion" that enveloped women "in the worship of and dialogue with God, as well as including a female representation in the Trinity" (p. 99). Her writing thus "expan[ded] the medieval rhetorical tradition" (p. 99).

Writing through vision or revelation not only enabled women to creatively address the issue of ethos, it allowed them to expand "what counts" as evidence in speaking and writing. Women during this time period were denied access to a university education where they may have learned traditional Greco-Roman forms of reasoning, so they established arguments based on personal experience and observation. One example is provided by the writings of Angela Merici, an Italian woman who wrote during the latter part of the medieval era. Much as Hildegard of Bingen and Julian of Norwich, Angela quoted scripture to justify her writing and to establish a place for women in the church. She also relied extensively on experience to justify her writings on roles for women in the church and the broader community (Dietrich 2005).

Medieval women's visionary writings often drew on allegory as a literary device to convey religious and scientific narratives. Allegories—used by male and female writers alike—are stories in which the characters often symbolize or stand in for larger universal ideas or concepts. Allegory was an apt device for women visionaries as it is often used to convey a universal truth or moral that is hidden or obscured; thus, it enabled women writers to establish arguments for women's moral authority in the church even in the midst of widely accepted church practices that excluded or demeaned women. For Hildegard, allegory provided a way to argue in favor of women's religious authority, and provided a "medium in which spiritual reality is given visual form" (Dietrich 1997, p. 205). Two hundred years later, as the medieval era was transitioning to the Renaissance, Christine de Pizan relied on allegory to speak out against misogynist representations of women in art and literature and to illustrate women's intellectual and moral capacities. The rhetorical contributions of Hildegard of Bingen and Christine de Pizan are detailed in "Unit 3" readings.

Medieval Women and Letter Writing

Just as the church provided an unlikely starting point for women's rhetorical contributions during the medieval era, so too did the practice of letter writing, or *ars dictaminis*, which grew to an established form of communication during this period. "Unit 2" briefly introduced us to women who wrote personal correspondence during the classical era. The medieval rhetorical scholar James Murphy (1974) notes that by the seventh century CE, formulas for writing letters had become widespread (p. 200). By the 1080s, books instructed would be letter writers in the practice, drawing upon Cicero's ideas for style and structure written centuries earlier. Letter writers or scribes played a very important role in taking down and transmitting the ideas of kings and politicians who may not have been able to write themselves. Letters were used by religious and political leaders to make proclamations, establish contracts, and to conduct business.

Hildegard of Bingen utilized the letter format for reporting her visions to both male and female religious figures (Ahlgren 1993). A detailed examination of Hildegard's more than two hundred letters shows that when Hildegard communicated with men she was aware of the need to use bolder claims to legitimate her visions and establish her authority. Her letters to women were more intimate in nature.

Not only women of the church, but those from middle- and upper-class families drew on letter writing as a means of communicating during this period. It was not unusual for medieval women of the propertied classes to wield considerable power within the family estate, particularly when husbands were away on business or military outings. If a woman were widowed, running the family affairs may have fallen to her completely. Women's business correspondence can be found in collections of letters from wealthy English families, such as the Paston family (Richardson 1997; Watt 1993). These letters reveal a number of interesting points. First, it was often the case that women wrote letters in a style and structure no different from their fellow male correspondents. This was the case, at least in part, because most often letters were dictated to male scribes. Additionally, however, women's letter writing sounded like a man's because women were no doubt aware of the *ars dictaminis* formula that would grant their voice authority and put them on equal footing with men (Richardson 1997, p. 146). Margaret Paston's letters show she wrote with authority and used written correspondence to arrange educational and marriage prospects for her children, to maintain the extensive family properties, and to collect rents (Watt 1993, p. 134).

Christine de Pizan's letters show a progression over time. Her letters from 1401–1403, in which she challenged the misogynist portrayals of women in a popular poem, followed the traditional formulas of *ars dictaminis*. In her 1410 publication, *Lamentation on the Evils of Civil War*—an open letter written to royalty—de Pizan "cultivates and thematizes a specifically female voice" that she uses to argue for peace (Richards 1993, p. 139).

Preview of Unit Readings

The readings in "Unit 3" provide us examples of the primary writings of two medieval women, Hildegard of Bingen and Christine de Pizan. It is important to note these women were not rhetorical theorists, per se, as we understand Aristotle or Cicero to be. That is, they did not explicitly theorize public speaking or writing. Still, they warrant inclusion in a study of rhetoric and the medieval era for a number of reasons. First, given the cultural, religious, and legal sanctions against women during this period, it is remarkable the extent to which women produced written works. Hildegard and de Pizan were prolific writers whose letters and books often go unnoticed in studies of this period. Second, both women were aware of and addressed the obstacles they faced as women who communicated publicly. They were acutely aware of the need to establish authority, or ethos, in the eyes of a male audience/reader. They were aware of and spoke to widespread beliefs that situated them as irrational, unreasonable, or otherwise untrustworthy persons. By studying their writings, we may glean the rhetorical decisions they made—regarding word choice, structure, etc.—and thus how they strategized to gain a hearing.

References

Ahlgren, Gillian T. W. 1993. "Visions and Rhetorical Strategy in the Letters of Hildegard of Bingen." In Karen Cherewatuk and Ulrike Wiethaus (eds.), *Dear Sister: Medieval Women and the Epistolary Genre*, pp. 46–63. Philadelphia: University of Pennsylvania Press.

Dietich, Julia. 1997. "The Visionary Rhetoric of Hildegard of Bingen." In Molly Meijer Wertheimer (ed.), *Listening to Their Voices: The Rhetorical Activities of Historical Women*, pp. 199–214. Columbia, SC: University of South Carolina Press.

——. 2005. "Women and Authority in the Rhetorical Economy of the Late Middle Ages." In *Rhetorical Women: Roles and Representations*, pp. 21–43. Tuscaloosa, AL: University of Alabama Press.

Dronke, Peter. 1994. *Women Writers of the Middle Ages: A Critical Study of Texts from Perpetua to Marguerite Porete.*" Cambridge: Cambridge University Press.

Glenn, Cheryl. 1997. *Rhetoric Retold: Regendering the Tradition from Antiquity Through the Renaissance.* Carbondale, IL: Southern Illinois University Press.

Murphy, James J. 1974. *Rhetoric in the Middle Ages: A History of Rhetorical Theory from Saint Augustine to the Renaissance.* Berkeley: University of California Press.

Richardson, Malcolm. 1997. "Women, Commerce, and Rhetoric in Medieval England." In Molly Meijer Wertheimer (ed.), *Listening to Their Voices: The Rhetorical Activities of Historical Women*, pp. 133–149. Columbia, SC: University of South Carolina Press.

Thiébaux, Marcelle. 1994. *The Writings of Medieval Women: An Anthology.* New York: Garland Publishing.

Watt, Diana. 1993. "No Writing for Writing's Sake: The Language of Service and Household Rhetoric in the Letters of the Paston Women." In Karen Cherewatuk and Ulrike Wiethaus (eds.), *Dear Sister: Medieval Women and the Epistolary Genre*, pp. 122–138. Philadelphia: University of Pennsylvania Press.

A Benedictine Visionary in the Rhineland

by Marcelle Thiébaux

Hildegard of Bingen (1098–1179)

Abbess, preacher, prophet, poet—Hildegard revealed in her writings an extraordinary genius and personal energy. The power and variety of her works are unparalleled among medieval women writers: she produced works of drama and lyric, music, mysticism, and cosmology. She made forays into scientific fields: the lore of animals and gems, and medicine (some of it admittedly folkloric). To accompany her three books of dazzling and encyclopedic allegorical visions, she left directions for the artistic illuminations that would elucidate her meaning.

Much of what Hildegard wrote contains autobiographical information. She dispatched hortatory letters, carrying on a voluminous, sometimes vehement correspondence with notable people of her day, among them Eleanor of Aquitaine and Henry II of England; Bernard of Clairvaux; popes Eugenius III, Anastasius IV, Adrian IV, and Alexander III; and the emperors Conrad III and Frederick Barbarossa.

After German emperors had appropriated vast powers in the previous century, and princes of state became guardians of the papacy, there followed a new period of unrest. During Hildegard's lifetime, the Church now wanted more control. Hildegard's contemporary, Pope Gregory VII, won supporters to his cause, and a schism developed. When Emperor Frederick Barbarossa endorsed one pope and Hildegard another, Hildegard unleashed a letter of rage against Frederick. "Listen to this, O King, if you wish to live," she threatened, "or else my sword will strike you!" Another of her scathing letters to the archbishop of Mainz proved astoundingly oracular, for soon after she foretold his doom the archbishop was deposed and banished.

Other gentler letters passed between Hildegard and the neighboring Benedictine mystic, Elisabeth of Schonau. An important letter to Guibert of Gembloux, who served as her secretary, vividly describes the workings of Hildegard's visions, and the appearance in them of a mirroring "shadow of the Living Light." Further sources on her life emerge from two contemporary biographies by the monks Godefrid and Theodoric, for which Hildegard herself wrote a dozen passages. A later inquiry into her life and miracles, conducted in the thirteenth century for Pope Gregory IX, adds to her *Vita*.

The woman who would be known as the "Sybil of the Rhine" was born into a noble family at Bermersheim near Alzey. Hildegard recalls that her visions of great light began when she was five. From the age of eight, she lived at Disibodenberg, founded by the 7th-century Irish bishop, St. Disibod. The convent had stood for four centuries, but the admitting of women was recent. There her parents, Hildebert and Mechthild, had placed her, their tenth and last child, under the tutelage of the anchoress Jutta of Sponheim. The monk Volmar was another teacher, later to be her friend and secretary. The Benedictine house of Disibodenberg emphasized prayer and study, the reading of scripture and psalms, together with physical labor. For women this meant nursing, spinning, and weaving, but Hildegard's spiritual daughters also attained high skill in copying and illuminating manuscripts. Despite Hildegard's protestations of ignorance, she certainly studied Latin, although she may not have had the same kind of classical education in Ovid, Horace, Terence, and Virgil as Hrotswitha had in the Ottonian renaissance of the tenth century.

Hildegard reluctantly succeeded her beloved Jutta as *magistra* of the community in 1136. She was thirty-eight. Five years later, when she was nearly forty-three, she experienced a vision of stunning radiance in which a heavenly voice commanded her to write what she saw. She resisted, however, until sickness compelled her to record the succession of visions she experienced over the next ten years.

Sickness was for many mystics a fruitful source and accompaniment of their visionary life, as it would be for Elisabeth of Schonau and, in fifteenth-century England, for Julian of Norwich. Hildegard describes her bodily pains "in all her veins and flesh to the marrow," declaring that from her birth she was "entangled as it were in a net of suffering."[1] Debility would prevent the mystic from performing her usual tasks and serve to separate her from others. If sickness befell the woman who was unwilling to write or dictate her visions, relief came only when she finally consented to record them. Hildegard's visions formed the beginning of her first book, *Scivias* (*Know the Ways*), short for *Scito vias domini*, "Know the ways of the Lord." Pope Eugenius read parts of the *Scivias* before the Synod of Trier in 1147. He also examined Hildegard, ascertaining the authenticity of her visions. She answered his interrogations with truth and simplicity. Once she gained papal approval, she began to be famous.

The next year, 1148, Hildegard wished to found her own convent, a move that would give her greater independence. She was refused permission by Kuno, abbot of Disibodenberg, who probably intended to retain control over a community that was gaining renown. Hildegard's temper flared. She was adamant, "a rock of stone." She bitterly upbraided Kuno, calling him an "Amalekite," a member of the bedouin tribe named in Exodus 17.8 as enemies of the Israelites in the desert. Her further enfeebling sickness persuaded Kuno that divinity had a hand in Hildegard's affairs, and she was allowed to begin building the independent convent of Rupertsberg near Bingen on the Rhine. She moved with fifty nuns, all noblewomen, to the new site in 1150.

During this same period Hildegard was completing the *Scivias* with the aid of Volmar. She also had the help of her secretary-companion Richardis von Stade, to whom she was intensely devoted. When a transfer for Richardis was proposed to a position of authority in another convent, Hildegard wrote letters denouncing Richardis's brother, the archbishop Hartwig, who had sought the promotion for his sister. Hildegard wrote to Pope Eugenius as well, but did not succeed in stopping Richardis's departure. She suffered. When Richardis died within a few years, Hildegard, now submissive to God's will, wrote a sympathetic letter to Hartwig.

She began her second book of visions, the *Liber vitae meritorum* (*The Book of Life's Rewards*) (1158–1163), while traveling and preaching throughout towns and cities in Germany. Though chronically ill she made four preaching journeys from the ages of sixty to seventy-two, not shrinking from contact with large numbers of people. She visited Cologne on three occasions and was very taken with the St. Ursula legend, then at its height with the discovery of what appeared to be bones belonging to the saint and her companions. Hildegard composed thirteen lyrics honoring the saint. Her admirer and correspondent Elisabeth of Schönau, recorded her own visions of Ursula's band [...], refashioning the legend in what would be its most influential form.

Hildegard wrote her third and final book of visions, the *Liber divinorum operum* (*The Book of Divine Works*) between 1163 and 1173. In it she suggests a human microcosm, mapping the interconnections between humanity and the cosmos; between the human and divine Christ; between the physical body, with its humors, and the soul, with its emotions and capacity for salvation. An in-dwelling fiery force, the *ignea vis*, unites all aspects of the universe in a way that is tranquil, rational, and harmonious. The composing unity of this work contrasts with the swirling commotion of the *Scivias*.

In the last year of her life when she was over eighty, Hildegard became embroiled in a controversy when she agreed to the burial of a nobleman, said to be excommunicated, at Rupertsberg. She insisted that the dead man had been sanctified at the end. All the same, her convent was placed under episcopal interdict. Hildegard refused to yield, she appealed to a powerful ally, and the interdict was lifted. On September 17, 1179, according to her biographer, she went to meet her Celestial Bridegroom in a blessed death. The sky was said to be illuminated with circles of light and shining red crosses, as if to reveal to her sisters the visions she had received.

Hildegard's visions, converted into marvelous, even hallucinating poetry and prose, are characterized by lights, fires, smokes, and stenches. Her universe abounds in geometric forms—circle, square, and oval. Cosmic elements of earth, air, fire, and water are manifest through suns and stars, skies and winds, lights and shadows, mountains and grottoes. Society is represented by kings and soldiers and hunters. Edifices rear up with their stone columns and balustrades, towers and temples, altars and crosses. Birds, fish, and animals appear that are naturalistic or monstrous. Speaking or trumpeting through clouds, fogs, and winds are vivid human forms: men and women with massive body, feet, hands, head, and hair. Hildegard's womanly presences are august and potent, with intensely feminine bodies, breasts, and wombs. A pregnant Ecclesia continually teems with offspring. The Cosmic Egg, filled with stars, similarly imparts a sense of female fertility. For Hildegard, the feminine divinity in her writing is represented with maternal fecundity and procreative force, not—as among later German mystics like Mechthild of Magdeburg—with the bridal and erotic imagery of the celestial marriage.

In a characteristic vision, a light will pour over some central scene (such as a mountain, a river, or an abyss) while an apocalyptic human presence, a beast, or an architectural structure materializes. Following the revelation will be an explanation of its meaning. Colors are conspicuous. Christianity and holy scripture are associated with the redness of the Savior's blood. White is the color of martyrs, and the dove of the holy spirit. Greenness and greening—*viriditas*—have a peculiar meaning for Hildegard, associated with the divinely energetic life-force that pulses through all being. "The soul is the body's green life-force," states *The Book of Divine Works*.[2]

Hildegard's visions—startling, even hallucinating, in their brilliance—have attracted the notice of modern pathologists, who trace their source in her lifelong illnesses.[3] And yet, the effective power of her visions, like those of seers from Elisabeth of Schonau to Joan of Arc, remains undiminished by scientific diagnosis. The mystic's gift was in some way dependent upon her physical suffering.

Passages 1–4, translated here from Hildegard's works, include her "Solemn Declaration" (*Protestificatio*) and selections from the first three visions in Book I of the *Scivias*. The *Scivias* comprises twenty-six visions. The six visions of Book I trace the history of God, humankind, and the world from the Creation and Fall to the promise of a Savior. In seven visions, Book II describes the redemption through Christ, as the Sun, and his mystic marriage with the Church at the foot of the Cross. Book III, in thirteen visions, represents through architectural imagery the rebuilding of salvation by divine powers, or virtues; the last days of the world; the last struggle against Satan; and the Church's entrance into the apocalypse of Eternity.

Passages 5–7 are taken from the *Liber Vitae Meritorum*. The *Book of Life's Rewards* is a vast cosmic psychomachia of verbal battles. Vices and Virtues, represented as universal forces, confront one another, using words as weapons. These verbal battles culminate in the triumphs of human goodness, with the Church's entrance into eternal glory. The book opens with a central figure of God. Hildegard's dazzled eyes behold him as a powerful, perfect, and transcendant Man, who reaches from the clouds to the depths of the abyss. He is the principle of all being, who guides human salvation on its course. Hildegard observes his cloud-shaped trumpet that blasts forth three winds. Above these hover three clouds: one fiery, one turbulent, and one luminous. These trumpeted winds of God's blowing invite comparison with Chaucer's windy, smoky trumpets in *The House of Fame*. Now Hildegard's verbal psychomachia unfolds. The book also dramatizes eternity's punishments and rewards. The last selection tells of the heavenly virgins, ecstatic companions of the Lamb. The scene is reminiscent of the biblical Book of Revelations, and anticipates the procession of 144,000 maidens in the fourteenth-century English *Pearl*.

A sample of Hildegard's gem lore appears in passages 8 and 9, from the book commonly known as *Physica*, or *Liber Simplicis Medicinae* (*The Book of Simple Medicine*). This work, together with her *Causae et Curae*, or *Liber compositae medicinae* (*The Book of Advanced and Applied Medicine*), belongs to Hildegard's great work on the natural sciences, the *Liber subtilitatum diversarum naturarum creaturarum*. The *Physica* lists in nine sections the basic and curative properties of plants, the elements, trees, stones, fish, birds, animals, reptiles, and metals. In the fourth book of the *Physica*, called *De lapidibus*, Hildegard composed twenty-six short chapters on precious stones: emerald, jacinth, onyx, beryl, sardonyx, sapphire, sard, topaz, chrysolite, jasper, prasius, chalcedony, chrysophrase, carbuncle, amethyst, agate, diamond, magnet, ligurius, crystal, pearl—both true and false—camelian, alabaster, chalk, and a category of "other gems."

Section 10 includes seven lyrics from the *Symphonia harmoniae caelestium revelationum* (*Symphony of the Harmony of Celestial Revelations*). The first two honor the Blessed Virgin Mary, the third celebrates St. Maximinus, and the fourth consists of an antiphon and responsory to St. Ursula, to whom Hildegard was especially devoted. There is a love song chanted to Christ by his virgin brides, written for the spiritual daughters of her convent. On ceremonial occasions, the nuns were permitted to wear bridal white, veils, and coronets, a custom that brought a rebuke from one of Hildegard's male critics. The last two lyrics are hymns to the green life-force, that *viriditas* which is one of Hildegard's pervasive presences.

In addition to these works, the letters, and the three visionary books mentioned above, Hildegard's opus includes her drama (the *Ordo Virtutum*), two books on her secret language (the *Lingua ignota* and the *Litterae ignotae*), a book of exegesis on the Psalms, the *Expositio Evangeliorum*, and two works of hagiography, honoring St. Rupert and St. Disibod.

1. A Solemn Declaration Concerning the True Vision Flowing from God: *Scivias*. Protestificatio

Lo! In the forty-third year of my temporal course, when I clung to a celestial vision with great fear and tremulous effort, I saw a great splendor. In it came a voice from heaven, saying:

"O frail mortal, both ash of ashes, and rottenness of rottenness, speak and write down what you see and hear. But because you are fearful of speaking, simple at expounding, and unlearned in writing—speak and write, not according to the speech of man or according to the intelligence of human invention, or following the aim of human composition, but according to what you see and hear from the heavens above in the wonders of God! Offer explanations of them, just as one who hears and understands the words of an instructor willingly makes them public, revealing and teaching them according to the sense of the instructor's discourse. You, therefore, O mortal, speak also the things you see and hear. Write them, not according to yourself or to some other person, but according to the will of the Knower, Seer, and Ordainer of all things in the secrets of their mysteries."

And again I heard the voice from heaven saying to me: "Speak these wonders and write the things taught in this manner—and speak!"

It happened in the year 1141 of the Incarnation of the Son of God, Jesus Christ, when I was forty-two years and seven months old, that a fiery light of the greatest radiance coming from the open heavens flooded through my entire brain. It kindled my whole breast like a flame that does not scorch but warms in the same way the sun warms anything on which it sheds its rays.

Suddenly I understood the meaning of books, that is, the Psalms and the Gospels; and I knew other catholic books of the Old as well as the New Testaments—not the significance of the words of the text, or the division of the syllables, nor did I consider an examination of the cases and tenses.

Indeed, from the age of girlhood, from the time that I was fifteen until the present, I had perceived in myself, just as until this moment, a power of mysterious, secret, and marvelous visions of a miraculous sort. However, I revealed these things to no one, except to a few religious persons who were living under the same vows as I was. But meanwhile, until this time when God in his grace has willed these things to be revealed, I have repressed them in quiet silence.

But I have not perceived these visions in dreams, or asleep, or in a delirium, or with my bodily eyes, or with my external mortal ears, or in secreted places, but I received them awake and looking attentively about me with an unclouded mind, in open places, according to God's will. However this may be, it is difficult for carnal man to fathom.

Once the term of my girlhood was completed, and I had arrived at the age of perfect strength which I mentioned, I heard a voice from heaven saying:

"I am the Living Light who illuminates the darkness. I have, according to my pleasure, wondrously shaken with great marvels this mortal whom I desired, and I have placed her beyond the limit reached by men of ancient times who saw in me many secret things. But I have leveled her to the ground, so that she may not raise herself up with any pride in her own mind. The world, moreover, has not had any joy of her, or sport, or practice in those things belonging to the world. I have freed her from obstinate boldness; she is fearful and anxious in her endeavors. She has suffered pain in her very marrow and in all the veins of her body; her spirit has been fettered; she has felt and endured many bodily illnesses. No pervading freedom from care has dwelt within her, but she considers herself culpable in all her undertakings.

"I have hedged round the clefts of her heart, so that her mind will not elevate itself through pride or praise, but so that she will feel more fear and pain in these things than joy or wantonness.

"For the sake of my love, therefore, she has searched in her own mind as to where she might find someone who would run in the path of salvation. And when she found one and loved him,[4] she recognized that he was a faithful man, one similar to herself in some part of that work which pertains to me. Keeping him with her, she strove at the same time with him in all these divine studies, so that my hidden wonders might be revealed. And the same man did not place himself above her. But in an ascent to humility, and with the exertion of goodwill when he came to her, he yielded to her with many sighs.

"You, therefore, O mortal, who receive these things—not in the turmoil of deception but in the clarity of simplicity for the purpose of making hidden things plain—write what you see and hear!"

But although I was seeing and hearing these things, I nevertheless refused to write for such a long time because of doubt and wrong thinking—on account of the various judgments of men—not out of boldness but out of the duty of my humility.

Finally, I fell to my sickbed, quelled by the whip of God. Racked by many infirmities, and with a young girl[5] of noble blood and good character as witness—as well as a man I had secretly sought out and discovered, as I have already said—I put my hand to writing.

While I was doing this, I sensed the profound depth of the narration of these books, as I have said. And despite the strength I experienced when I was raised up from my sickness, I carried out that work with difficulty to the end, completing it after ten years. These visions and these words took place during the days of Heinrich, Archbishop of Mainz;[6] Conrad, Emperor of the Romans;[7] and Kuno,[8] abbot of Mount St. Disibodenburg under Pope Eugenius.[9]

I have spoken and written this, not according to the invention of my heart, or of any man, but as I saw these things in the heavens and heard and perceived them through God's sacred mysteries. And again I heard a voice from the sky saying to me, "Shout, therefore, and write this way!"

2. The Iron-Colored Mountain and the Radiant One: *Scivias.* Book I, Vision 1

I saw what seemed to be a huge mountain having the color of iron. On its height was sitting One[10] of such great radiance that it stunned my vision. On both sides of him extended a gentle shadow like a wing of marvelous width and length.[11] And in front of him at the foot of the same mountain stood a figure full of eyes everywhere.[12] Because of those eyes, I was not able to distinguish any human form.

In front of this figure there was another figure, whose age was that of a boy, and he was clothed in a pale tunic and white shoes.[13] I was not able to look at his face, because above his head so much radiance descended from the One sitting on the mountain.[14] From the One sitting on the mountain a great many living sparks cascaded, which flew around those figures with great sweetness.[15] In this same mountain, moreover, there seemed to be a number of little windows, in which men's heads appeared, some pale and some white.[16]

And see! The One sitting on the mountain shouted in an extremely loud, strong voice, saying: "O frail mortal, you who are of the dust of the earth's dust, and ash of ash, cry out and speak of the way into incorruptible salvation! Do this in order that those people may be taught who see the innermost meaning of Scripture, but who do not wish to tell it or preach it because they are lukewarm and dull in preserving God's justice. Unlock for them the mystical barriers. For they, being timid, are hiding themselves in a remote and barren field. You, therefore, pour yourself forth in a fountain of abundance! Flow with mystical learning, so that those who want you to be scorned because of the guilt of Eve may be inundated by the flood of your refreshment!

"For you do not receive this keenness of insight from man, but from that supernal and awesome judge on high. There amidst brilliant light, this radiance will brightly shine forth among the luminous ones. Arise, therefore, and shout and speak! These things are revealed to you through the strongest power of divine aid. For he who potently and benignly rules his creatures imbues with the radiance of heavenly enlightenment all those who fear him and serve him with sweet love in a spirit of humility. And he leads those who persevere in the path of justice to the joys of everlasting vision!"

3. The Fall of Lucifer, the Formation of Hell, and the Fall of Adam and Eve: *Scivias*. Book I, Vision 2

Then I saw what seemed to be a great number of living torches, full of brilliance. Catching a fiery gleam, they received a most radiant splendor from it. And see! A lake appeared here, of great length and depth, with a mouth like a well, breathing forth a stinking fiery smoke. From the mouth of the lake a loathsome fog also arose until it touched a thing like a blood vessel that had a deceptive appearance.

And in a certain region of brightness, the fog blew through the blood vessel to a pure white cloud, which had emerged from the beautiful form of a man, and the cloud contained within itself many, many stars. Then the loathsome fog blew and drove the cloud and the man's form out of the region of brightness.

Once this had happened, the most luminous splendor encircled that region. The elements of the world, which previously had held firmly together in great tranquillity, now, turning into great turmoil, displayed fearful terrors.

[Hildegard hears a voice explaining the meaning of what she has seen:]

The "great number of living torches, full of brilliance" refers to the numerous army of heavenly spirits blazing forth in their life of blessedness. They dwell with much honor and adornment, for they have been created by God. These did not grasp at proudly exalting themselves, but persisted steadfastly in divine love.

"Catching a fiery gleam, they received a most radiant splendor from it" means that when Lucifer and his followers tried to rebel against the heavenly Creator and fell, those others who kept a zealous love of God came to a common agreement, and clothed themselves in the vigilance of divine love.

But Lucifer and his followers had embraced the sluggardly ignorance of those who do not wish to know God. What happened? When the Devil fell, a great praise arose from those angelic spirits who had persisted in righteousness with God. For they recognized with the keenest vision that God remained unshaken, without any mutable change in his power, and that he will not be overthrown by any warrior. And so they burned fiercely in their love for him, and persevering in righteousness, they scorned all the dust of injustice.

Now "that lake of great length and depth" which appeared to you is Hell. In its length are contained vices, and in its deep abyss is damnation, as you see. Also, "it has a mouth like a well, breathing forth a stinking, fiery smoke" means that drowning souls are swallowed in its voracious greed. For although the lake shows them sweetness and delights, it leads them, through perverse deceit, to a perdition of torments. There the heat of the fire breathes forth with an outpouring of the most loathsome smoke, and with a boiling, death-dealing stench. For these abominable torments were prepared for the Devil and his followers, who turned away from the highest good, which they wanted neither to know nor to understand. For this reason they were cast down from every good thing, not because they did not know them but because they were contemptuous of them in their lofty pride.

"From that same lake a most loathsome fog arose, until it touched a thing like a blood vessel that had a deceptive appearance." This means that the diabolical deceit emanating from deepest perdition entered the poisonous serpent. The serpent contained within itself the crime of a fraudulent intention to deceive man. How? When the Devil saw man in Paradise, he cried out in great agitation, saying, "O who is this that approaches me in the mansion of true blessedness!" He knew himself that the malice he had within him had not yet filled other creatures. But seeing Adam and Eve walking in childlike innocence in the garden of delights, he—in his great stupefaction—set out to deceive them through the serpent.

Why? Because he perceived that the serpent was more like him than was any other animal, and that by striving craftily he could bring about covertly what he could not openly accomplish in his own shape. When, therefore, he saw Adam and Eve turn away, both in body in mind, from the tree that was forbidden to them, he realized that they had had a divine command. He realized that through the first act they attempted, he could overthrow them very easily.

The line "in this same region of brightness he blew on a white cloud, which had emerged from the beautiful form of a man, and the cloud contained within itself many, many stars" means this: In this place of delight, the Devil, by means of the serpent's seductions, attacked Eve and brought about her downfall. Eve had an innocent soul. She had been taken from the side of innocent Adam, bearing within her body the luminous multitude of the human race, as God had preordained it.

Why did the Devil attack her? Because he knew that the woman's softness would be more easily conquered than the man's strength, seeing, indeed, that Adam burned so fiercely with love for Eve that if the Devil himself could conquer Eve, Adam would do anything she told him. Therefore the Devil "cast her and that same form of a man out of the region." This means that the ancient seducer, by driving Eve and Adam from the abode of blessedness through his deceit, sent them into darkness and ruin.

4. The Cosmic Egg: *Scivias*. Book I, Vision 3

After this I saw a huge creation, rounded and shaded and shaped like an egg.[17] It was narrow at the top, wide in the middle, and compact below. At the circumference was a blazing fire[18] that had a kind of shadowy membrane beneath it. Within that fire was an orb of glittering red flame,[19] of such great size that the whole creation was illuminated by it. Above it were aligned in a row three little torches[20] that steadied the orb with their fires so that it would not fall. Sometimes the orb reared itself upwards, and many fires rushed to meet it, so that it then further lengthened its own flames.[21] At other times it sank downwards and a great cold obstructed it, and the glittering red orb quickly retracted its own flames.[22]

But from the fire around the circumference of that creation, a wind gusted forth with its tornadoes.[23] And from the membrane that was under the fire another blast boiled up with its whirlwinds, and they spread here and there throughout the creation. In that same membrane there was a dark fire so horrifying that I was not able to look at it.[24] This fire tore through the entire membrane with its force, full of thundering, storms, and the sharpest stones, both large and small. As long as it raised up its thunder, the brilliant fire and the winds and air were thrown into a turmoil,[25] and lightning flashes outdid the thunder. For that brilliant fire was the first to feel the thunder's commotion.[26] Below that membrane was the purest ether, which had no membrane under it. In the ether I saw an orb of dazzling white fire,[27] very great in size. Two little torches[28] were set brightly above it, steadying the white orb so that it would not swerve from its course. And in that ether, many bright spheres[29] were placed everywhere. Into these spheres the dazzling white orb emptied some portion of itself from time to time, sending out its radiance. And so, the white orb, hastening back toward the glittering red orb and renewing its own flames there, breathed forth those flames among the spheres. And from that ether, a wind blasted forth with its tornadoes, and it whirled everywhere through that creation I spoke of.[30]

Below that same ether I saw a watery air that had a white membrane under it. This air, blowing here and there, provided moisture to the entire creation. Now and then it would suddenly gather itself together, and with a great spattering spew forth a sudden torrent. Then it would softly spread itself and drop a caressing, gently falling rain. But from this place too, a wind gusted forth[31] with its whirling force, and blew everywhere throughout that creation I spoke of.

In the midst of these elements was a sandy globe[32] of great size, and the elements enveloped it in such a way that it could slip neither here nor there. But occasionally, when the elements clashed together in alternation with the winds I mentioned, they caused the sandy globe to be moved to some degree by their force.[33]

And I saw between the North and the East what seemed to be a huge mountain. Toward the North it had much darkness, and toward the East it had much light, so that the light was unable to extend to the shadows, nor could the shadows extend to the light.[34]

5. The Three Trumpeted Winds of God: *Liber Vitae Meritorum*. Vision I, Part 1

I saw a man of such height that he touched everything from the summit of heaven's clouds down to the abyss. From his shoulders upward he was above the clouds in the clearest ether. From his shoulders down to his thighs, he was below the clouds, and in the midst of another white cloud. From his thighs to his knees he was in terrestrial air, and from the knees to his calves, in the earth. From his calves downward to the soles of his feet he was in the waters of the abyss, so that he was standing above the abyss. And he turned toward the East so that he was gazing both East and South. His face flashed forth with such brightness that I could not look at him completely.

At his mouth he had a white cloud shaped like a trumpet, which was full of a rapidly ringing din. When he blew the trumpet it blasted three winds. Each wind had a cloud above it: a fiery cloud, a turbulent cloud, and a luminous cloud. The winds were holding those clouds up. But the wind that had the fiery cloud above it remained in front of the man's face. The other two winds, with their clouds, descended to his chest, and there they spread their blasts. The wind before his face stayed there, and blew from the East to the South.

In the fiery cloud was a living fiery multitude, who were all together in one will and one con-joined life. And before them was spread a tablet full of wings everywhere, which flew with God's commands. When God's commands lifted that tablet on which the Wisdom of God had written its secrets, this multitude zealously examined it together. When they had examined these writings, the power of God rewarded them, so that they resonated together in a single chord of music like that of a mighty trumpet.

The wind that had the turbulent cloud above it blew with the cloud from the South to the East, so that the length and breadth of the cloud were like an open city square. Because of its extent, it could not be grasped by the human intellect. On that cloud was an enormous crowd of the blessed, who all possessed the spirit of life, and who were too numerous to count. Their voices were like the rushing of many waters, and they said: "We have our dwelling places according to the pleasure of the One who has brought forth these winds. And when shall we receive them? For if we were to have our clouds, we would rejoice more than we do now."

But the crowd that was in the fiery cloud responded to them in voices full of psalms: "When the Divinity takes hold of his trumpet he will breathe forth lightning and thunder and burning fire toward the earth. And he will touch the fire that is in the sun, so that all the earth will be moved; and it will come about that God will make manifest his great sign. And then in that trumpet all the tribes of earth and all the families of tongues will shout, as well as all who are inscribed in that trumpet, and here you will have your dwelling place.

The wind over which the luminous cloud was hovering, together with that same luminous cloud, spread itself from the East to the North. But very great shadows, thick and horrible, were coming from the West, and spreading themselves toward the luminous cloud. But the shadows were unable to proceed beyond the luminous cloud.

Within that luminous cloud a Sun [Christ] and a Moon [the Church] appeared. In the Sun there was a lion, and in the Moon a horned goat. The Sun shone above the heavens and through the heavens, and on the earth and beneath the earth, and so it proceeded in its rising and returned to its setting. But as the Sun was moving, the lion advanced with it and in it, plundering and despoiling as they went. When the Sun returned, the lion went back with it and in it, and roared greatly for joy. The Moon, too, in which there was a horned goat, gradually followed the rising and setting of the sun. Then the wind blew and said, "A woman will bear a child, and the horned goat will fight against the North."

In the shadows there was a crowd of lost souls beyond number. When they heard the sound of those singing from the South, they turned away, since they did not wish their society. The leader of these lost souls was called the "Deceiver," for they all follow his works and have been smitten by Christ, so that they are powerless. And all of these were crying in sorrowful voices, saying, "Woe, woe to the injurious and dreadful deeds that flee from life and travel with us toward death."

Then I saw a cloud coming from the North, which extended itself toward these shadows. This cloud was barren of all joy and happiness, for even the Sun did not touch it or extend to it. It was full of evil spirits, who were drifting here and there on it, and contriving to set traps for me. These spirits began to blush with shame on account of the Man. And I heard the old serpent saying among them, "I will make my strong men ready for the bulwarks, and I will fight with all my strength against my enemies."

Then among the men he spat out of his mouth a foamy froth, full of filth with all the vices, and puffed them up with mockery and said, "Ha! Those who are named suns because of their luminous deeds, I will drive them to the baleful, horrible shadows of night." And he blew out a loathsome fog which covered all the earth like the blackest smoke, and from it I heard a great roaring that thundered forth. It roared, "No man will worship another God unless he sees and knows him. What is this, that man cherishes what he does not recognize?" In that same cloud I saw different kinds of vices, each in its own image.

6. Worldly Love and Celestial Love: *Liber Vitae Meritorum.* Vision I, Part 1

The Words of Worldly Love:

The first figure had the form of a man and the blackness of an Ethiopian. Standing naked, he wound his arms and legs around a tree below the branches. From the tree all kinds of flowers were growing. With his hands he was gathering those flowers, and he said:

"I possess all the kingdoms of the world with their flowers and ornaments. How should I wither when I have all the greenness? Why should I live in the condition of old age, since I am blossoming in youth? Why should I lead my beautiful eyes into blindness? Because if I did this I should be ashamed. As long as I am able to possess the beauty of this world, I will gladly hold on to it. I have no knowledge of any other life, although I hear all sorts of stories about it."

When he had spoken, that tree I mentioned withered from the root, and sank into the darkness of which I spoke. And the figure died along with it.

The Reply of Celestial Love:

Then from that turbulent cloud of which I spoke I heard a voice replying to this figure:

"You exist in great folly, because you want to lead a life in the cinders of ashes. You do not seek that life which will never wither in the beauty of youth, and which will never die in old age. Besides, you lack all light and exist in a black fog. You are enveloped in human willfulness as if enwrapped with worms. You are also living as if for the single moment, and afterward you will wither like a worthless thing. You will fall into the lake of perdition, and there you will be surrounded by all its embracing arms, which you with your nature call flowers.

"But I am the column of celestial harmony, and I am attendant upon all the joys of life. I do not scorn life, but trample underfoot all harmful things, just as I despise you. I am indeed a mirror of all the virtues, in which all faithfulness may clearly contemplate itself. You, however, pursue a nocturnal course, and your hands will wreak death."

7. The Celestial Joys of the Virgins: *Liber Vitae Meritorum.* Book VI, Part 6

In that same brightness I looked, as if through a mirror, upon air having the purity upon purity of the most transparent water, and radiating from itself the splendor upon splendor of the sun. The air held a wind which contained all the green life-force of the plants and flowers of paradise and earth, and which was full of all the scent of this greenness, just as summer has the sweetest scent of plants and flowers.

In that air, which I regarded as if through a mirror, were those beings arrayed in the most gleaming robes, seemingly interwoven with gold; they had long sashes encrusted with the most precious stones, that hung from the breast to the foot. From them, moreover, breathed forth the intensest fragrance like that of spices. And they were girded round with belts ornamented with what seemed to be gold, gems, and pearls beyond human understanding.

Encircling their heads they wore crowns of gold intertwined with roses and lilies and stems studded with the most precious stones. When the Lamb of God called to them, the sweetest breath of wind, coming from the mysteries of Divinity, touched those stems so that every kind of lyre song, and lyre and organ music, rang out from them, together with the voice of the Lamb. No one else sang except for those wearing the crowns. Indeed the others were listening to it and rejoicing in it, just as one rejoices in beholding the splendor of a sun not seen before.

And their slippers were so transparent, so bathed in light that they seemed to be shod with a living fountain. Sometimes they stepped forth as if walking on wheels of gold, and then they were carrying their lyres in their hands and playing the lyres. Then they understood and knew and spoke a strange tongue that no one else knew or could speak. I was not able to see the rest of their ornaments, of which there were more.

For while they had lived in the world in their bodies, they had acknowledged their faith in the Creator, and had performed good works. They now, therefore, existed in this blessed tranquillity of bright joy. And since, in the purity of their minds, they had eschewed the fleeting vanities of fleshly delights and had ascended by the Law's commands into the love of the true, burning sun above, they possessed the air having the purity upon purity of the most limpid water, and the splendor upon splendor of the sun radiating forth.

Because of their most sweet desires, which they had proven to God and mortals through the green life-force of their virginity, and the flower-bloom of their minds and bodies when they poured forth the good savor of many virtues—for they had been kindled with ardor by the Holy Spirit—they felt that breath which contained all the green life-force of the plants and flowers of paradise and earth, and which was full of the scent of all greenness, just as summer has the sweetest scent of plants and flowers.

8. Preface on Precious Gems: *Physica*

All stones contain fire and moisture. But the Devil abhors precious stones. He hates and despises them, because he remembers that their beauty shone within him before he fell from the glory that God had given him, and also because precious stones are born of fire, and fire is where he receives his punishment. For he was defeated by God's will and plummeted into the fire. Just so, he was conquered by the fire of the Holy Spirit, when humanity was snatched from his jaws by the Holy Spirit's first breath.

Precious stones and gems arise in the East and in those regions where the sun is especially hot. For the mountains that are in those zones contain a very high temperature like that of fire because of the sun's heat. The rivers in those regions flow and boil continuously because of the sun's excessive heat. Occasionally, a flood gushes forth from those rivers and, swelling, flows upward toward those burning mountains. When the same mountains, burning because of the sun's heat, are touched by those rivers, they hiss wherever the water touches fire or the rivers splash their foam, like a fiery iron or fiery stone when water is poured on it. In that place the foam sticks like a burdock. In three or four days it hardens into stone.

But after the flood of these waters subsides so that the waters return again to their streambed, the foam which had clung in several places to the mountains becomes thoroughly dry, depending on the various hours of the day and the temperature of those hours. And, depending on the temperature of those hours, they acquire their colors and their virtues. As they dry they harden into precious stones. Then from various places they loosen like fish scales and fall into the sand.

When the flood of those running streams rises again, the rivers carry off many stones and conduct them to other countries, where they are found by men. The mountains I mentioned—on which gems of such quality and number are born in this manner—glitter like the light of day.

So precious stones are engendered by fire and by water, and therefore they contain fire and moisture within themselves. They possess many virtues and great efficacy so that many benefits can be brought about by their means. These are good and worthy effects and useful to mankind—not effects of corruption, fornication, adultery, hatred, murder, and similar things that lead to sin and are inimical to man. For the nature of precious stones procures the worthy and the useful, and wards off the perverse and evil, just as virtues cast down vices and just as the vices cannot operate against the virtues.

There are, however, other gems that are not born of those mountains or in the manner described. They arise from certain other, harmful things. From these, according to their natures, good or evil can be brought about with God's permission. For God beautified the foremost angel as if with precious stones. He, Lucifer, seeing them glitter in the mirror of divinity, gained knowledge from this. He recognized that God wished to create many wonderful things. Then his spirit grew proud because the beauty of the gems in him shone forth against God. He thought his power was equal to God's, even greater than God's. For that reason his splendor was extinguished.

But just as God saved Adam for a better destiny, so God did not abandon the beauty and virtue of those precious stones, but desired them to remain on earth with honor and praise, and for medical use.

9. The Emerald: *Physica*

The emerald is formed in the morning of the day and in the sunrise, when the sun is powerfully situated in its sphere and about to set forth on its journey. Then the greenness of the earth and the grasses thrives with the greatest vigor. For the air is still cold and the sun is already warm. The plants suck the green life-force as strongly as a lamb sucks its milk. The heat of the day is just beginning to be adequate for this—to cook and ripen the day's green life-force and nourish the plants so that they will be fertile and able to produce fruit.

It is for this reason that the emerald is powerful against all human weaknesses and infirmities; because the sun engenders it and because all of its matter springs from the green life-force of the air.

Therefore, whoever suffers a malady of the heart, the stomach, or the side, let that person carry an emerald so that the body's flesh may be warmed by it, and the sick one will be healed. But if diseases so overwhelm the patient that their tempest cannot be resisted, then let the patient place an emerald in the mouth so that it may be wetted by the saliva. Let the body frequently absorb the saliva, warmed by the stone, and then spit it out. The sudden attack of those diseases will then in all likelihood cease.

If a person falls down, stricken by epilepsy, place an emerald in the patient's mouth while he is still lying down, and presently the spirit will revive. After the patient is raised up and the emerald is removed from the mouth, let the patient look attentively and say, "Just as the spirit of the Lord fills up the earthly sphere, so let his mercy fill the house of my body so that it may never again be shaken." Let the patient do this for nine consecutive days, in the morning, and the cure will follow. But the patient should always keep the same emerald and gaze at it daily in the morning, all the while saying these words. And the sick person will be made well.

Anyone who suffers especially from headache should hold the emerald before the mouth and warm it with his breath, so that the breath moistens it. The sufferer should then rub the temples and forehead with the moisture. Let it be placed in the mouth and held there for a little while, and the patient will feel better.

Whoever has much phlegm and saliva should heat up a good wine, and then place a linen cloth over a small vessel and the emerald upon the cloth. Pour the warm wine so that it flows through the cloth. This should be done again and again, as if one were preparing lye. Then consume at frequent intervals a mixture of that wine with bean flour, and drink the same wine prepared this way. It purges the brain so that the phlegm and saliva will be lessened.

And if one is gnawed by worms, place a linen cloth on the sore, and on this the emerald, and tie another strip of cloth over it like a poultice. Do this so that the stone may thus grow warm. Keep it there for three days, and the worms will die.

10. *Lyrics: Symphonia Harmoniae Caelestium Revelationum*

O tu, suavissima virga

O you, most delightful branch,
putting forth leaves from the rod of Jesse,
O what a great splendor it is
that Divinity gazed at a most beautiful girl
—just as the eagle fixes his eye on the sun—
when the heavenly Father strove toward
the Virgin's brightness
and he wanted his word to be made flesh in her.

Now when the Virgin's mind was illuminated
by God's mystical mystery,
miraculously a bright flower sprang forth
from that Virgin—
with the celestial!

Glory to the Father and the Son
and to the Holy Spirit,
as it was in the beginning—
with the celestial!

O splendidissima gemma

O brightest jewel,
and serene splendor of the sun,
the fountain springing from the Father's heart
has poured into you.
His unique Word,
by which he created the primal matter of the world
    —thrown into confusion by Eve—
the Father has forged this Word, as humanity,
for you.

Because of this, you are that lucent matter, through
    which that same Word
breathed all the virtues—

just as it drew forth all creatures
from primal matter.

Columba aspexit per cancellos

The dove gazed through the latticed window screen:
before her eyes, the balsam's fragrant moisture
flowed from the luminous Maximinus.

The sun's heat flamed forth
and glittered among the shadows;
from them arose the jewel
of which the purest temple was built
in the virtuous heart.

He stands, a lofty tower made of
the tree of Lebanon, of cypress,
and ornamented with carnelian and jacinth;
he is a city surpassing the arts of all artificers.

He runs, the swift stag, to the fountain
of purest water, flowing
from the most potent stone,
which has refreshed with sweet perfumes.

O makers of unguents and colors, who dwell
in the sweetest greenness
of the gardens of the king,
you rise up to perfect the holy sacrifice
among the rams.

Among you shines this artificer,
this rampart of the temple,
he who desired the wings of an eagle
so that he might kiss Wisdom, his nurse,
in the glorious fecundity of Ecclesia.

O Maximinus, you are the mountain and the valley:
In both you appear, a high edifice,

where the horned goat sprang forth
with the elephant,
and Wisdom dwelled in delight.

You are strong and sweet in sacred ceremonies:
in radiance you ascend the altars
as a smoke of spices
to the pillar's summit of praise.

There you intercede for the people,
who reach to the mirror of light—
to whom there is praise on high.

Antiphon: O rubor sanguinis

O crimson blush of blood,
you who have streamed from that eminence
bordering on divinity,
you are a flower
which the wintry serpent's blast
has never withered.

Responsory: Favus distillans

A trickling honeycomb
was the virgin Ursula;
she yearned to clasp the Lamb of God.
Honey and milk are beneath her tongue—
for she gathered to herself
a garden yielding fruit, and the flower of flowers
in a throng of virgins.

And so, in the most noble morning light,
be glad, Daughter Zion,
that she gathered to herself
a garden yielding fruit, and the flower of flowers
in a throng of virgins.

Glory be to the Father and the Son

and the Holy Spirit,
for she gathered to herself
a garden yielding fruit, and the flower of flowers
in a throng of virgins.

O dulcissime amator

O sweetest lover,
O sweetest embracing love,
help us to guard our virginity.

We have been born out of the dust, ah! ah!
and in the sin of Adam:
most harsh is it to deny
one's longing for a taste of the apple.
Raise us up, Savior Christ.

Ardently we desire to follow you.
O how difficult it is for us, miserable as we are,
to imitate you, spotless and innocent
king of angels!

Yet we trust you,
for you desire to recover a jewel
from what is rotten.

Now we call on you, our husband and comforter,
who redeemed us on the cross.
We are bound to you through your blood
as the pledge of betrothal.
We have renounced earthly men
and chosen you, the Son of God.

O most beautiful form,
O sweetest fragrance of desirable delights,
we sigh for you always in our sorrowful
    banishment!
When may we see you and remain with you?
But we dwell in the world,

and you dwell in our mind;
we embrace you in our heart
as if we had you here with us.
You, bravest lion, have burst through the heavens
and are descending to the house of the virgins.
You have destroyed death, and are building life
in the golden city.
Grant us society in that city,
and let us dwell in you,
O sweetest husband,
who has rescued us from the jaws of the Devil,
seducer of our first mother!

O viriditas digiti Dei

O green life-force of the finger of God,
through which God sets his planting,
you gleam with sublime radiance
like an upright column.
You are full of glory
in the completion of God's work.

O mountain's height,
you will never be overthrown
because of God's indifference.

Solitary you stand
from ancient times as our defense.
Yet there is no armed might
that can drag you down.
You are full of glory.

Glory be to the Father and the Son
and the Holy Spirit.
You are full of glory!

O nobilissima viriditas

O noblest green life-force,
you are rooted in the sun
and in pure white serenity.
You illuminate in a wheel
what no excellence on earth can encompass.
You are encircled in the embrace
of the divine retinue.

You redden like the morning
and bum like the flame of the sun.

Notes

1 Richard Kieckhefer, *Unquiet Souls: Fourteenth-Century Saints and Their Religious Milieu* (Chicago: U of Chicago P, 1984), p. 57, remarks on the mystic's "heaven-sent affliction" of illness and its role in achieving ecstasy.

2 See Marie-Helene Moya, "Le Symbolisme sacré des couleurs chez deux mystiques médiévales: Hildegarde de Bingen; Julienne de Norwich," *Les Couleurs au Moyen* Age, Sénéfiance No. 24 (Aix-en-Provence: Université de Provence, 1988): 255–272; Peter Dronke, "Tradition and Innovation in Medieval Western Colour-Imagery," *Eranos Jahrbuch*, 1972.

3 Oliver Sacks, *Migraine: Understanding a Common Disorder*, (Berkeley, 1985); John F. Benton, "Consciousness of Self and Perceptions of Individuality," in *Renaissance and Renewal in the Twelfth Century*, ed. Robert L. Benton and Giles Constable (Cambridge: Mass., Harvard UP, 1982), pp. 267–268. Sabina Flanagan discusses Hildegard's migraines in her chapter "Potent Infirmities," in *Hildegard of Bingen: A Visionary Life* (London: Routledge, 1989), pp. 200–206.

4 The monk Volmar of Disibodenberg, Hildegard's secretary.

5 This was Richardis von Stade, toward whom Hildegard felt deep affection.

6 Heinrich I of Wartburg, archbishop between 1142 and 1153.

7 Conrad III (1138–1152), who died on crusade in the Holy Land.

8 It was Kuno (fl. c. 1136–1155) who had attempted to bar Hildegard's move to Rupertsberg.

9 Eugenius III (1145–1153). After examining Hildegard, Eugenius gave her permission and encouragement to continue writing her books. This authorization proved a stroke of inspiration or good fortune during a time when it was possible for popes and councils to condemn and bum such books.

10 Notes 10 through 16 represent in abbreviated form the explanations Hildegard receives from the One sitting on the mountain. The iron-colored mountain signifies the strength and immutability of God's eternal realm. The One who has stunned Hildegard's vision is the same One who, reigning over all the spheres of earth and heavenly divinity in unwavering brightness, is incomprehensible to the human mind.

11 The shadow is the sweet, gentle protection of the blessed Defense. It both admonishes and chastises, justly and affectionately, showing the way to righteousness with true equity.

12 This figure is Fear of the Lord (*Timor Domini*). Armored by the keen sight of good and just intentions, he inspires in human beings his own zeal and steadfastness. His acute vigilance drives away that forgetfulness of God's justice that often afflicts mortals.

13 The boylike figure in white shoes is the poor in spirit. In pale submission to God, it puts on a white tunic and faithfully follows the gleaming white footsteps of the Son of God.

14 The radiance descending from the One on the mountain is the shining visitation from that One who governs all creatures, pouring down the power and strength of his blessedness.

15 The living sparks cascading down from the One on the mountain are the many potent virtues that emanate from him. These virtues ardently embrace and soothe those who truly fear God and love poverty of spirit, enfolding them with their aid and protection.

16 The men's heads, some pale and some white, appearing in the little windows, show that human actions cannot be hidden. The pale, dull-colored ones indicate those who are lukewarm and sluggish in their deeds, and therefore dishonorable. The white and shining ones are those who are vigilant.

17 Notes 17 through 34 represent in abbreviated form Hildegard's allegorizations of what she sees. The firmament is Almighty God, incomprehensible in his majesty and unfathomable in his mysteries, the hope of all the faithful.

18 In this fiery circumference, God consumes those who are outside the true faith with the fire of his vengeance, but those remaining within the Catholic faith he purifies with the fire of his consolation.

19 The sun, explained allegorically as the solar Christ, or the Sun of Justice, whose fiery love illumines all things.

20 Mars, Jupiter, and Saturn represent the Trinity, their descending order showing the earthward descent of Christ.

21 The Sun's lengthened rays signify the fecundating power of the Father, at the time of Christ's incarnation, by which the heavenly mystery was effected in the Virgin Mary.

22 This sinking indicates Christ's descent to earth to put on wretched human form and physical suffering, after which he ascended again to the Father, as the Scriptures record.

23 Each of the four speaking winds carries a specific report. The first wind, coming from the South and located in the fiery circumference, is God's word. God the Father reveals his power through the just words of his truth.

24 The North wind, boiling up from the dark region of fire, is the Devil's insane and futile speech.

25 Cosmic storms are provoked by the sin of murder, which brings on heavenly retribution. These storms pelt creation with thunder, lightning, and hail.

26 Divine majesty foresees the crime of murder and punishes it.

27 The Moon, to be understood also as the unconquered Church.

28 Venus and Mercury, to be understood also as the Old and New Testaments guarding the Church.

29 The stars in the ether signify the many splendid works of piety appearing everywhere in the purity of the faith.

30 The West wind, emanating from the purest ether, spreads the strong and glorious teachings of the faith.

31 The East wind, blowing from the humid, airy region, brings salvation through true speech and sermons, with the inundation of baptism.

32 The globe is earth, surrounded by the elements in commotion. Human beings on earth, though connected to the elements, are meant to rule over them.

33 These are divine miracles that shake the bodies and minds of mortals.

34 The mountain is the great fall of man. It stands between diabolical wickedness and divine goodness, between the Devil's deceit— which leads toward damnation—and the light of redemption. The peak of the mountain points downward into the earth's green-growing particles, or grains; its base is rooted in the white membrane of air.

Further Reading

Anton Brück, ed. *Hildegard von Bingen 1179–1979: Festschrift zum 800. Todestag der Heiligen.* Mainz, 1979.

Peter Dronke. "Hildegard of Bingen as Poetess and Dramatist: The Text of *The Ordo Virtutum,*" in *Poetic Individuality in the Middle Ages.* Oxford: Clarendon P, 1970.

_____. "Problemata Hildegardiana." *Mittellateinisches Jahrbuch: Internationale Zeitschrift für Mediävistik/ International. Journal of Medieval Studies* 16 (1981): 97–131.

Sabina Flanagan. *Hildegard of Bingen: A Visionary Life.* London: Rout-ledge, 1989.

Mary Ford-Grabowsky. "Angels and Archetypes: A Jungian Approach to Saint Hildegard." *American Benedictine Review* 41 (1990): 1–19.

Hildegard of Bingen. *Hildigardis abbatissae opera omnia. Patrologiae cursus completus: series latina.* Ed. Jacques-Paul Migne, 221 vols. (Paris, 1841–1868), Vol. 197.

_____. Lyrics. Pudentiana Barth, Maria-Immaculata Ritscher, and Joseph Schmidt-Görg, eds. *Lieder: Nach den Handschriften heraus-gegeben.* Salzburg: Otto Müller, 1969.

_____. Audrey Ekdahl Davidson, ed. *The Ordo Virtutum of Hildegard of Bingen: Critical Studies*. Kalamazoo: Medieval Institute Publications, 1984.

_____. Letters. Adelgundis Führkotter, ed. and trans. *Briefwechsel: Nach den ältesten Handschriften übersezt und nach den Quellen erläutert*. Salzburg, 1965.

_____. Adelgundis Führkötter and Angela Carlevaris, eds. *Scivias*. Corpus Christianorum, Continuatio Mediaevalis 43–43a. 2 vols. Turnhout: Brepols, 1978.

_____. Adelgundis Führkötter, ed. *The Miniatures from the Book Scivias of Hildegard of Bingen from the Rupertsberg Codex*. Trans. Fr. Hockey. Turnhout: Brepols, 1978.

_____. Columba Hart and Jane Bishop, trans. *Scivias*. With an introduction by Barbara Newman. New York: Paulist Press, 1990.

_____. Bruce W. Hozeski, trans. *Book of the Rewards of Life (Liber Vitae Meritorum)*. New York: Garland, 1993.

_____. Bruce Hozeski, trans. "'Ordo Virtutum': Hildegard of Bingen's Liturgical Morality Play." *Annuale Medievale* 13 (1972): 45–69.

_____. Paul Kaiser, ed. *Hildigardis Causae et Curae*. Leipzig, 1903.

_____. Lyrics. Barbara Newman, ed. and trans. *Symphonia: A Critical Edition of the Symphonia Armonie Celestium Revelationum [Symphony of the Harmony of Celestial Revelations]*. Ithaca: Cornell UP, 1988.

_____. J.B. Pitra, ed. *Sanctae Hildigardis Opera. Liber vitae meritorum*. Analecta Sacra, 8. Monte Cassino, 1882. Repr. Farnborough: Gregg Press, 1966.

Barbara Lachman. *The Journal of Hildegard of Bingen: Inspired by a Year in the Life of the Twelfth-Century Mystic*. New York: Bell Tower, 1993.

Werner Lauter. *Hildegard-Bibliographie*. Alzey, 1970.

Barbara Newman. *Sister of Wisdom: St. Hildegard's Theology of the Feminine*. Berkeley: U of California P, 1987.

Miriam Schmitt. "Blessed Jutta of Disibodenberg: Hildegard of Bingen's Magistra and Abbess." *American Benedictine Review* 40 (June 1989): 170–189.

Bernhard W. Scholz. "Hildegard von Bingen on the Nature of Woman." *American Benedictine Review* 31 (1980): 361–383.

Charles J. Singer. *From Magic to Science: Essays on the Scientific Twilight*. Repr. New York: Dover, 1958.

Carolyn Wörman Sur. *The Feminine Images of God in the Visions of Saint Hildegard of Bingen's Scivias*. Lewiston, N.Y.: Edwin Mellen, 1993.

Ingeborg Ulrich. *Hildegard of Bingen: Mystic, Healer, Companion of the Angels*. Trans. by Linda M. Maloney. Collegeville, MN: Liturgical Press, 1993.

Ulrike Wiethaus. "Cathar Influences in Hildegard of Bingen's Play 'Ordo Virtutum.'" *American Benedictine Review* 38 (1987): 192–203.

Emilie Zurn Brunn and Georgette Epiney-Burgard. "Hildegard of Bingen." In *Women Mystics in Medieval Europe*. Trans. Sheila Hughes, pp. 3–38. New York: Paragon House, 1989.

CHRISTINE AND THE ROSE BEFORE THE DEBATE

Christine de Pizan

1. From Christine de Pizan, *The God Of Love's Letter (L'epistre Au Dieu D'amours*, May 1, 1399)[1]

French Verse (Rhyming Decasyllabic Couplets)

[*Cupid, the god of love, addresses this letter to all who are in his service. Presiding over his court, he has received a complaint from an unspecified group of women, concerning the large number of insincere and devious men who attempt to get their favors but who do nothing but slander women, whatever the outcome. Cupid condemns such men but praises those who are loyal and sincere in their love. He then launches into the more general topic of how men treat women.*]

Still I say that a man who says defamatory, offensive, or disgraceful things about women in an effort to scold them (be it one woman, or two, or categorically) is acting contrary to nature. And even if we assume that there are some foolish ones or ones full of many vices of different sorts, lacking faith, love, or any loyalty, domineering, wicked, or full of cruelty, or with little sense of constancy, fickle and changeable, crafty, furtive, and deceptive, must one, on that account, challenge all of them[2] and assert that they are all worthless? When God on high created and formed the angels, the cherubim, seraphim, and the archangels, were there not some of them whose acts were evil? Must one for that reason call the angels wicked? Instead, if someone knows an evil woman, let him watch out for her, without defaming one-third or one-fourth of them, or reprimanding all of them without exception and besmirching their female behavior; for there have been, are, and will be many of them[3] who, kindly and beautiful, are to be praised and in whom virtuous qualities are to be found, their discernment and merit having been proven by their benevolence.

But as concerns those who scold those women who are of but little worth, I still say that they are at fault if they name them and say who they are, where they live, what their deeds are, and of what sort. For one must not defame the sinner, this God tells us, or reprimand him in public. As the text where I read this asserts, one can certainly blame vices and sins harshly, without naming those who are tainted by them or defaming anyone. There are large numbers of people who speak like this, but such a vice is disgraceful in noble men. I say this to those who are guilty of it and not at all to those who have not sinned in this way, for there are many noble men so worthy that they would rather forfeit their possessions than in any way be accused or reproached for such deeds or be caught in the act of performing them.

But the injurious men I am talking about, who are good neither indeed nor in intention, do not follow the example of the good Hutin de Vermeilles,[4] in whom there was such an ample measure of goodness that no one ever had any reason to reproach him, nor did he ever value a slur meant to defame. He was exceptional in the honor he bestowed upon women, and he was incapable of listening to accusatory or dishonorable things said about them. He was a brave, wise, and beloved knight, and this is why he was and will continue to be glorified. The good, the valiant Oton de Grandson,[5] who ventured out exerting himself so much for military causes, was in his time courtly, noble, brave, handsome, and kind—may God receive his soul in heaven!—for he was a knight with many good qualities. Whoever acted ill toward him I consider to have committed a sin; Fortune, however, did him harm, but she commonly brings suffering to good men.[6] For in all circumstances I consider him to have been loyal, and braver in military deeds than Ajax, son of Telemon. He never took pleasure in defaming anyone, he strove to serve, praise, and love women. Many others were good and valiant and ought to serve as examples for those who fall short; there still are many of them, there truly is need of them, those who follow the good paths of valiant men. Honor trains them, virtue leads them there; they put effort into acquiring renown and praise; they take pride in the noble manners with which they are endowed; their merits are manifested in their brilliant deeds in this kingdom, in others, and beyond the seas. But I will refrain from naming their names here, for fear that someone might say this was meant to flatter, or that it risk turning into a boast.[7] And this is indeed how men of noble breeding must by right behave. Otherwise that very nobility would be lacking in them.[8]

But the above-mentioned ladies complain of several clerics[9] who accuse them of blameworthy conduct, composing literary works, lyric poems, works in prose and in verse, defaming their behavior with a variety of expressions; then they give these materials to beginning students—to their new, young pupils—to serve as a model and as instruction, so that they will retain such advice into their adulthood. They say in their poetry, "Adam, David, Samson, and Solomon, along with a mass of others, were deceived by women morning and night. What man will manage to protect himself from this?" Another cleric says that they are most deceitful, wily, treacherous, and of little value. Others say that they are exceedingly mendacious, fickle, unstable, and flighty. Others accuse them of several serious vices and blame them ceaselessly, never excusing them for anything. It is in this manner that day and night clerics compose their poems, now in French, now in Latin, and they base themselves upon I don't know what books that tell more lies than a drunken man.

Ovid said a lot of nasty things about them (I consider that he did much harm by this) in a book he wrote, which he called the *Remedia amoris* (Remedies for Love)[10] and in which he accuses them of repulsive behavior—foul, ugly, and full of disgrace. That they might possess such vices, this I dispute with him, and I make my pledge to defend this in battle against all those who would like to throw down the gauntlet; I am of course referring to honorable women, for I do not take any account of worthless ones. Thus the clerics have studied this little book since their childhood in their earliest learning of grammar,[11] and they teach it to others with the goal that their pupils not endeavor to love a woman. But as far as this is concerned, they are foolish and wasting their time: to prevent such love would be nothing if not futile. For between myself and Lady Nature, as long as the world lasts we will not allow women not to be cherished and loved, in spite of all those who would like to reproach them, nor will we prevent them from seizing, removing, and making off with the hearts of several of those very people who rebuke them the most[12]—this without any deceit and without any blackmail, but just by ourselves and the impression we make on the mind: men will never be so informed by skilled clerics [as to resist it], not even for all their poems, notwithstanding the fact that many books speak of women and blame them, for they have very little effect in this matter.

And if someone says that one must believe the books that were made by men of great renown and of great learning, who did not give their consent to lies—those who proved the wickedness of women—I respond to them that those who wrote this down in their books did not, I think, seek to do anything else in their lives but deceive women; these men could not get enough of them, and every day they wanted new ones, without remaining loyal, even to the most beautiful of them. What was the result for David and King Solomon? God became angry with them and punished their excess. There have been many others, and especially Ovid, who desired so many of them and then thought he could defame them. Indeed, all the clerics who have spoken so much about them were wildly attracted to them much more than other people—not to a single one, but to a thousand! And if people like this had a mistress or a wife who did not do absolutely all they wanted or who might have attempted to deceive them, what is surprising about that? For there is no doubt that when a man thrusts himself into such an abject state, he does not go looking for worthy ladies or good and respected noblewomen. He neither knows them nor has anything to do with them. He does not want any others than those who are of his station: he surrounds himself with strumpets and commoners. Does such a man deserve to possess anything of value, a skirt chaser who adds all women to his list and then, when he is no longer capable of anything and is already an old man, thinks he can successfully cover up his shame by blaming women with his clever arguments? However, were someone to blame only those women who have given themselves over to vice and who have led a dissolute life, and advise them not to continue as they have done, he could truly succeed in his enterprise; and it would be a very reasonable thing, a worthy, just, and praiseworthy teaching, devoid of defamatory statements about all women indiscriminately.

And to say something about trickery, I am incapable of imagining or conceiving how a woman could deceive a man: she neither goes looking for him nor hunts him down; she does not go to his home to beg him or woo him; she does not think of him or even remember him when the man comes to deceive and tempt her. To tempt her how? Truly, he gives the appearance that there is no torment that is not easy for him to endure, nor burden to bear. He doesn't take pleasure in any other activity than in striving to deceive them, having committed his heart, his body, and his wealth to it. This suffering, along with the pain, lasts a long time and is often repeated, even though such lovers' plans often fail, in spite of their effort. And it is of these men that Ovid speaks in his treatise on the art of love; for on account of the pity that he had for these men he compiled a book in which he writes to them and teaches them clearly how they will be able to deceive women with tricks and obtain their love. And he called the book *The Art of Love;* however, he does not teach behaviors or morals having to do with loving well, but rather the opposite. For a man who wants to act according to this book will never love, however much he is loved, and this is why the book is poorly named. For it is a book on the *Art of Great Deception*—this is the name I give it—*and of False Appearances.*

How is it then—since women are weak and frivolous, easy to sway, naïve and scarcely upright, as some clerics claim—that these men have need for so many ruses in their effort to procure this goal? And why do these women not give in instantly without there being any need for skill or cunning in order to capture them? For once a castle has been taken there is no need to start a war. And especially for a poet as clever as Ovid, who was later exiled, and Jean de Meun in the *Romance of the Rose*—what a drawn-out affair! what a difficult thing! He puts in it much erudition, both clear and obscure, and impressive stories! But how many characters are introduced into it and consulted, and so many exertions and tricks invented, in order to deceive just one young girl—and that's the goal of it, by means of fraud and ruse! Is a great assault thus necessary for an unprotected place? What's the use of making a great leap when one is so close? I do not see or understand why great effort, skill or wit, or great cunning would be necessary to take an undefended site. It thus necessarily follows from this that since skill, great ingenuity, and considerable effort are needed to deceive a noble or common woman, they are not at all so fickle as some say or so changeable in their affairs.

Yet if people tell me that the books are full of these things—this is a response that many make and that I deplore—I respond to them that women did not make the books and that they did not put in them the things that we read there against women and their morals; and those who plead their case without an opponent go on talking to their hearts' content, make no concessions, and take the lion's share for themselves, for combative people easily injure those who do not defend themselves. But if women had written the books, I know in truth that the facts would be different, for they know well that they have been wrongly condemned and that the shares have not been divided equitably: the stronger ones take the biggest portion and he who slices the pieces keeps the best for himself ...

2. From Christine de Pizan, *Moral Teachings (Les Enseignemens Moraux*, 1399 Or 1402?)*[13]

French Verse (Rhyming Octosyllabic Couplets Organized In Quatrains)

[*Christine wrote this work to provide teachings to her young son, who had a lengthy stay in England from 1399 to 1402; it is normally assumed that she either gave it to him before his departure or wrote it after he returned in the spring of 1402. In any event, it was written before June 1402, inasmuch as it is included in Christine's first manuscript collection, which was completed in that month. The work consists of a sequence of 113 quatrains, each providing a specific moral lesson or bit of advice concerning such things as dress, speech, charity, and so forth.*]

XXXVIII. Do not believe all the defamatory statements that some books make about women, for there exist many good women; this, experience shows you.

XLI. Flee rowdy company and women who lack modesty, deceivers, people who ridicule and slander, as well as those who harm others.

XLIV. Listen to this lesson and note it down. Do not fall madly in love with a stupid woman if you want true love, for your moral fiber would be degraded by it.

XLVII. Do not be a deceiver of women; honor them and do not defame them. Limit yourself to loving a single one and do not quarrel with any.

LI. If you wish to take a woman as a wife, observe the mother and you can ascertain her moral qualities; this said, there are undoubtedly few rules that do not on occasion prove wrong.

LV. If you have a good and wise wife, believe her on the state of the household and trust her word, but do not speak in confidence to a foolish one.

LXVII. Do not reveal your secret to anyone without cause, and do not tell tales of others when there is no point in doing so, for he who reveals his thoughts is enslaved.

LXXIII. Flee idleness if you want to acquire honor, possessions, a reputation, and land; beware of worthless pleasures, and avoid disreputable deeds.

LXXVI. If you wish to flee the domination of love and totally cast it away, distance yourself from the person to whom your heart is most inclined.

LXXVII. If you wish to live well and chastely, do not read the book of the *Rose* or Ovid's *Art of Love*, for their example merits reproach.

LXXX. If your desire is pointed toward love and you wish to love in order to be more worthy, do not work up such a passion in your heart that you might end up being worth less.

LXXXV. If you feel your passions making you impulsive, have Reason take you into her school and teach you to put your feelings in order; in this way you can restrain yourself.

XCI. To the extent that you can, clothe your wife honorably and let her be next to you as the lady of the house, not a servant; make your household serve her.

XCIV. Make your wife fear you as necessary, but make sure never to beat her, for if she's good it would make her resentful, and if she's bad, she'd just get worse.

3. From Christine De Pizan, *The Debate Of Two Lovers* (*Le Débat De Deux Amans*, 1400?)[14]

French Verse (Quatrains Formed By Three Decasyllables Followed By A Four-Syllable Line, With The Rhyme Scheme *Aaab, Bbb, Cccd*, Etc.)

[*The first-person narrator, identifiable with Christine, presents to Louis, duke of Orléans, this debate between two lovers that she claims to have witnessed, and she asks him to offer his judgment of it. At a gracious party in a Parisian dwelling in the month of May, the narrator begins a conversation on the topic of love with a knight and a squire. In order to be able to talk more privately, they go outside to an orchard, but the narrator insists on having a "lady ... who hates slander and reproach" (l. 386) and a bourgeois woman accompany them, so that there will be no possibility for slanderers to wag their tongues. The debate, on whether love brings happiness or sorrow to lovers, is opened by the knight, who provides a lengthy exposé on the torments of love.*]

When the affable and courtly knight had finished his noteworthy speech, which most people would take to be the truth, and expertly delivered, expressed with some nice touches, neither too slow nor too hurried, the lady, who had listened closely to the speech, then started afresh and said:

"If I have understood your discourse, the god of Love provides harsh schooling to lovers, neither soothing nor tender, or so it seems to me; without reason, he drives many a man mad. But as for me, I do not think that there are hordes of lovers trapped in such a prison, in spite of the fact that many go around delivering this line to women, sometimes here, sometimes there; nonetheless, their heart is not in it nor do they ever pause in one single place,[15] however much they go on thoroughly wasting their words with endless speeches. But I do not believe that a single one is so seriously enslaved by it nor that he would ever serve Love and his lady so loyally and with such submissive hope. And, begging your pardon, I do not believe, by my soul, that any man is so inflamed by such a fire that he would experience such painful suffering for a woman; rather, it is a quite a common tale that men tell women in order to inspire trust, whereas the whole thing amounts to nothing. But she who lends credence to such a discourse is in the end held to be rather unwise. As for me, I maintain that it has just become a habit to speak of love in this way, in jest and to pass the time.

And if what I have just heard were true, that lovers in ancient times were sincere in the way you describe, then to my mind it has been more than a hundred years since this has happened, for neither today nor yesterday have lovers been thus afflicted. However, lovers do know how to satisfy their needs through argumentation and eloquence. And even if long ago they died and languished on account of love and endured many painful ills—even the most fortunate of them, as you tell[16]—I believe that nowadays their pains are slight. In spite of this, these pains continue to be found written down in abundance in romances and meticulously described at length. The *Romance of the Rose* spoke of it well in drawn-out expositions, and thus provided something of a gloss on the sort of love you have just expressed here, in the chapter of Reason, who forcefully gives directives to the foolish lover, who has been ensnared by such a love. She states all too well that the greatest joy arising from this love is worth little and passes quickly; she gives him advice on the path one must take in order to extricate oneself from it and likewise says that it is a thing that leads lovers astray, a severe affliction, adding that it is loyal disloyalty, and loyalty that is very disloyal,[17] a great peril for noblemen and royalty: all people are doomed if they approach it. That's what she said, but I think that few people are caught up in this kind of feeling;[18] rather, all desire nothing except money and living comfortably. But also who could live in the wretchedness that you have described? I believe, by Saint Nicaise, that there is not a man alive (may no one be displeased by this) who, however sturdy he might be, would be able to bear the ills that I hear you tell of here without tasting death.

But I have never heard tell where the cemeteries are in which are buried those whom pure love has put to death and who, for such a reason, have been confined to bed or might be carried in a stretcher to the saint from whom the illness comes.[19] So, whatever many people say, I believe that no one loves unless it is for his pleasure. I do not say this to contradict your statement and your lament, with all due respect, nor am I debating that this could not be, but I believe that those who have such a poor recovery from having loved too much are few and far between."

[The squire follows with an impassioned response in which he speaks of the joys of love. After a brief restatement of their irreconcilable positions, the two men attempt to find a judge who will decide the dispute, but since it is impossible to pick a judge, it is left in the hands of the narrator (Christine), who proposes to turn the decision over to the duke of Orléans. The two debaters ask Christine to make a poem of the event, and that is the form in which she presents it to the duke.]

Notes

1   This passage has been translated from *Œuvres poétiques de Christine de Pisan,* ed. Maurice Roy, 3 vols., SATF (Paris: Firmin Didot, 1886–96; rpt. New York: Johnson Reprint Corporation, 1965), 2:7–14 (ll. 181–422). English translations of the complete work are available in *Poems of Cupid, God of Love: Christine de Pizan's Epistre au Dieu d'Amours and Dit de la Rose, Thomas Hoccleve's The Letter of Cupid, with George Sewell's The Proclamation of Cupid,* ed. and trans. Thelma S. Fenster and Mary Carpenter Erler (Leiden: Brill, 1990), 34–75; and *The Selected Writings of Christine de Pizan,* ed. Renate Blumenfeld-Kosinski, trans. Renate Blumenfeld-Kosinski and Kevin Brownlee, 16–29.

2   The expression used here is *mettre en fermaille,* the meaning of which is not immediately obvious, although the general sense of the sentence is clear, referring to the idea, repeated elsewhere, that all women are being slandered and mistreated indiscriminately by men. In its literal sense, a *fermaille* is a buckle or a clasp; the few uses of the word I have found in a figurative sense provide the sense of an agreement or an accord (such as a marriage betrothal) or, more frequently, a wager of some kind, typically involving some kind of dispute or challenge. The online Middle French Dictionary (ATILF, Nancy Université and CNRS, Dictionnaire du Moyen Français, http://www.atilf.fr/dmf, hereafter DMF) provides one example of the reflexive verb *soi mettre en fermaille,* meaning "to engage oneself, to bind oneself by one's word." I have translated the expression according to the latter sense, which suggests that men make all women prove their innocence by swearing to it or by putting up some kind of defense.

3   This is a tacit rejoinder to the famous, highly misogynistic, couplet attributed to the Jealous Husband in the *Rose:* "Toutes estes, serez et fustes, / de fet ou de volenté, pustes" (All you women are, will be, or have been, indeed or intention, whores) (*Rose,* ed. Lecoy, ll. 9125–26; trans. Dahlberg, 165 [altered]).

4   Hutin de Vermeilles was a well-known figure in the late fourteenth century, renowned for his chivalric deeds and his courtly qualities; he is best represented in the *Cent Ballades* (One Hundred Ballads), a poetic narrative written in 1389 by a small group of nobles, of whom Jean Le Sénéchal was the principal poet. Hutin is there portrayed as a wise, older knight who gives advice on chivalry and on manners to a younger knight identified as Jean Le Sénéchal. In addition to having had a brilliant military career (he was at the battle of Poitiers in 1356 and fought other battles against the Black

Prince), he was related to the royal family through his marriage to Marguerite de Bourbon and served as a chamberlain to the king until his death in 1390.

5 Oton de Grandson (1340 / 1350–1397) was the emblematic figure of the knight/poet in the late fourteenth century. He had a very full military career during the Hundred Years' War. A noble from Savoy whose earlier allegiances were with the kings of England, Oton was later pardoned by the king of France. His fame as a love poet was even greater than that as a knight, and his works remained popular to the end of the fifteenth century. Hutin de Vermeilles and Oton de Grandson are also mentioned by Christine in the *Débat de deux amants* (Debate of Two Lovers), in *OEuvres poétiques de Christine de Pisan*, 2:97 (ll. 1615–19).

6 Oton de Grandson did indeed come to a tragic end. Caught up in some complicated political maneuvers in the 1390s, he was accused of being an accomplice to murder, and, ultimately sentenced to participate in a judicial duel in order to prove his guilt or innocence, he was killed in 1397.

7 One can sense here the dual presence of Christine and the God of Love in this fictional letter. Christine has reason to be sensitive about flattery, an issue that will be brought out later in the debate, but it is the God of Love who is cautious about boasting (worthy men in love being a sign of Cupid's success).

8 What I have translated as "in them" is the indirect object pronoun *y*, which can in Old and Middle French refer to animate or inanimate nouns. It could conceivably be referring to the aforementioned "kingdom" or more generally to the "world," meaning that if noble men do not act in this way nobility would disappear. However, a form of the same word is being used for "noble"/ "nobility" (*gentil/gentillece*) in the last two sentences of this paragraph, which would suggest that this sentence is referring pointedly back to the statement in the previous one.

9 Here and elsewhere in this volume, I translate the French term *clerc* as "cleric," which indicated throughout the Middle Ages a man who had received some measure of learning (in matters both secular and religious) and had some connection with a religious institution, typically marked by the tonsure. The words "lay" and "cleric" designated a major social distinction, the former often associated with a lack of learning and illiteracy (but incorrectly so, as many aristocrats knew how to read but were members of the laity), while the latter (as a group, known as the *clergie*) formed the intelligentsia, functioning not only in religious circles but in the secular world, as teachers, for instance, or as bureaucrats within the royal administration. All of the men participating in the debate with Christine are members of this group.

10 Although it is Ovid's *Art of Love* that is usually cited for its misogynistic perspectives, as later in this passage, here Christine has the God of Love refer to Ovid's retraction of his earlier text. Part of the advice Ovid gives to the lover who wishes to rid himself of his feelings is to disparage his lady's physical charms and behavior, which is undoubtedly what is being referred to here.

11 The study of grammar, one of the three sciences of language, along with logic and rhetoric, known throughout the Middle Ages as the *trivium*, had become a very sophisticated discipline in the universities, stretching into the domains of philosophy and epistemology. Here, Christine is thinking of the

more modest place of grammar in pre-university training, which often used snippets of classical Latin texts as exemplars.

12 The syntax of this very long sentence is tricky. The God of Love's point is that whatever the clerics say, he and Nature will prevail: men will love women and women will steal men's hearts, in spite of what they read. The sentence reads in the original: "we will not allow them not to be cherished ... and not to seize the hearts." Since this is rather awkward, I have reformulated the second part with the verb "prevent" and a positive verb, which says roughly the same thing.

13 Translated from *Œuvres poétiques de Christine de Pisan*, 3:33–41.

14 Translated from ibid, 2:76–79 (ll. 909–1000). A complete English translation is available in *An Anthology of Medieval Love Debate Poetry*, ed. and trans. R. Barton Palmer and Barbara K. Altmann (Gainesville: University Press of Florida, 2006), 257–305.

15 Not pausing or stopping in a single place, or not depositing one's heart there, is a common way of referring to the lover's fickleness.

16 In his discourse, the unhappy lover had provided a list of unhappy lovers from myth, romance, and history: Paris and Helen; Pyramus and Thisbe; Hero and Leander; Achilles and Po lixena; Essacus, son of Priam, and Hesperia; Iphis and Anaxarete; Tristan and Iseut; Cahedin, also from the *Tristan;* the Châtelain de Coucy and the dame de Faël; the Châtelaine de Vergy.

17 Christine here quotes from Reason's list of contraries, itself translated from Alan of Lille's *Complaint of Nature,* that articulates the paradoxical nature of love (*Rose,* ed. Lecoy, ll. 4265–66; trans. Dahlberg, 94: "Love is ... disloyal loyalty and loyal disloyalty").

18 Thus, according to this lady, Reason's cautions are unnecessary, for no one loves in this way.

19 There would seem to be here a reference to a tradition used by Achille Caulier, a poet who followed upon the success of Christine's contemporary, Alain Chartier, probably in the 1430s. In his *Cruelle femme en amour* (Cruel Lady in Matters of Love), he speaks of a temple of Venus where sick lovers go to be cured, next to which is a cemetery of great lovers; he expands this vision in his later *Hospital of Love,* which has still another famous cemetery scene (cf. Alain Chartier, Baudet Herenc, Achille Caulier, *Le cycle de* La Belle Dame sans Mercy, ed. David F. Hult, with the collaboration of Joan E. McRae, Champion Classiques, 8 [Paris: Hon-oré Champion, 2003], 260–65 and 362–69). On the cemetery of love as an important image characteristic of fourteenth- and fifteenth-century literature, see Jacqueline Cerquiglini-Toulet, *The Color of Melancholy,* trans. Lydia G. Cochrane (Baltimore: Johns Hopkins University Press, 1997), 127–40.

CONCLUSION

Comprehension Questions

1. Explain how the Christian church influenced views of women during the medieval era.

2. Explain what life was like for women and girls during the medieval era.

3. How did the use of visionary writing enable women such as Hildegard of Bingen to obtain a voice?

4. Identify the characteristics of women's letter writing during the medieval era.

Critical Thinking Questions

1. Given what you learned about women who wrote during the medieval era, identify at least two contributions they made to our understandings of public communication.

2. Do you believe women who speak in public settings in the twenty-first century are discriminated against due to their sex, as were women during the medieval era? What has changed and what, if anything, has remained the same?

Unit Summary

"Unit 3" provided a look into life during the medieval era, a period spanning the fifth to fifteenth century CE. The establishment of the Christian church greatly influenced life during this period and further solidified the ancient Greco-Roman belief that women were inferior and irrational and thus unfit for public participation and decision making; however, convents provided a cloistered space where women and girls could obtain a modest education and engage in charity work.

Despite sanctions against women's public speaking and education, women persisted in writing books, plays, poems, and letters. Their writings show they relied on both traditional rhetorical structures and styles (e.g., allegory, letter writing) and also at times devised unique ways to express their ideas, such as through visionary tracts, so as to establish their ethos.

The next unit explores the Enlightenment, a period known for substantial political and intellectual advancements. We will continue our endeavor to situate theories on rhetoric within the larger context marked (in the case of the Enlightenment) by the transatlantic slave trade and continued exclusion of women from public participation.

UNIT 4

ENLIGHTENMENT PRINCIPLES APPLIED UNEVENLY

Consider

1   What do you know about the time period of the Enlightenment?

2   Given that literacy was becoming more widespread during this period, how might that have influenced issues concerning public speaking and civic participation?

3   What role does literacy play in present-day democratic efforts?

In units II and III, we contextualized theories on public speaking and debate by describing the social, political, and economic context of the time period that undoubtedly shaped how thinkers conceptualized civic participation, governance, and public and personal relationships. We begin "Unit 4" by describing life during the Enlightenment, a period spanning the seventeenth through eighteenth centuries. We will briefly describe what life was like for marginalized groups—specifically, women and non-Western peoples—barred from public activity and/or subjected to colonization and the transatlantic slave trade. We will then get an idea of the main tenets of Enlightenment thought and how this body of knowledge shaped understandings of public speaking and civic participation. Finally, we will explore how disenfranchised groups used Enlightenment ideals toward their own ends as they sought economic and political equality. We will see that marginalized groups faced many of the same obstacles as those who lived in previous centuries and they developed and adapted strategies for public speaking that warrant inclusion in our understandings of rhetorical theory.

A Day in the Life ...

People living during the early 1600s through the end of the 1700s witnessed a great deal of change, innovation, discovery, and advancements in the areas of science, astronomy, physics, philosophy, and governance; hence, the term "enlightenment" is used to describe this era. In the 1500s, Copernicus challenged the belief that the earth was the center of the universe; in the 1600s, Isaac Newton advanced universal laws of motion; and in the 1700s, the world witnessed American and French revolutions and such inventions as the steam engine (1698) and the flushing toilet (1775). Literacy—although still not widespread during this time—was reaching to those of the middle and poorer classes. Throughout England and Europe, women were still less likely than men to be literate or to have access to an education. And for enslaved people, literacy was outlawed. But, similar to eras studied in previous units, women and slaves advocated and struggled for their rights through public expression. For example, Mary Astell, in her work, *A Serious Proposal to the Ladies, For the Advancement of Their True and Great Interest*, proposed a school for girls, a forward-thinking idea given its date of publication, 1694.

A central part of the historical context during this period was the growth and spread of the international slave trade, which was justified by writings on race that suggested a hierarchy of races. This body of thought is referred to as scientific racism and was reflected in the works of anthropologists, biologists, and philosophers. Scientific racism asserted persons of white, European descent were superior intellectually and physically to non-Europeans, who were deemed "others," subordinate, and/or inferior. This hierarchy of the races—a theory that developed over centuries—was used to justify colonization of African nations, widespread subjugation, and the transatlantic slave trade—and, as Parris (2015) notes, "reached a peak in the eighteenth-century scientific concept of race" (p. 27). These racist beliefs clearly influenced philosophical thought on the human condition along with civic participation and public expression.

What Were the Main Ideas of the Enlightenment?

Enlightenment thinkers include men such as Immanuel Kant, Georg Hegel, René Descartes, John Locke, Jean-Jacques Rousseau, and David Hume. Their writings on human nature and the mind were considered radical for the time insofar as they challenged the authority of the church that held sway throughout the medieval era (see "Unit 3"). Specifically, these thinkers emphasized reason, rationality, progress, and individualism as key concepts that would advance the human condition. They suggested society is best organized according to individual rights and rational principles rather than authority based on a church, deity, or monarchy. For instance, Locke (1632–1704) suggested individuals are naturally endowed with the rights to life, liberty, and property, and Kant emphasized progress through reason. Enlightenment thought influenced those we consider the "founding fathers" of the United States, such as Thomas Jefferson. The ideas of Enlightenment thinkers such as Hume and Giambattista Vico are particularly relevant for us as rhetorical theorists insofar as they advanced thought on human knowledge and how we come to know what we know. These epistemological questions are intimately entwined with language and public expression.

Recall an important point made in the "Unit 1" introduction concerning theory building: Theories and bodies of knowledge (whether they center on the human condition or the nature of communication) take shape within and are influenced by the political, economic, and cultural contexts in which they reside. Thus, our understandings of these theories should be grounded in historical contexts and understood as shaped by the particular power dynamics and disparities of a given period. The prevailing cultural beliefs of the period that justified the economic and political marginalization—even enslavement—of women and persons of non-European descent were part and parcel of the writings of Enlightenment thinkers. Therefore, as students/scholars of rhetoric, we should don our critical/cultural lens to get a more incisive look at theories of rhetoric and the human mind that led to different applications for persons occupying different political/economic spaces. *It is important to call attention to and tease out the sexism and racism in the works of these well-known writers because it bears directly on how they conceptualized the right to citizenship, public expression, and civic participation.*

Highlighting Sexism and Racism in Enlightenment Thought

John Locke's ideas on the natural rights of all persons (e.g., to life and liberty) did not extend to women. Locke believed women's subordinate position to their husbands was a natural condition. His writings did not engage at all on the position of women as citizens. Rousseau wrote about the importance of education for boys in his book, *Emile*. But he did not extend his beliefs to girls and women whose education, he believed, should center on how to tend to and please the men in their lives (Lerner 1993, p. 211). Kant was similarly skeptical of women's rights to education, believing it was not suited to their nature. According to Kant (2006/1785), women were naturally timid, weak, and in need of male protection.

In addition to suggesting women were naturally inferior to men—a belief we saw embedded in writings dating back to rhetorical theorists of ancient Greece and Rome—many Enlightenment thinkers embraced the ideas of scientific racism, which purported that black people from African nations were naturally lazy, untamed, and inferior to those of European descent. Kant, Hume, and Hegel are a few Enlightenment theorists whose writings embraced such racist notions (Farr 2004; Mills 1998; Parris 2015). In a famous essay written in 1753, Hume included a footnote elaborating on the natural inferiority and uncivilized nature of African peoples, asserting erroneously that they have "no arts, no sciences" in their cultures. Noted Hume: "such a uniform and constant difference could not happen in so many countries and ages, if nature had not made an original distinction betwixt these breeds of men ... there are Negroe slaves dispersed all over EUROPE, of which none ever discovered any symptoms of ingenuity" (quoted in Parris 2015, p. 29). Hegel (1944/1837) delineated a hierarchy of races wherein African peoples, deemed naturally wild and barbarous, were situated at the bottom. These writings influenced the thinking of America's founding fathers, including Thomas Jefferson who wrote extensively about the inferiority of black skin and who referenced Locke's notion of property rights to justify owning Africans as property (Parris 2015). In short, the ideology of scientific racism, a set of beliefs that developed over centuries, was woven throughout the writings of Enlightenment thought and used to justify the dehumanization and enslavement of non-Europeans.

Using Enlightenment Principles for Their Own Ends

So, you may have observed contradictory currents in Enlightenment thinking; namely, the espousal of the principles of equality and liberty—but only for men of European descent. This point was not lost on women and abolitionists of the period who saw Enlightenment ideals as an entry for arguing a more inclusive form of equality and justice. The contemporary scholar Jane Donawerth (2000) reminds us "women did participate in the development of philosophies of rhetoric" during the Enlightenment (p. 243). Mary Wollstonecraft, an influential writer and a feminist ahead of her time, penned *The Vindication of the Rights of Women* (1792), in which she drew on Lockean ideals to argue for the natural rights of women alongside men and made a case for the education of girls and women. In her 1795 essay, "An Essay on the Noble Science of Self-Justification," Maria Edgeworth drew upon—but also poked fun at—Enlightenment ideas of scientific rhetoric and empiricism. Her essay is a satire of the nagging housewife or "shrew," which conveyed a broader critique of the prevailing notion in Locke's and Rousseau's writings that wives should remain subservient to husbands (Donawerth 2000).

In the late 1700s to early 1800s, as slavery was becoming an entrenched feature in the development of the United States as a nation, with capitalism as its significant feature, abolitionists—free and enslaved Americans—drew upon Enlightenment ideals as a way to call out the hypocrisy in this philosophical body of thought. David Walker's *Appeal in Four Articles; Together with a Preamble, to the Coloured Citizens of the World, but in Particular, and Very Expressly, to Those of the United States of America* (1829) directly confronted scientific racism and "casts a critical reflection on the democratic, enlightened, Christian slaveholding nation so that its citizens could see their nation for what it truly was" (Parris 2015, p. 45). Specifically, Walker pointed out how Enlightenment ideals were selectively applied and he condemned scientific racism particularly as it was used to justify slavery as a central feature of American capitalism. Into the nineteenth century, as the United States was transitioning to a period known as the Industrial Age, a former slave and widely known abolitionist public speaker, Frederick Douglass, continued in the same vein as Walker by challenging racism in philosophy and political thought and calling on white America to apply the ideals of freedom and equality to all persons without exception. Parris (2015) explains that the racist philosophy of Hume, Hegel, Kant, and Jefferson served as a catalyst for the "epistemological resistance in which Africana thinkers pondered questions of Being and Freedom" toward the end of racial equality and an end to slavery (p. 64).

The Enlightenment period was not without philosophers who continued to draw upon more traditional sources for their ideas. For instance, as we will learn in one of this unit's readings, Margaret Fell and Madeleine de Scudéry drew upon religious discourses and classical Greco-Roman concepts to theorize women and public speaking. Fell was a Quaker who was imprisoned in the mid-1660s for holding church services in her home. In *Women's Speaking Justified* (1666), Fell adopted a strategy for establishing ethos used by her medieval era sisters before her. She quoted extensively from the Bible those passages that illustrated or advocated women's speaking. As Donawerth (1993) explains, "since the Word of God is irrefutable, her quotations buttress her own authority as speaker and become at the same time an extrinsic argument from testimony" (p. 109). Fell adopted a "collaborative voice" (Donawerth 1993) that suggests a new way to conceptualize ethos, one that takes account of the epistemological position of the speaker. In the 1680s, de Scudéry published dialogues, in the tradition of Plato's dialogues of the 300s BCE, in which she outlined a theory of conversation, grounded in the ancient Roman concept of sermo (see "Unit 2"). Her grounding in the classics enabled her to establish her authority on the subject matter, particularly important given her secondary status as a woman during the 1600s.

Why Does This Matter for Rhetorical Theory?

This brief background on the history of Enlightenment thought—fraught as it was by prevailing racist and sexist frameworks, beliefs, and values—suggests to us the importance of considering social location in how we conceptualize public speaking, civic participation, and related epistemological questions. For instance, for marginalized groups, the process of acquiring knowledge of the world was no doubt influenced by daily experiences of marginalization, degradation, and enslavement. The ways excluded "others" employed traditional Greco-Roman strategies such as ethos and logos was, as we have seen, influenced by women's and slaves' experiences of exclusion from education and enforced illiteracy. Finally, options for exercising leadership and civic participation were delimited or circumscribed by prevailing views on the nature of the human condition, human potential, and who is included in those renderings. The critical/cultural view of rhetorical theory elaborated in the "Unit 1" introduction reminds us that how we come to know or acquire viewpoints, values, and beliefs is shaped by our social location in terms of sex, race, class, etc. The issues addressed by theorists from Plato to Hegel are important. But if we wish to know about the human condition and what roles communication plays in how we understand and communicate about ourselves and our world, our endeavors "must acknowledge we are constituted as raced [and sexed] beings and that race [and sex] ... affect one's opportunities and the ways in which self-consciousness develops" (Farr 2004, p. 156).

Preview of Unit Readings

In "Unit 4's" first reading, "The Gender of Enlightenment," Robin May Schott furthers our understandings of the main tenets of Enlightenment, providing a more focused look at the writings of Immanuel Kant. The essay elaborates on what life was like for women during this period and provides insight on Kant's views on women, which shaped his thinking on education and social progress. The second reading, "Authorial Ethos, Collaborative Voice, and Rhetorical Theory by Women," focuses on the theoretical efforts of four women who lived and wrote between 1600 and 1900. The essay's author, Jane Donawerth, makes an important point regarding women's contributions to rhetorical theory—namely, that women's theories on speaking often came to us in nontraditional forms. Whereas theories advanced by men were directed toward teaching boys in a school setting, "women's theory instructed women reading at home, or addressed a mixed public audience and argued for women's education in some branch of rhetoric" (p. 107).

References

Donawerth, Jane. 1993. "Authorial Ethos, Collaborative Voice, and Rhetorical Theory by Women." In Hildy Miller and Lillian Bridwell-Bowles (eds.), *Rhetorical Women: Roles and Representations*, 107–124. Tuscaloosa, AL: University of Alabama Press.

——. 2000. "Poaching on Men's Philosophies of Rhetoric: Eighteenth- and Nineteenth-Century Rhetorical Theory by Women." *Philosophy and Rhetoric, 33*, 243–258.

Farr, Arnold. 2004. "Whiteness Visible: Enlightenment Racism and the Structure of Racialized Consciousness." In George Yancy (ed.), *What White Looks Like: African-American Philosophers on the Whiteness Question*, 143–158. New York: Routledge.

Hegel, Georg. 1944/1837. *The Philosophy of History*. Translated by J. Sibree. New York: Willey Book Co.

Kant, I. 2006/1785. *Anthropology from a Pragmatic Point of View*. Translated by Robert B. Louden. New York: Cambridge University Press.

Lerner, Gerda. 1993. *The Creation of Feminist Consciousness: From the Middle Ages to Eighteen-seventy*. New York: Oxford University Press.

Mills, Charles W. 1998. *Blackness Visible: Essays on Philosophy and Race.* Ithaca, NY: Cornell University Press.

Parris, LaRose T. 2015. *Being Apart: Theoretical and Existential Resistance in Africana Literature.* Charlottesville, VA: University of Virginia Press.

Perry, Ruth. 1990. "Mary Astell and the Feminist Critique of Possessive Individualism." *Eighteenth-Century Studies, 23,* 444–457.

The Gender of Enlightenment

by Robin May Schott

E nlightenment is one of the most debated themes of contemporary intellectual discourse. The eighteenth-century claim that progress is possible through the use of reason and the advancement and spread of knowledge is summed up in Kant's dictum, "Have courage to use your own reason!"[1] This view has been reiterated and updated by contemporary defenders of enlightenment such as Jurgen Habermas. In Habermas's view, the Enlightenment tradition is the only possible source of rational judgment in the face of the irrationality, prejudice, blind obedience to authority, and violence that characterized the darkest days of German history under Hitler. It is only through enlightenment that rational criteria for the critique of domination and for the possibility of emancipation is possible.[2]

Criticism of Enlightenment commitments have abounded in many diverse quarters. Earlier members of the Frankfurt School of social theory, such as Max Horkheimer and Theodor Adorno, argued that enlightenment represents Western culture's attempt to dominate sensuous existence by means of a controlling rationality, which finds its fullest expression in the historical period of the eighteenth century. Far from en-suring the progress of reason and emancipation, enlightenment reason has resulted in the return of the repressed, in the eruption of barbarism in twentieth-century Germany.[3] Recent writers such as Berel Lang have reiterated this thesis, arguing that the Enlightenment claims for universal truths and its extreme notions of the indi-vidual, autonomous, ahistorical self contribute directly to genocide.[4] In his view, the Enlightenment's insistence on the universality of rational judgment makes it unable to deal with any claims of particularism and any judgments influenced by historical factors. The obvious exclusion of women, servants, and Jews from the call to enlightenment coexisted with its principle of tolerance.[5] Ultimately, according to Lang, the inability of Enlightenment rationality to provide controls for determining the status of groups excluded from its domain leads to the possibility of unbounded destruction of these groups.[6]

Criticism of the project of the Enlightenment from postmodernist quarters has been just as intense. Writers such as Jean-François Lyotard, Jacques Derrida, and Michel Foucault, loosely grouped by others (though not by themselves) under the umbrella of postmodernism, have attacked the hegemony of enlightenment rationality, its claim to grasp universal truth, and the concomitant rejection of any form of historicity or particularism. Enlightenment, it might be said, disenfranchises not only other possible interpretations but also the groups that initiate these interpretations. It thus readily can be wielded as an instrument of power in the service of its own vision of scientific truth.[7]

Feminist theorists have a particularly embattled relation to the question of enlightenment. Some feminists argue that the Enlightenment tradition of individual reason, progress, and freedom is a precondition for the discourse of women's liberation, and for the political gains that women have won. Even feminists who have a qualified relation to the Enlightenment (i.e., who argue that its fulfillment would advance the historical task of self-scrutiny) suggest that women have not yet had their enlightenment.[8] On this view, even though women have been viewed by Enlightenment thinkers as not fully rational, and even though women have been severely restricted in their educational opportunities, which form a prerequisite for achieving the free use of reason, nonetheless one should demand that the Enlightenment be completed by incorporating previously excluded groups. It is appealing for many to use the Enlightenment tools of rationality and objectivity to argue the case for women's emancipation.[9]

By contrast, many feminist theorists argue that the fundamental commitments of the Enlightenment are antithetical to feminist politics and theory and that feminists must throw their caps in the ring with postmodern critics. Not only have enlightenment thinkers excluded women from the province of autonomy but feminist notions of self, knowledge, and truth are contradictory to fundamental enlightenment commitments as well.[10] Feminists, like postmodernists, are skeptical of all transcendental, transhistorical claims for truth and argue that "universality" is itself a reflection of the experience of the dominant social group. On this view, feminists are committed to showing that reason is not divorced from "merely contingent" existence, that the self is embedded in social relations, that the self is embodied and is thus historically specific and partial. Jane Flax writes, "What Kant's self calls its 'own' reason and the methods by which reason's contents become present or self-evident, are no freer from empirical contingency than is the so-called phenomenal self."[11] Moreover, feminists argue that this desire to detach the self from contingency and embodiment is itself an effect of particular gender relations, itself an expression of the flight of masculinity from the temporal, embodied, uncertain realm of phenomenal existence.

Before evaluating the claims laid on the present by the philosophical project emerging from the Enlightenment, in particular its implications for feminism, I will make some brief historical comments about the situation of women during the Age of Enlightenment. Although this discussion is best left to historians, it is an important context for understanding Kant's discussion of enlightenment. I will then discuss Kant's notion of self-imposed tutelage and emancipation in his essay "What Is Enlightenment?" and re-pose the questions of autonomy and heteronomy from a feminist perspective.

Historians are divided about the historical implications of the Enlightenment for women. It was certainly not a period of unambivalent progress for women. The most positive reading of this period is that the Enlightenment legitimized safeguards in theory which were not secured in practice for nearly another century.[12] Looking at the Age of Enlightenment in France, Claire Moses argues that the eighteenth century ended in repression. The uniform legal system enshrined the Rousseauian concept of the difference of women from men. The Civil Code recognized the rights of all citizens but excluded women from citizenship. Therefore, women's status worsened in relation to men's status. Moreover, some women's status worsened absolutely. Whereas earlier some noble women could escape the full harshness of patriarchal laws, these opportunities were now erased.[13] Moses argues that the eighteenth-century views of women were contradictory, providing both encouragement for the emergence of feminism and the weapons to gun it down. For example, the Civil Code served as a rallying point for women in enshrining the Rousseauian concept of the difference between women and men, in which women remained subordinate to men. Not only did it incite feminist protest because it discriminated against women, but, in proclaiming the political significance of sex, it also intensified women's sense of sex identification.[14]

The Enlightenment's theoretical legitimization of the rights to organize, lecture publicly, and publish freely were not secured for women in France until 1879. In the years that followed, women won the right to secondary education, the gradual opening of the university to them, and the right to practice "public" professions (newspaper publishing, medicine, law). In 1907, women were granted equal authority with the father over children and the right to control their own earnings, but women in France had to wait until 1944 to gain the right to vote.[15]

In terms of women's education in the Age of Enlightenment, it is clear that women's literacy in France lagged far behind men's.[16] The feminist political activist Olympe de Gouges dictated all her works to a secretary because she was unable to write. And the four youngest daughters of Louis XV, after several years at the convent, were still illiterate. Despite deficiencies in formal instruction, many women were able to complete their education independently.[17] Women's education in France varied significantly depending on their class and region. Upper-class girls and daughters of the bourgeoisie received their early education at home, and later were sent to a convent until they were to be married. Although there are idealized descriptions of the social life of convents, a more realistic picture includes harrowing practices such as girls being sent to pray alone, in the vaults where nuns were buried, as punishment.[18] The social function of the convents was most important; reading, writing, and catechism occupied a distant second place. Other "safe" subjects included the lives of the saints, needlework, and sewing, whereas novels, mythology, physical or natural sciences, ancient philosophy, and even history except in its most elementary form remained taboo.[19] Girls from impoverished families depended on charity schools for education, which provided training in manual skills and crafts. Although progress in the education of women in France was achieved in the eighteenth century (the level of literacy improved, the need for organized public education was recognized), women's exclusion from formal higher education and participation in the professions during this period continued to hamper their achievements.

Women were excluded from university education in Germany as well (including Konigsberg University where Kant studied and taught) during the Age of Enlightenment.[20] And although universities were not centers of cultural innovation during the eighteenth century, they remained the locus in Germany for philosophical and scientific work.[21] Women's exclusion from university life was considered so natural that only the most recent scholars of German education make note of it. By 1914, women constituted 7 percent of the student body in Prussia—marking a dramatic increase in their enrollment since 1900.[22] Women's absence from the academies ensured their exclusion from training in medicine, law, and government positions in Germany until the late nineteenth and twentieth century.[23]

It is in this historical context that Kant's view of women is situated. Far from challenging women's exclusion from education on egalitarian grounds, Kant mocks women's attempts at serious philosophical and scientific work. Kant asserts that women's character, in contrast to men's, is wholly defined by natural needs. Women's lack of self-determination, in his view, is intrinsic to their nature. He writes, "Nature was concerned about the preservation of the embryo and implanted fear into the woman's character, a fear of physical injury and a timidity towards similar dangers. On the basis of this weakness, the woman legitimately asks for masculine protection."[24] Because of their natural fear and timidity, Kant views women as unsuited for scholarly work. He mockingly describes the scholarly women who "use their books somewhat like a watch, that is, they wear the watch so it can be noticed that they have one, although it is usually broken or does not show the correct time."[25] Kant's remarks on women in the *Anthropology* echo his sentiments in *Observations on the Feeling of the Beautiful and the Sublime*. In that early work, Kant notes, "A woman who has a head full of Greek, like Mme. Dacier, or carries on fundamental controversies about mechanics, like the Marquise du Chatelet, might as well even have a beard, for perhaps that would express more obviously the mien of profundity for which she strives."[26] In Kant's view, women's philosophy is "not to reason, but to sense." And he adds, "I hardly believe that the fair sex is capable of principles."[27] No wonder that under these conditions the woman "makes no secret in wishing that she might rather be a man, so that she could give larger and freer latitude to her inclinations; no man, however, would want to be a woman."[28]

In providing the Marquise du Châtelet with a beard, Kant suggests that there is a contradiction between women and scholarship that is rooted in a natural condition, not a social one. Some biographical remarks about the Marquise du Châtelet help in evaluating Kant's views. By the time of her death in 1749, Emilie du Châtelet was not only well known in French intellectual circles but also had been elected to the Bologna Academy of Sciences. She had published on the metaphysics of natural science, on the nature of fire and heat, and on the nature of force. In addition, she had completed a translation of Newton's *Principia Mathematica* and had anonymously co-authored with Voltaire a popularization of Newtonian physics.

Despite her scientific vocation, Emilie du Châtelet was hampered throughout her life by her inability to obtain the systematic learning provided to boys, to be educated in an institutional context as opposed to a private tutoring situation, and to travel freely and to work undisturbed by household obligations. Thus she was hindered in carrying out anything like a long-term research program.[29] Because her intellectual training was limited to her relationship with a small set of famous figures (e.g., Voltaire), it was difficult for her to take the step from tutelage to independence. Her responsibilities for family, household, friends, and social duties made it impossible for her to lead the life of a full-time scientist. She was able to achieve as much as she did by functioning on four or five hours of sleep a night. When necessary, she survived on even less, dipping her arms in ice water to stay awake.[30]

Although the discipline required for the Marquise du Châtelet to accomplish scientific work matches Kant's own stern discipline in life, it is clear that Kant had little sympathy for the frustrations of intelligent women like her. His views are further illustrated by his correspondence with Maria von Herbert, an intelligent young aristocratic woman who had studied Kant's writings together with a male friend. In a letter to Kant dated January 1793, Maria von Herbert writes to Kant of her own personal despair and frustration with her life. "Even when I am not frustrated by any external circumstances and have nothing to do all day, I'm tormented by a boredom that makes my life unbearable."[31] Although Kant had responded to an earlier letter of Maria's discussing her moral failings, he failed to respond to this letter. Instead, he sent it on to another young lady as an example of "mental derangement" that occurs when young ladies succumb to "the errors of a sublimated fantasy."[32] He failed to consider the possibility that this young woman's despair may have arisen in part from external circumstances that smothered her urge to do something in the world. In my view, the lives of these two women provide counterexamples to Kant's view concerning the inverse relationship between civil freedom and freedom of mind, expressed in "What Is Enlightenment?" The restrictions placed on these women's lives did not encourage the flourishing of their intellectual development but rather furthered the very form of intellectual tutelage that Kant ostensibly deplored.

It is important to bear in mind concrete historical features when evaluating the philosophical work of the period. Social practices are not "outside" the sphere of culture in which philosophy operates. Rather, philosophy can be viewed as a reflective appropriation of cultural and historical traditions.[33] Therefore, in turning to Kant's essay "What Is Enlightenment?" new perspectives are disclosed if one asks: What could this conception of enlightenment have meant to women of the period, and how would women's experiences have challenged Kant's formulations?

Kant has only one reference to women in particular in this short essay. He writes, "the step to competence is held to be very dangerous by the far greater portion of mankind (and by the entire fair sex)."[34] His general indifference to differentiating the possibilities of enlightenment for men and for women appears to arise from his view that the subject of enlightenment (humanity) that is called on to free itself from self-imposed tutelage is a universal one. He never qualifies his claim by saying it is for masters and not their servants, men and not women, Christians and not Jews. Therefore, any reference to particular kinds of groups or classes of individuals in society seems out of place. Although Kant says "Have courage to use your own reason!"[35] where this courage comes from, what conflicts within individuals' lives it encounters, and what factors interfere with its realization—none of these are his concerns. Rather, Kant's project is to address enlightenment as a demand for the individual to use reason; and reason, as Kant's critical writings attest, is viewed as a universal, ahistorical faculty.[36]

And yet for the contemporary reader, the question of inclusion and exclusion of particular groups in the domain of enlightened thought becomes pressing. As the critics of enlightenment mentioned above have argued, the universal subject of enlightened thought had particular unacknowledged qualifications. As already noted, Kant claims that all women are afraid of enlightenment (he did not, however, turn his attention to how this fear might be counteracted). Similarly, it is difficult to see how Kant might include servants or domestics in his call for enlightenment, since these latter are, in Kant's view, a legal possession of the master. In his letter to C. G. Schutz dated 10 July 1797, Kant writes of this relationship as follows: "The right to use a man for domestic purposes is analogous to a right to an object, for which the servant is not free to terminate his connections with the household and he may therefore be caught and returned by force."[37] In Kant's claim that the servant "belongs" to the master just as an object does, it is difficult to see how there would be any domain left to the servant in which reason could be exercised freely. Historically, women of all classes and men of the servant class could not share equally with bourgeois men in the "public" exercise of reason, which Kant defines as the "use which a person makes of it as a scholar before the reading public."[38]

Similarly, Kant's discussion of self-incurred tutelage is not formulated with reference to women's experience. Kant begins his essay with the claim that "enlightenment is man's release from his self-incurred tutelage. Tutelage is man's inability to make use of his understanding without direction from another. Self-incurred is this tutelage when its cause lies not in lack of reason but in lack of resolution and courage to use it without direction from another."[39] In this context, it is helpful to recall the little we know about the lives of women like Emilie du Châtelet and Maria von Herbert. These women did apparently experience their education as being a form of tutelage. Emilie du Châtelet's self-doubt, self-deprecation, and tendency to choose safe, "dependent" research projects such as translation, criticism, and commentary may have been a result of her personal indebtedness to friends such as Voltaire who were already famous, which made it difficult for her to take the step from pupil to colleague, from tutelage to independence.[40] And one can imagine from Kant's response to Maria von Herbert's letters that for him, the only conceivable relation a woman could have to philosophy is to be tutored by a mentor. In his letter to Elizabeth Motherby, Kant notes that Maria refers to his writings as being "difficult to understand without an explanation."[41] The implication is with a proper explanation, Maria may have been saved from the reefs of her "sublimated fantasy."

Thus the extent to which these women's tutelage was self-imposed arose from their very desire to gain knowledge and to resist being defined by what is "pleasant and pointless."[42] But their difficulties in escaping from it cannot be explained by "laziness and cowardice" (the reasons Kant gives for mankind's tutelage).[43] Nor is it likely that they were "fond" of this state.[44] Rather, their state of tutelage seems to be a result of social forces and restrictions stronger than their power to change them.[45]

Just as Kant's discussion of tutelage does not explain obstacles to enlightenment faced by "humanity," but at best explains the obstacles faced by certain groups of people (e.g., middle-class men with education and civil office who could become, for example, military officers and clergymen), so too Kant's conception of enlightenment also has to be understood as a particular historical construction. For Kant, rationality is possible only on the basis of excluding emotion. He does invoke "courage" in the use of reason, just as elsewhere he invokes "respect" for the moral law. But only this kind of feeling that is "self-wrought by a rational concept" and is not rooted in inclination or fear can be praiseworthy.[46] But concerning emotion in general, Kant expresses only disdain. In the *Anthropology from a Pragmatic Point of View,* he writes, "To be subject to emotions and passions is probably always an illness of mind because both emotion and passion exclude the sovereignty of reason."[47] Similarly, "Passion, on the other hand, no man wishes for himself. Who wants to have himself put in chains when he can be free?"[48] Since emotion and passion threaten the sovereignty of reason, they must be excluded from ordinary consciousness.

Kant's attempt to exclude emotion from rationality is premised on the assumption that his rational posture is itself wholly nonemotional. Yet the emotional currents of Kantian rationality are clearly expressed in his personal correspondence. Maria von Herbert wrote to Kant during a personal crisis, in which she had revealed to a friend that she had formerly loved another man and this friend now treated her with coldness. Kant responds to Maria in a didactic manner. Although Kant acknowledges that in men there is a limit on candor (in some men more than in others) that interferes with the ideal of friendship, he distinguishes this lack of candor from lack of sincerity, from dishonesty in expressing one's thoughts.[49] Kant adjudicates Maria of being guilty of this latter sin and for rightly feeling the pains of conscience: "For conscience must focus on every transgression, like a judge who does not dispose of the documents, when a crime has been sentenced, but records them in the archives in order to sharpen the judgment of justice in new cases of a similar or even dissimilar offense that may appear before him."[50] Kant admits that he is answering her in the form of sermon: "instruction, penalty, and solace, of which I beg you to devote yourself somewhat more to the first two."[51]

In this letter, Kant epitomizes the ascetic priest described by Nietzsche: the inventor of bad conscience, the upholder of self-punishment, the antagonist of the fulfillment of sensual pleasures. Nietzsche writes in the *Genealogy of Morals,* "Every suffering sheep says to himself, 'I suffer; it must be somebody's fault.' But his shepherd, the ascetic priest, says to him, 'You are quite right, my sheep, somebody must be at fault here, but that somebody is yourself. You alone are to blame—you alone are to blame for yourself.'"[52]

Kant's response to Maria gives support to the view that his moral philosophy is an existential choice, a manner of living "with our eyes fixed on abstract, impartial principles,"[53] and not merely a position to be held in debates about rational principles. Kant's philosophy is paradigmatic of what contemporary critics call the perspective of impartial reason. As Iris Young writes, "Impartial reason must judge from a point of view outside the particular perspectives of persons involved in interaction, able to totalize these perspectives into a whole or general will. This is the point of view of a solitary transcendent God."[54] But this perspective is built on the assumption that the impartial self is a disembodied, disembedded self. As Seyla Benhabib notes in reference to the impartial self in the theories of Rawls and Kohlberg, "this is a strange world: it is one in which individuals are grown up before they have been born; in which boys are men before they have been children; a world where neither mother, nor sister, nor wife exist."[55] It is a self that abstracts from concrete individuality and identity and thus ultimately makes the concept of the Other as different from oneself incoherent.[56]

One may object that an argument proving Kant's exclusion of emotion from morality does not argue for the role of emotions in ethics. This objection exemplifies the commitments of the Kantian paradigm, to which much contemporary academic discourse is heir. My claim, however, is that this rational detachment is already an emotional posture with consequences for human relations (witness Kant's letter to Maria von Herbert and his refusal to respond to her subsequent letters). But the failure to acknowledge the emotional content of detached impartiality precludes the possibility of evaluating how we are to use emotions, which emotions are positive and which are negative. As Young notes in reference to the exclusion of desire, affectivity, and need from deontological reason, "Since all desiring is equally suspect, we have no way of distinguishing which desires are good and which bad, which will expand the person's capacities and relations with others, and which stunt the person and foster violence. In being excluded from understanding, all desiring, feeling, and needs become unconscious, but certainly do not thereby cease to motivate action and behavior."[57] Nietzsche notes in the *Genealogy* of *Morals* that human beings have the capacity of oblivion, by which "what we experience and digest psychologically does not ... emerge into consciousness. ... The role of this active oblivion is that of a concierge: to shut temporarily the doors and windows of consciousness; to protect us from the noise and agitation with which our lower organs work for or against one another; to introduce a little quiet into our consciousness so as to make room for the nobler functions and functionaries of our organism which do the governing and planning. This concierge maintains order and etiquette in the household of the psyche."[58] But as Nietzsche and, following him, Freud, Horkheimer, and Adorno have argued, this edifice remains harnessed to the noise and agitation of the psyche. In refusing to acknowledge the existence of nonrational motivations, one forfeits the possibility of self-understanding.

Much contemporary debate in moral theory revolves around the paradigm of autonomy that Kant articulated. Autonomy, in Kant's view, is the moral equivalent of the Enlightenment motto "Have courage to use your own reason!" In the *Foundations of the Metaphysics of Morals*, Kant defines the principle of autonomy in which man is "subject only to his own, yet universal legislation, and that he is only bound to act in accordance with his own will, which is, however, designed by nature to be a will giving universal laws."[59] Just as enlightened reason must exclude the influence of emotions, so moral behavior "wholly excludes the influence of inclination" such as sympathy and sensual love.[60] Only then can rational judgments be universalizable and detachable from the concrete context in which they are made.

Many feminists have vociferously criticized this model of autonomy because of its presumption of detachment, universality, and disembeddedness. Writers such as Carol Gilligan, and those following in her wake, advocate the legitimacy of an alternative to this Kantian model of autonomy that they call the care perspective. The care perspective, evident in many women's responses to moral dilemmas, emphasizes the individual's connectedness with others. In this perspective, individuals make moral choices by concretely assessing who will be hurt and who will be helped by particular decisions.[61]

The viability of a care perspective has been heatedly debated both within feminist and non-feminist circles. Feminists such as Claudia Card criticize this conception on the grounds that it presumes traditional gender dualism, itself the product of patriarchal history. They argue that the care perspective advocates traditional feminine virtues that may be survival strategies for women in forced relations of dependencies but are hardly an emancipated vision for the future. Many feminists, however, defend this posture as an alternative conception of moral autonomy, as a form of reasoning motivated by persons' sense of their own concrete identity that also acknowledges human connectedness.[62] Others, like Benhabib, seek to integrate Kantian moral autonomy with care, a position that "allows us to recognize the dignity of the generalized other through an acknowledgment of the moral identity of the concrete other."[63]

The attention given to the debate about impartiality versus care in academic journals as well as popular ones attests to the historical nerve that it has touched. To some extent, interest in this debate has been sparked by the problematizing of gender identity in contemporary culture. But its significance is also connected to a paradigm shift in contemporary intellectual discourse—across fields such as psychology, moral philosophy, and literary analysis—a shift that challenges the notion that there is individual, subjective identity that exists as a deep self, a unified whole, an isolated ego. Challenging the Kantian conception of the subject is certainly not unique to the present debate. It finds historical antecedents in Hegel's concept of reciprocal recognition and in Marx's concept of the fundamentally social character of human identity. But the question of intersubjectivity has achieved a certain historical urgency today, in light of the crisis of the philosophy of the subject.

The phrase "care perspective" may in fact be a misnomer for the analysis of human interrelatedness. "Care" seems too thin, mild, and one-dimensional to account for the dynamics of human connectedness. As experience of intimacy teaches, relations may include feelings of love and anger and resentment simultaneously. Relatedness might express the possible depth of harmony between two individuals, as well as the cruelty that individuals can exercise against each other; and these different dynamics can coexist within the same relationship. Therefore, "care" cannot be taken as descriptive of the range of emotions involved in human connectedness. Moreover, the care perspective cannot be formulated by the normative principle "Be compassionate" or "Take responsibility."[64] The care perspective is committed to concrete, individual decision making as opposed to abstract, universal rules, which cannot help in deciding between conflicts of responsibilities.

But I would suggest that the radical potential within "care" theories, which go beyond what many of these theorists themselves argue, is to challenge the primacy of the category of autonomy that has prevailed since Kant. In discussing the Kantian subject, Lucien Goldmann once wrote, "That it could never pass from the *I* to the *we*, that in spite of Kant's genius it always remained within the framework of bourgeois individualist thought, these are the ultimate limits of Kant's thought."[65] In our times we may need to perform another conceptual revolution, as Kant did with previous philosophers and as Marx did with Hegel, to reverse the moral weight given to autonomy and heteronomy and to argue for a concept of moral and political theory that is premised on the heteronomy, the interdependence of individuals.[66] Individuals who have close friends, lovers, children, or parents do need to make decisions on the basis of what is best for the "we" of which they form a part. Why shouldn't this acknowledgment of relations be a starting point for moral philosophy, as opposed to beginning with the model of the individual as cut off from intimacy, which Kant personified in his own life and which has become the paradigm of moral philosophy? The health and happiness of these collectivities depend, of course, on balancing to the greatest extent possible the conflicting needs of individuals involved in these relationships. From this perspective, heteronomy includes respect for individuals' integrity and desire to make their own decisions; but individual priorities cannot be absolute. Moreover, these groups do change: children grow up, partners separate, individuals die, interests and needs change with personal development. However, to privilege the autonomy of the individual as the primary factor in moral thinking makes human separateness and detachment morally normative.

A number of objections may be raised to these suggestions. For example, one might argue that even recognizing the primacy of heteronomy in the moral domain does not undercut the need for a Kantian principle of rational autonomy in the political domain, in order to protect individuals' rights against violent encroachment. A principle that validates the group per se over the individual might pose an even greater danger of exclusion, harassment, and violence than has occurred under the inheritance of the Enlightenment. If radical Right, homophobic, antiabortion advocates achieved their "we" as the primary political agenda, imagine what would happen to individual women, lesbian and gay activists, and AIDS research and support groups.

A number of responses to this objection are in order. First of all, it is important to point out the discrepancy between Kant's moral theory and a political recognition of equal rights. For example, in the *Metaphysical Elements of Justice,* Kant argues "that one ought to obey the legislative authority that now exists, regardless of its origin" and adds that there can be "no legitimate resistance of the people to the legislative chief of the state."[67] Because Kant viewed legislative authority as grounded in the law-giving form of the will, the particular laws in society are viewed as morally binding. Thus Kant's moral theory offers no political protection for, for example, women, servants, or Jews, who might have been discriminated against in existing law. As Young argues, in modern normative political theory and practice, impartiality in the public realm is attained by the exclusion of those linked to particular interests, needs, and concrete identities. The notion of the impartial public domain assumes a "homogeneity of citizens.... It excludes from the public those individuals and groups that do not fit the model of the rational citizen who can transcend body and sentiment."[68]

If one were interested in developing the political implications of moral heteronomy, I think it would be fruitful to look at examples such as the Scandinavian welfare states, which have a basic commitment to providing fundamental conditions of human dignity, including money, housing, and health care, to all the members of the community.[69] One might also consider the political party for women in Iceland, a path the National Organization of Women is seeking to pursue. These political parties seek recognition for a particular group in society. Political conflicts between different groups obviously entail negotiation and compromise, to achieve a "rational consensus." But such a consensus can never be achieved, or considered fully rational, if it is cut off from concrete identities, needs, interests, and emotions of the individuals within these groups.

How then does one assess the significance of Kant's essay "What Is Enlightenment?" for the contemporary world? With many of the critics of the Enlightenment, I challenge its fundamental conception of rationality, autonomy, and freedom. This philosophical position has been the hallmark of a historical period in Western European and American society characterized by imperialism, the hegemony of dominant groups over other groups excluded from wealth, political power, and often basic human respect. And yet it would be naive to think that we can free ourselves of this heritage merely by intellectual critique. Even in reacting against Enlightenment assumptions, postmodern and feminist critics are determined by these assumptions, often using the very tools they seek to reject. We may be heir to a tradition that constrains our ability to think the unthought, but nonetheless we must respond to the demand to create a new future, shaped by the contributions of women and Third World people, whose history is the underside of Enlightenment tolerance. We must find a way of living the practical contradiction between the past from which we seek to free ourselves and the future that we desire to create.

Notes

1 Immanuel Kant, "What is Enlightenment?" in *Kant on History*, trans. Lewis White Beck (New York, 1963), 3.

2 Habermas argues for "the way back" to enlightenment, in contrast to Horkheimer's and Adorno's efforts to show its self-destruction. *The Philosophical Discourses* of *Modernity*, trans. Frederick Lawrence (Cambridge, Mass., 1987), 128.

3 See Max Horkheimer and Theodor Adorno, *Dialectic* of *Enlightenment*, trans. John Cumming (New York, 1972), xi.

4   Berel Lang, *Act and Idea in the Nazi Genocide* (Chicago, 1990), 179ff.

5   I will discuss Kant's lack of egalitarianism regarding women and servants below. Lang also notes that few figures in the Enlightenment extended their tolerance to Jews. Kant did not view Judaism as having the status of a true religion but considered it rather a cult based on external rituals and therefore removed from the moral domain. Voltaire repeated many of the conventional slurs from the past (e.g., his reference to Jews as "the most contemptible of all nations ... robbers, seditious") and clearly considered the Jews to be themselves intolerant (by maintaining their separateness), thereby exempting them from the privilege of being tolerated by others. (Lang, *Act and Idea*, 185).

6   Lang, *Act and Idea*, 188.

7   In Foucault's essay "Kant on Enlightenment and Revolution," trans. Colin Gordon, *Economy and Society* 15, no. 1 (1986), 88–96, he argues that Kant develops an "ontology of the present" in "What Is Enlightenment?" which should be distinguished from the "analytic of truth" that Kant develops in his critical philosophy. However, Foucault's critique of Kant does extend to this "analytic of truth."

8   See Christine di Stefano, "Dilemmas of Difference," in *Feminism/Postmodernism*, ed. Linda J. Nicholson (New York, 1990), 75. Di Stefano's suggestion that postmodernism may be a theory whose time has come for men, but not for women, implies that women still need to carry out the Enlightenment tasks of developing a centered self and a coherent system of truth.

9   See Jane Flax's discussion of this position in "Postmodernism and Gender Relations," in *Feminism/Postmodernism*, 42.

10 Jane Flax, "Postmodernism and Gender Relations," in *Feminism/Postmodernism,* 42. Flax writes, "The way(s) to feminist future(s) cannot lie in reviving or appropriating Enlightenment concepts of the person or knowledge."

11 Ibid., 43.

12 Claire G. Moses, "The Legacy of the Eighteenth Century: A Look at the Future," in *French Women and the Age* of *Enlightenment,* ed. Samia I. Spencer (Bloomington, 1984), 413.

13 Ibid., 409–4 10.

14 Ibid. In terms of the view from Germany, one should note Kant's enthusiasm for the French Revolution and the political constitution that emerged from it. See Foucault, "Kant on Enlightenment and Revolution," 94.

15 Ibid., 413–414.

16 For example, between 1719 and 1730, a teacher in the Vosges region asked thirty-six couples to sign the marriage register. Although twenty-three men would write their names, thirty-two of the women were unable to write a cross, much less their names. Jean Larnac, *Histoire de la litterature feminine en France* (Paris, 1929), 132. Cited in Samia I. Spencer, "Women and Education," in *French Women and the Age of Enlightenment,* 95.

17 Spencer, "Women and Education," 83–84.

18 Ibid., 86.

19 Ibid., 84.

20 Some few aristocratic women in Prussia, such as Dorothea von Schlozer, were able to acquire a university education in the eighteenth century. However, they were also frustrated by their inability to use their education. But university education did not open up for women more generally until the twentieth century. As in France, the professions of medicine, teaching, and law began to open up gradually to women in the 1880s and 1890s. James C. Albisetti, "Women and the Professions in Imperial Germany," in *German Women in the Eighteenth and Nineteenth Centuries,* ed. Ruth-Ellen B. Joeres and Mary Jo Maynes (Bloomington, 1986), 96.

21 Wolff, Kant, Fichte, Schelling, Hegel, and Schleiermacher were all university professors. By contrast, in England scholars such as Darwin, Spencer, Mill, Bentham, Ricardo, Hume, Locke, Hobbes, and Bacon were not connected with university life. See Friedrich Paulsen, *The German Universities and University Study,* trans. Frank Thilly and William W. Elwant (New York, 1906), 4–5.

22 Charles E. McClelland, *State, Society, and University in Germany, 1700–1914* (Cambridge, 1980), 250.

23 The difficulty women have in gaining access to education and cultural authority remains an issue today. Michele Le Doeuff notes that although creative areas in philosophy today do not lie in the area of academic work, it is still crucial to note that since 1974 the number of women who pass selective examinations for teaching jobs has been very small ("Women and Philosophy," in *French Feminist Thought,* ed. Toril Moi [Oxford, 1987], 200–201). She explains this phenomenon in part by differences between men's and women's philosophical writing: "Men treat the text familiarly and knock it about happily; women treat it with a politeness for which girls' education has its share of responsibility. If the timidity and the desire to flatter are not too strong, this form of reading can, I think, produce great successes, a distanced kind of reading which enables one to see what is implicit in the text or to pick out the 'gaps' in theorization. The question is whether it is because this kind of reading is not highly valued that the women fail, or whether it is not highly valued just because it is evidently feminine. I prefer the second hypothesis, and would add that the feminine is excluded because it is associated with the idea of lack of authority" (p. 205).

24 Kant, *Anthropology from a Pragmatic Point of View,* trans. Victor Lyle Dowdell (Carbondale and Edwardsville, 1978), 219.

25 Ibid., 221.

26 Kant, *Observations on the Feeling of the Beautiful and Sublime,* trans. John T. Goldthwait (Berkeley, Los Angeles, and London, 1960), sec. 3, p. 78.

27 Ibid., 132–133.

28 *Anthropology,* 222.

29 Linda Gardiner, "Women in Science," in *French Women and the Age of Enlightenment*, 184ff.

30 Ibid., 189.

31 Immanuel Kant, *Philosophical Correspondence 1759–99*, ed. and trans. Arnulf Zweig (Chicago, 1967), 201.

32 Letter to Elisabeth Motherby, 11 February, 1793, in *Philosophical Correspondence*, 204.

33 Hans-Georg Gadamer, *Philosophical Hermeneutics*, ed. and trans. David E. Linge (Berkeley, Los Angeles, and London, 1976), 28.

34 "What Is Enlightenment?" 3.

35 Ibid.

36 See my book *Cognition and Eros: A Critique of the Kantian Paradigm* (Boston, 1988), for a discussion of Kant's conception of rationality. In particular, see chap. 9.

37 *Philosophical Correspondence*, 236.

38 "What Is Enlightenment?" 5. Although Kant did not express particular interest in extending Enlightenment ideas to women, a few of his contemporaries did—notably Theodor Gottlieb von Hippel. Hippel called for improving women's education and giving women opportunities for meaningful activity. Ruth P. Dawson, "'And This Shield Is Called Self-Reliance': Emerging Feminist Consciousness in the Late 18th Century," in *German Women in the Eighteenth and Nineteenth Centuries*, 158. There were many women writers of the eighteenth and nineteenth centuries who have been "unjustly forgotten." However, these women had to struggle against enormous social forces that prescribed women's "proper" role in the home and family. Women writers were not taken seriously. They appeared in the shadows of men, and they often wrote pseudonymously or anonymously in order to get published. Moreover, they faced a certain "vacuum of experience" because of their exclusion from education, government, military office, and business. Patricia Her-minghouse, "Women and the Literary Enterprise in Nineteenth-Century Germany," in *German Women in the Eighteenth and Nineteenth Centuries*, 79–90.

39 "What Is Enlightenment?" 3.

40 Gardiner, "Women in Science," 187.

41 *Philosophical Correspondence*, 204.

42 Maria's letter to Kant, January 1793, in *Philosophical Correspondence*, 201.

43 "What Is Enlightenment?" 3.

44 Ibid., 4.

45 Maria von Herbert did commit suicide, nine years after her last letter to Kant *(Philosophical Correspondence*, 26).

46 Immanuel Kant, *Foundations of the Metaphysics of Morals*, trans. Lewis White Beck (Indianapolis, 1959), 17.

47 *Anthropology*, par. 73, p. 155.

48 Ibid., par. 74, p. 157.

49 *Philosophical Correspondence*, 188–189.

50 Ibid., 189–190.

51 Ibid., 190.

52 Friedrich Nietzsche, *The Genealogy of Morals*, in *The Birth of Tragedy and the Genealogy of Morals*, trans. Francis Golffing (New York, 1956), 264.

53 Thomas E. Hill, Jr., "The Importance of Autonomy," in *Women and Moral Theory*, ed. Eva Feder Kittay and Diana T. Meyers (Totawa, NJ., 1987), 132. Although Hill is seeking to defend a view of Kantian autonomy as part of a debate about moral principles, not a way of living life, he acknowledges that Kant conflated the two and thus seems to undercut his own thesis.

54 Iris Young, "Impartiality and the Civic Public: Some Implications of Feminist Critiques of Moral and Political Theory," in *Throwing Like a Girl and Other Essays in Feminist Philosophy and Social Theory* (Bloomington, 1990), 96.

55 Seyla Benhabib, "The Generalized and the Concrete Other: The Kohlberg-Gilligan Controversy and Moral Theory," in *Women and Moral Theory*, 162.

56 Benhabib notes that "Rawls recapitulates a basic problem with the Kantian conception of the self, namely, that noumenal selves cannot be *individuated*. If all that belongs to them as embodied affective, suffering creatures, their memory and history, their ties and relations to others, are to be subsumed under the phenomenal realm, then what we are left with is an empty mask that is everyone and no one" (p. 166).

57 Young, "Impartiality and the Civic Public," 98.

58 Nietzsche, *Genealogy of Morals*, 189.

59 *Foundations*, 51.

60 *Foundations*, 17.

61 Carol Gilligan, *In a Different Voice: Psychological Theory and Women's Development* (Cambridge, Mass., 1982). See also articles debating Gilligan's work in *Women and Moral Theory*.

62 Diana T. Meyers, "The Socialized Individual and Individual Autonomy: An Intersection between Philosophy and Psychology," in *Women and Moral Theory*, 139, 152.

63 Benhabib, "Generalized and Concrete Other," 169.

64 Thomas Hill suggests that these rules are what attentiveness to a "caring" solution implies. "The Importance of Autonomy," 132.

65 Lucien Goldmann, *Immanuel Kant,* trans. Robert Black (London, 1971), 170.

66 *The* meaning of heteronomy has also to *be* redefined. In Kant's view, heteronomy refers to everything outside of the universal legislation of reason. All of *these* other factors were subsumed under the concept of nature *(Foundations,* 51). Kant's concept of heteronomy provides no tools for analyzing and distinguishing the nature of one's own emotions, the influence of other persons, or the impact of physical constraints on an individual. Therefore, he has no means of acknowledging the possibility of mutuality between persons, other than a shared abstract respect for the moral law.

67 Immanuel Kant, *The Metaphysical Elements* of *Justice,* trans. John Ladd (Indianapolis, 1959), 85–86.

68 Young, "Impartiality and the Civic Public," 98, 100.

69 Unfortunately, *the* commitments of the social welfare state in Scandinavia are now in jeopardy: witness recent significant cutbacks in social services in both Denmark and Sweden.

Authorial Ethos, Collaborative Voice, and Rhetorical Theory by Women

by Jane Donawerth

Women who wrote rhetorical theory between 1600 and 1900 did so in forms quite different from the textbooks and treatises of the men's rhetorical tradition.[1] One reason for this difference is audience: men's theory instructed boys in school or college; women's theory instructed women reading at home, or addressed a mixed public audience and argued for women's education in some branch of rhetoric.

A second reason that women wrote theory in forms different from men's, however, is the difficulty women had—and still have—in establishing ethos with the authority to construct a theory and persuade readers of its value. European and American culture of the seventeenth to nineteenth centuries prescribed silence as a virtue for women and promoted a gender ideology that relegated women to a naturally inferior position.[2] As a result, in their theoretical writings on communication, women often employed collaborative voice to establish authority and to suppress the obvious secret that a lone woman was producing theory. This was especially true when the intended audience of the work was both men and women. By "collaborative voice" I mean not "group writing," as Lisa Ede and Andrea Lunsford define it in their study of collaboration (14–16), but rather something like "dialogic" rather than "hierarchical" collaboration as they describe it (133–36). I will return to this matter of definition in my con-clusion. In this essay I examine works by four women who use collaborative voice: from seven-teenth-century England, Margaret Fell; from seventeenth- century France, Madeleine de Scudéry; from nineteenth-century United States, Frances Willard; and from early-twentieth-century United States, Mary Augusta Jordan.[3]

Margaret Fell, presently known as "the mother of Quakerism," was an early convert of George Fox, and her house became the center for early Quaker meetings, correspondence, appeals to the king, rest and recreation for traveling preachers, and childcare for women preachers on the road (many of Fell's daughters were preachers). Fell wrote *Women's Speaking Justified* in prison in 1666 after being found guilty of holding church services in her home.[4] She interweaves scriptural language with scriptural quotation to argue that women have been and should be preachers—she collaborates with God.

We can see how this interweaving of biblical and authorial language works at the level of diction in the following passage:

> It was Mary Magdalene, and Joanna, and Mary the mother of James, and the other women that were with them, which told these things to the Apostles. *And their words seemed unto them as idle tales, and they believed them not.* Mark this, ye despisers of the weakness of women, and look upon yourselves to be so wise: but Christ Jesus doth not so, for he makes use of the weak: for when he met the women after he was risen, he said unto them, *All Hail,* and they came and held him by the feet, and worshipped him, then said Jesus unto them, *Be not afraid, go tell my brethren that they go into Gallilee, and there they shall see me* [Matthew 28:10, Mark 16:9]. And John saith, when Mary was weeping at the sepulchre, that *Jesus said unto her, Woman why weepest thou? what seekest thou? And when she supposed him to be the gardener, Jesus saith unto her, Mary; she turned herself, and saith unto him, Rabboni, which is to say master; Jesus saith unto her, Touch me not, for I am not yet ascended to my Father; but go to my brethren, and say unto them, I ascend unto my father and your Father, and to my God, and your God* [John 20:16–17]. Mark this, you that despise and oppose the Message of the Lord God, that he sends by women; what had become of the Redemption of the whole body of mankind, if they had not believed the Message that the Lord Jesus sent by these women, of and concerning his Resurrection?[5]

Here Fell slyly points out that it is the women, the Marys who stayed with Jesus during the crucifixion while the men hid, who first preach the good news of Jesus' death for all.

In this passage Fell begins in her own words, and then inserts a scriptural quotation—"*And their words seemed to them as idle tales*"—to mark the men's misogynist assumption that women cannot be preachers.[6] She continues in her own words, but flavors them with biblical diction and allusion: the clause "Christ Jesus ... makes use of the weak," for example, is an allusion to a scriptural passage from Paul's letters (1 Corinthians 1:27) about the reversal of low to high in Christian values. Fell ends her historical narrative in support of women's preaching by quoting Jesus' own words telling the women to carry the message (from Matthew 28:10, Mark 16:7, and John 20: 15–17). Since the Word of God is irrefutable, her quotations buttress her own authority as speaker and become at the same time an extrinsic argument from testimony. She thus presents her very language as a summary of and collaboration with scripture.

In addition, Fell bases each of the major arguments in her pamphlet in favor of women's preaching on scriptural passages, a hermeneutic approach to argumentation common in sixteenth- and seventeenth-century Reformation Europe. Her overall argument is more a reinterpretation of scripture than a set of assumptions drawn out to conclusions (although it is also that). Fell begins by proposing, from scriptural examples, that God sees men and women as equal, citing the creation in Genesis 1:27–29, revising the story of Eve so that Eve and Adam are equal in blame and repentance, and referring to 1 Corinthians 1:27–28, where Paul proclaims that God chooses the weak to do his work. She then marshals instances in the Bible where the church is spoken of metaphorically as a woman, using them to argue that women are a God-ordained part of the church, citing an impressive array of passages from Isaiah, Jeremiah, the Psalms, the Song of Solomon, and Revelations. She also lists examples where Jesus speaks directly to women rather than through male intermediaries: the Samarian woman, Martha, Joanna, and the repentant prostitute usually assumed *to* be Mary Magdalene. Fell concludes, "Thus we see that Jesus owned the love and grace that appeared in women,"[7] using this recognition not only as support for her argument but also to build ethos.

In a long section Fell refutes the passages where Paul commands that women will not speak in church and that women will learn from their husbands (1 Corinthians 14 and 1 Timothy 2). To do this, Fell adopts a Protestant hermeneutic that requires scripture to be read in its historical context and according to the intent of its human speaker: Fell supposes that Paul means to exclude not *all* women, but only women not yet released from the law, who cannot yet trust in the inspiration of the Inner Light. It is these "indecent and unreverent women" who should be silent, she explains, not those women who "had union and fellowship with the Spirit of God."[8] Fell cites other passages from Paul where the Apostle welcomes or praises women: in quoting from 1 Corinthians 11:4–13, for example, Fell skips the verses that enjoin female subservience and cites only those verses that support her argument.

Fell demonizes the Catholic and Anglican Churches and their policy of excluding women from priesthood through interpreting the "Whore of Babylon" passages in Revelations as references to Catholics and nonreformed Anglicans (Revelations 17:6, for example). She returns to this refutative condemnation of priests in her postscript on the hypocrisy of blind priests who use women's words from the Bible as texts for their sermons, to get money, but then tell women that they may not preach. In a final passage, Fell lists almost every woman in the Bible who speaks—Aquilla and Priscilla, Deborah, Huldah, Sarah, Anna, Martha and Mary, Miriam, Esther, Judith, and even Mary, Jesus' mother—as preachers and prophets, inventing (Fell would see it as recovering) a Judeo-Christian history of women preachers. Fell can do this because the Quakers have redefined preaching more democratically, to include the testifying and witnessing on which they center their church services (rather than only formal public speaking). As Fell explains, again using scriptural words, and as she carries out in the collaborative form of her pamphlet, "your sons and daughters shall prophesy" (Acts 2:27 and Joel 2:28).

While Fell's collaboration with scripture in *Women's Speaking Justified* is hierarchical in the sense that she appeals to a superior authority, it is collaborative in the sense that she feels free to adapt and appropriate scriptural language, and to argue with the pronouncements of men in the Bible by citing their own words against them (especially Paul). In other of her pamphlets, she explains further the basis for her and other women's authority to preach. The biblical scripture is not itself the authority, but rather "the Word that is nigh, in the Heart, which is the Word of Faith which we preach" ("An Epistle to Convinced Friends" 95). And this Word is available to all who have true faith: "The word in *Davids* heart was a light unto him, and so it is unto all, whose heart is upright, who is guided by the light, which is the word, which is the Spirit" (*A Loving Salutation* 15). Thus Fell's hermeneutic justifies her adopting scriptural language to her own ends, for scriptural authority does not end with the printed text, but rather resides in the conscience of each believer.

A very secular version of collaboration appears in Madeleine de Scudéry's rhetorical works contemporary to Fell. Madeleine de Scudéry was born into an impoverished gentry family and made her own way (and that of her brother, Georges) through her education and writing after they were orphaned. Their conversational skills at Mme. de Rambouillet's salon, as well as their writings, gained Georges a diplomatic post and, later, Madeleine her own household and salon in Paris and a pension from the king.[9] In dialogue essays published in the 1680s in France (some adapted from dialogues taken from her romance novels published in the 1650s), Scudéry constructs a rhetoric for salon conversation that models the advice she gives, adapting the classical rhetorical dialogue as a vehicle for her own theories of domestic discourse—conversation and letter writing. She provides dialogues on conversation, speaking too much or too little, invention, and wit in her 1680 *Les Conversations sur Divers Sujets* and "The Manner of Writing Letters" in her 1684 *Conversations Nouvelles sur Divers Sujets*.[10]

Following Plato in the *Gorgias* and the *Phaedrus*, Cicero in *De Oratore*, and Augustine in *De Magistro*, Scudéry uses the dialogue to promote her rhetorical theory. In the essays in her first volume, she appropriates classical principles to establish standards for salon conversation. In "Of Conversation," for example, she adapts the conception of speech as civilizing, which Cicero had imported from the Sophists, and the sophistic idea that the goal of speech is pleasure (which she renames *"l'agréable"*) to conversation. In another dialogue, "Of Speaking Too Much or Too Little, and How to Speak Well," Emile lists the major qualities of the ideal speaker as those possessed by Plotine, and the list Scudéry gives him runs through the Roman five divisions of oratory adapted to conversation: invention is spontaneous, arrangement is clear, style is "noble and natural," and memory and delivery, with "no hesitation," are at the service of invention. In these dialogues Scudéry further adapts Aristotle's twofold division of sophistries into those of words and those of matter to an analysis of mistakes in conversation, and offers advice on wit and the relation of art versus nature that she appropriates from Cicero and Quintilian. She is thus using a standard Renaissance technique for establishing authority by working within tradition, by alluding to the classics, and by recovering ancient knowledge for contemporary uses, the knowledge itself helping to establish the authority of the speaker.

Now let us look closely at one dialogue, "On Wit," to see how Scudéry performs collaborative ethos. This dialogue begins as a narrative, but we never learn who the "I" is, male or female, and so both male and female readers may identify with the speaker's point of view. In addition, the group holding the discussions is almost exactly gender balanced: the speaker is traveling with two gentleman cousins and two ladies; the family they visit is a Spanish count, his newly returned son, and the sea-captain friend who has just brought him home, but the count has invited several ladies from the area as local guests to help make his visitors feel welcome. The dialogue is addressed to "Madame," as if telling a travel story. So the dialogue frame, which encloses several conversations, is also set as a dialogue, but a dialogue in which the reader is free to take the positions of speaker and listener.

The dialogue pays detailed attention to the ceremonious luxury of its setting, sounding very much like the famous Versailles entertainments, although with far fewer guests. The guests are treated to a symphony during the carefully arranged themed dinner, cannons and trumpets when they toast the king, cedar-wood caskets perfuming the air, formal gardens, and an outdoor opera in an arbor.

The dialogue is staged as an elaborate collaboration, a conversation among the elegant guests, and falls roughly into three sections: a friendly debate between Clarice and Melinta about the topic of conversation, Clarice voting for an account of the son's travels and Melinta despising such stories; a discussion of the nature of wit; and an epideictic portrait of a judicious king. In the first debate most of the guests participate, choosing sides between Clarice and Melinta about the value or interest of travel stories, and the outcome is a negotiated compromise: Clarice will get her travel story only after Melinta gets a discussion of wit, and Melinta gets to choose the form—a portrait of a famous person, not simply a list of waterfalls and rivers.

The discussion on wit arises out of a digression from this debate, a guest asking the travelers whether or not wit is the same in all places and countries. The travelers (and of course the author, Scudéry) give a sophisticated, materialist answer: wit "varies according to the diversity of nations, of temperaments, and of customs.... For according to the temperament of a people and the customs of nations, wit is rude or tactful, nasty or agreeable; it is mocking among some people and among others a simple playfulness that makes society more pleasant." But even this answer, accommodating to all people, is turned over and examined: Clearchus refutes with the example that some individuals don't joke, but Melinta defends the universality of wit by analogy to reason—some people are stupid, but we still say that all humans have the faculty of reason. Clarice, a sore loser in the debate about travel stories, gets in a dig at Melinta, suggesting that she carries her teasing to the point of injustice at times, Melinta defends herself, and the rest of the group line up, not around liking or disliking Melinta, but around the nature of wit. Melinta proposes that wit must include "agreeable malice" and some agree, while Clarice and Euridamia suggest that there is no innocent teasing and that even "gallant teasing" is like "walking along a precipice—you may fall into the pit of rude insult."

Proposing and agreeing to the kinds of behaviors that do not belong in witty conversation: one should not mock friends, enemies, oneself (because immodest), inferiors or superiors, crimes, evil, or foreigners, and one must always pay attention to decorum (occasion and audience); one must avoid vulgarity, repetition, long stories, proverbs, and joking about everything; one should follow only the court as a model for wit; and one must never say terrible things about someone as if it is a joke. After reaching this negative consensus, the group appoints Euridamia to set up a list of rules for wit,[11] since by this point she has won over even Melinta to her side. Euridamia, however, refuses the role of judge and states the principle of consensus that the group has been working under all along: "I wish only to tell you my opinion and to submit it to your judgment." The group, led by Euridamia, agrees that wit is brief, original, not too cruel, "bold familiarity," and has a twist at the end; wit speaks the "language of well-bred people," avoids satire or cutting remarks, and a true wit never says anything to friends that amuses the speaker more than the person being made fun of. Antigene astutely adds the social purpose of wit: with wit one may tell the truth to people whom one cannot politely criticize.

The long praise of the king, although viewed as a model of elegant language during Scudéry's own time, is actually an example of wit that breaks some of the rules the group has agreed upon. It is a very long praise of the speaker's king but disguised as a character sketch of a famous long-dead Egyptian monarch; consequently, it is a joke at Clarice's expense, not the travel story she desired. The speaker signals that he is teasing Clarice with this story by warning the group, "Do not laugh at this," and by his exaggeration of the evidence for the story's authenticity. While the story is too long and too much a travel story to be counted as wit by the terms of the dialogue, it has a twist at the end, and it allows the speaker (and Scudéry herself) to tell a truth without offending: she praises the monarch—and so Louis XIV, her own king—for never allowing his ministers too much power, which is actually a warning against trusting too much in ministers. Finally, Clarice is as pleased by the trick, the shift to praise of her current monarch, as the speaker is himself, so he does not offend his friend.

So this dialogue is not only truly collaborative, representing a group coming to a consensus through debate and accommodation, but also multi-layered in its collaboration: a conversation, framed by a conversation, and finally, a joke at the author's expense—Scudéry has written a long travel story as her example of wit, which is forbidden as dull in the dialogue. Scudéry moves to this self-mockery near the end, by suggesting that no proper courtier of her time would read the dialogues of Plato or Xenophon, and "if he should come upon a book in which the natural manner of living of well-bred people is painted, ... he could hardly be made to open the volume ... [after he found out] that it was printed by Barbin or Courbé." Scudéry thus concludes with a joke she and the reader share: Barbin and Courbé were the printers who published Scudéry. Scudéry's witty self-mockery establishes herself-as-author in ironic collaboration with the reader, both knowing what the characters in the dialogue do not.

Frances Willard, for a while Dean of Women at Northwestern University, was a nineteenth-century social reformer and suffragette, who helped organize and eventually headed the Women's Christian Temperance Union (WCTU). With other women in the WCTU, Willard helped to invent techniques of social protest and public demonstration that we still use, and promoted public speaking for women, training them in parliamentary procedure.[12] Willard published *Woman in the Pulpit* in 1888. Weaving together her own words with letters and essays from male and female preachers, she argues for women's right to preach. Whereas Fell had adopted collaboration with scripture to achieve authority, Willard drew on the republican authority of testimony by the best citizens, quoting long passages from twenty-one men and eleven women in defense of women preaching.

Willard introduces her topic through the words of men praising her defense. T. De Witt Talmage agrees with Willard's defense of women's preaching, because women's voice, he claims, will bring tenderness, pathos, and sympathy to religion. Joseph Cook, in a second letter, himself provides testimony from a woman, quoting a letter from a woman missionary whose teaching has gradually moved from women's meetings in her parlor to public speaking in church. He further argues that if the women who wrote *Uncle Tom's Cabin* and *Aurora Leigh* can preach so notably in print, there is no reason women should not preach orally in churches; that he does not name these writers (Harriet Beecher Stowe and Elizabeth Barrett Browning) increases the force of his argument, for he expects every reader to know these texts. He concludes with an analogy linking the nineteenth-century conception of women's domestic sphere to men's public roles: "Hand in hand, man and woman build the home; hand in hand they ought to build the state and the church" (Willard 14). Again, he expects his readers to collaborate with him in constructing his argument, for "Hand in hand" is an allusion to the end of Milton's *Paradise Lost,* thus also an interpretation of that poem and of Genesis to suggest divine approbation for equality between men and women. A third letter, by Joseph Parker, makes the standard essentialist argument, but with irony: men, Parker suggests, have the ability to make scripture difficult to understand, but women bring pathos and sympathy to its interpretation and dissemination. These prefatory letters, like the epideictic poems at the beginning of Renaissance books, or the blurbs from reviews on the front pages of our own culture's paperbacks, advertise the contents through approval of famous men. Willard shows herself, through this means, in conversation and collaboration with the famous divines of her day.

Willard also constructs her own argument in support of women's preaching. Chapter 1 of *Woman in the Pulpit* is a refutation of Paul's proscriptions against women speaking or teaching in church. Willard argues that the "rules" of Paul and of scripture in general are culture bound, demonstrating that current pastors follow only a selection of these rules: Protestants don't require celibacy of the clergy or unleavened bread at communion, for example. Thus, she concludes, scripture should *not* be taken literally, and she sets out a table that juxtaposes the strictures restricting women against words by Paul or Jesus to show that even these early Christians did not really require silence of women. Like Fell, Willard reinterprets biblical women who are prophets, judges, or who record their prayers as preachers, listing Miriam, Deborah, Hannah, Esther, Judith, and the Marys. Willard ends with a bold reversal: "The whole subjection theory [of women being subject to men's governance] grows out of the one-sided interpretation of the Bible by men" (37). Men and women need to collaborate to get the interpretation right.

In chapter 2 of *Woman in the Pulpit,* Willard sets up a positive argument for women's preaching: women demonstrate their faith as apostles in the scriptures, so there is historical precedent for women preaching; preaching is particularly appropriate to women, who by their natures appeal to moral sentiment; with proper training, women's voices are physically sufficient to be heard; motherhood fits women for a life of spiritual guidance of others; and God calls women as well as men to preach—women are already preaching as missionaries and in the WCTU. Here Willard steps back from the social constructionist argument she uses for scriptural interpretation, relying on an essentialist view of gendered spheres: "Men preach a creed; women will declare a life.... Men's preaching has left heads committed to a catechism, and left hearts hard as nether millstones.... [But] Religion is an affair of the heart" (47).

But the bulk of Willard's argument is founded on testimony from many supporters. Chapter 3 is a refutation of the argument that women cannot be preachers because their vocation must be "mother." While Willard frames the chapter with her own arguments, most of the chapter is lengthy quotation, first from an anonymous woman preacher and then from Senator Henry Blair. The woman argues that motherhood as a spiritual state prepares women to be preachers if we just relieve them of the irrelevant jobs of "cook, laundress, seamstress, and nurse-maid" (68); Senator Blair, in his book on temperance and the right to vote, suggests that motherhood prepares women to be good citizens and to vote in the best interest of their children. Chapters 4 and 5 offer testimony from male and female preachers (each in their own chapter). From the men we hear that one has been "converted" from his "bitterest prejudices" against women's preaching by his more enlightened reading of Saint Paul (73–74); that the Bible cannot be fully understood until "men and women work it out together" (76); that since men have successfully converted many women, we should allow women to convert the men (76); and that there exists insufficient evidence that God has *not* called women to preach to refuse them this right (82). From the women we hear that it is right for women to preach because "it is surely right for a messenger to give a message of truth" (96); that women are natural preachers because of their "sympathetic and intuitional nature, ... [and their] high moral sense" (97); that raising well-cared-for children does not prevent women from being available and effective ministers (from twenty-five years' experience by a woman preacher) (98–99); and that women have the "reason," the "voice," the persuasive "eloquence," and the "religious sense" to give them an "advantage in winning souls" (133). Willard concludes with a debate between two men resulting from a shorter defense she had published in a journal.

Willard thus recapitulates her society's gendered spheres in the design of her book, allowing men and women to make different but equally well-reasoned arguments in support of women's preaching (and even one argument against it), demonstrating the consensus of a multivoiced community. She assumes an audience that is hostile to the practice of women's preaching. She constructs her argument in collaboration with her audience, both hostile and supportive, interweaving refutation and what Aristotle calls "inartistic proofs"—testimony from witnesses. She lets other voices speak along with her in order to be heard. Willard separates men and women into their own chapters—creating quite literally in her book the separate spheres of nineteenth-century Anglo-American social life. Yet she argues against this doctrine for preaching, demonstrating a tension between her commitment to social change, and an essentialist view of women's gender as naturally nurturant.

Mary Augusta Jordan was educated at Vassar College and was a professor of English at Smith College from 1884 to 1921. Influenced by ideals of progressive education, she stood against the turn-of-the century trend in favor of correctness.[13] In 1904 Jordan published *Correct Writing and Speaking* in the Woman's Home Library series, and her book seems to be based on her lectures from Smith College rhetoric courses.

Whereas the other theorists I have talked about adopted collaboration as a means to gain the authority to address a public audience, Jordan is ostensibly addressing an audience of women. Yet she inserts her theories on women's speech and letter writing in between lengthy quotations from learned progressive men. Jordan has imported this collaborative technique that previous women theorists used for mixed audiences for a different purpose—to address the issue of what type of education women should have. In the late nineteenth century, as women colleges were created, educators debated what should constitute college education for women—should women be taught men's learning, or should they be taught knowledge appropriate for women?[14] Jordan chooses to do both, by "collaborating" with men.

Jordan "collaborates" with men by including long quotations from men—men in their own voices—in her textbook. She is thus offering men's knowledge to women students, showing she is certain that women are capable of understanding such knowledge. But she is not so certain that this knowledge is "correct" or that it is appropriate to women students. We see these reservations in the dialogic ways she uses her male collaborators, and in the knowledge she adds in her own voice.

Jordan does use quotations from male experts to establish authority, quoting approvingly A. J. Ellis, Robert Louis Stevenson, and H. G. Wells.[15] But she criticizes the "great man" theory of the history of English language (14), and in most instances she modifies or even perverts the original intentions of the great man she quotes. Quoting John Walker's against Richard Sheridan's views of English pronunciation, then A. J. Ellis's against Sheridan's (34–35), she sets experts against each other so that she can reinforce her thesis—that there is no single "correct" English, since great men cannot agree on a standard. She quotes Matthew Arnold only to critique him: "The weakness of this description [of criticism] is the weakness, however, of Arnold's entire conception of the relation of human beings to culture ... [for this] false distinction [between what is known and what is thought] opens the door to all sorts of intellectual tyranny" (74). And she makes fun of Sir Thomas More, quoting him not only for his argument in favor of the common reader's good sense but also for his nonstandardized English: "The most superficial examination of this fearless expression of opinion," mocks Jordan, "makes it clear that the bold champion of the freedom of the reader allowed himself extensive liberty of grammar and construction" (23). Jordan introduces men's voices into her textbook in order to discuss the matters of language, rhetoric, and literary criticism with them, not simply as authority. She thus creates for herself a kind of dialogic ethos, depending partly on the authority of these male experts, but partly, also, on overturning this authority.

The knowledge Jordan adds in her own voice is the kind of rhetorical theory that women had been writing for the two hundred years before Jordan's textbook: advice on conversation and letter writing. [16] Jordan examines the requirements for conversation and presents it as a collaborative venture, where the speaker is more interested in furthering other speakers' goals of self-expression than her own (229–37). Jordan treats letters as the most frequent literary expression of the common person, and especially addresses the faults that her "girl" students might succumb to—fancy paper and colored ink. She is especially interested in letters as gifts, establishing a conversation between people, especially women, over long distances (60–64, 237–42). Finally, Jordan also adds, to the tradition of women's rhetoric, advice on public speaking for women—assuming that what most women are required to do is after-dinner speaking for social or moral causes. She is especially concerned that the public speaker should not impose ideas on her audience but instead should gather up the spiritual forces of the audience and express them (64–71). "The audience is not to be dominated, cajoled, or bullied," Jordan instructs: "It is to be interpreted, and made to know its own self in terms of something else than prejudice, or passion, or lazy self-indulgence.... The successful speaker of the present will use all his art to enable him to discern the signs of the spiritual *forces* coming into action in his presence. His aim will be to conserve them, to let as little as possible real energy go to waste" (69).

These women theorists center their theories on conversation rather than on public discourse. Like all Quakers, Fell believes that preaching should be replaced by testimony from the Inner Light by all Friends, a conversation with each other and God. Scudéry is a founder of the *precieuse* salon culture in France and offers a theory adapting classical dicta on effective persuasion and style to conversation. Willard advocates the public speech of preaching for women, but does so within the women's club movement and the WCTU, based on parlor entertainment and conversation circles. And Jordan includes advice on conversation in her textbook on "correct" speaking and writing. Basing their theories conceptually on conversation, these women also make a conversation in their writings, building authority out of imagined collaboration.

Having traced the construction of imagined collaboration in four instances, we can now return to Ede and Lunsford's definitions in their study of collaboration. None of the women examined in this essay seem to have published as authorial collaborators in the works we examined, although Frances Willard comes closest to it, with her collection of letters from other people. Margaret Fell frequently collaborated with other Quaker Friends in other pamphlets. But all of these women did use what I have been calling "collaborative voice." In their conclusion, Ede and Lunsford declare that their "study of collaborative writing has led [them], finally, to embrace the full complexity of collaborative acts and, as a result, to dissolve the traditional boundaries between collaborative writing and writing" (137). At the very least, they discern two modes of collaboration. "Hierarchical collaboration" is a mode of efficiently completing writing tasks in the professions, where each participant is assigned a portion; it is a highly structured form, where goals are specific and each person's task explicitly limited, under the leadership of a senior group member. This form of writing works because the goal is limited to pragmatic problem solution or information delivery (133). A second mode, however, "dialogic collaboration," involves more fluid roles and less structured process, according to Ede and Lunsford. In this mode all group members participate in defining goals, and one goal is often the production of knowledge (rather than the simpler delivery of information). This mode, Ede and Lunsford claim, can be "deeply subversive" (133) because it can better acknowledge the reality of "a plurality of voices" in any cultural production of knowledge (135).

This mode, "dialogic collaboration," is quite close to the "collaborative voice" employed by the women I have studied in this essay. They complicate the definition of collaboration yet further, however, because their collaboration is imagined and constructed rather than a result of multiple authors. Even in the case of Frances Willard, who includes whole letters, the structure is an imagined written dialogue of collected pieces rather than a hierarchical process of multiple authors writing to order—it is Willard's means of demonstrating the consensus of her community in favor of women's preaching. In addition, the arguments of all of these women then become layered: the words of others are embedded in their own arguments, creating an ethos based on self-in-relation-to-others rather than a self-sufficient authorial self. Such an ethos is not an essentialist reflection of women's gendered role, but is instead a carefully constructed rhetorical implement, depending on the ironic complexity resulting from the juxtaposition of diverse voices.

Notes

1 For more information on women rhetorical theorists, see Patricia Bizzell and Bruce Herzberg, *The Rhetorical Tradition*; Joy Ritchie and Kate Ronald, *Available Means*; and Jane Donawerth, *Rhetorical Theory by Women before 1900: An Anthology*.

2 On silence as a requirement of the ideal woman in Renaissance and nineteenth-century conduct books, see Suzanne W. Hull, *Chaste, Silent & Obedient, English Books for Women, 1475–1640*; and Nan Johnson, "Reigning in the Court of Silence: Women and Rhetorical Space in Postbellum America," and *Gender and Rhetorical Space in American Life, 1866–1910*.

3 Although not much work has been done on women rhetorical theorists, a great deal has now been accomplished on the history of women's rhetoric. See especially Karlyn Kohrs Campbell, ed., *Man Cannot Speak for Her*; Carole Levin and Patricia A. Sullivan, eds., *Political Rhetoric, Power, and Renaissance Women*; Andrea Lunsford, ed., *Reclaiming Rhctorica: Women in the Rhetorical Tradition*; Molly Wertheimer,

ed., *Listening to Their Voices: Essays on the Rhetorical Activities of Historical Women;* Christine Mason Sutherland and Rebecca Sutcliffe, eds., *The Changing Tradition; Women* in *the History of Rhetoric;* Cheryl Glenn, *Rhetoric Retold: Regendering* the *Tradition from Antiquity through the Renaissance;* Catherine Hobbs, ed., *Nineteenth-Century Women Lean to Write;* Lucille M. Schultz, *The Young Composers: Composition's Beginnings in Nineteenth-Century Schools;* Shirley Logan, ed. *With Pen and Voice: A Critical Anthology of Nineteenth-Century African-American Women,* and Logan, *"We Are Coming": The Persuasive Discourse of Nineteenth-Century Black Women;* Carla Peterson, *"Doers of the Word": African-American Women Speakers and Writers* in *the North (1830–1880);* Jacqueline Jones Royster, *Traces of a Stream: Literacy and Social Change among African American Women;* Nan Johnson, "Reigning in the Court of Silence" and *Gender and Rhetorical Space* in *American Life, 1866–1910;* Carol Mattingly, *Well-Tempered Women;* Susan Kates, *Activist Rhetorics and American Higher Education, 1885–1937;* Bizzell and Herzberg, eds., 2nd ed. *The Rhetorical Tradition;* and Janet Carey Eldred and Peter Mortensen, *Imagining Rhetoric: Composing Women of the Early United States.*

4   On Fell's life, see Isabel Ross, and Bonnelyn Young Kunze. On Fell as a rhetorical theorist, see Donawerth, "The Politics of Renaissance Rhetorical Theory," 261–63, and Bizzell and Herzberg, 748–52.

5   The quotations from Fell are taken from my edition of Margaret Fell, *Women's Speaking Justified, Proved and Allowed of by the Scriptures…* (London, 1666), Folger Shakespeare Library F642 (copy 1), in my anthology, *Rhetorical Theory by women before 1900;* I modernize spelling and punctuation, but not grammar—in this passage there are *very* few changes.

6   See Luke 24:11. Fell follows the King James Version, the version that Fell and other Quakers generally used, but here and elsewhere she seems to be quoting from memory, for her quotations are slightly off—one preposition substituted for another, verb tenses changed, phrases transposed. See my essay "Margaret Fell's Reading and Writing Practices."

7   In Donawerth, *Rhetorical Theory,* 63.

8   Ibid., 65.

9   On de Scudéry's life, see Nicole Aronson. On de Scudéry as a rhetorical theorist, see Elizabeth Goldsmith, 41–76; Donawerth, "As Becomes a Rational Woman to Speak'"; and Bizzell and Herzberg, 761–66, as well as the introduction to the March 2004 edition of Scudéry's rhetorical writings, translated by Donawerth and Strongson.

10 All quotations from Scudéry's work are the translations from *Letters, Orations, and Dialogues of Madeleine de Scudéry,* translated by Julie Strongson and me, from the University of Chicago Press in March 2004. For more on Scudéry's theory, see my essay in *Rhetorica.*

11 As Elizabeth Goldsmith observes, the group dynamic in de Scudéry's conversations moves from a negative survey of what other speakers do wrong to positive praise of one of themselves as a model for speaker; see ch. 2, pp. 41–75.

12 On Willard's life, see Ruth Bordin. On Willard's rhetoric, see Bonnie J. Dow; Richard W. Leeman; Carolyn DeSwarte Gifford; Carol Mattingly; and Martha Watson. On Willard as a rhetorical theorist, see Donawerth, "Poaching on Men's Philosophies of Rhetoric" and "Conduct Book Rhetoric by Women."

13 On Jordan's life, see Kathleen Perkins. On Jordan as a rhetorical theorist, see Donawerth, "Textbooks for New Audiences," and Susan Kates, "Subversive Feminism" and *Activist Rhetoric.*

14 On issues in women's higher education during Jordan's tenure at Vassar, see Solomon, esp. ch. 6, pp. 78–93.

15 Jordan quotes A. J. Ellis, for example, 54–56; H. G. Wells, 113–18; and Robert Louis Stevenson, 91–97.

16 See my essay on nineteenth-century conduct book rhetoric by women.

Works Cited

Aronson, Nicole. *Mademoiselle de Scudéry.* Trans. Stuart R. Aronson. Boston: Twayne, 1978

Bizzell, Patricia, and Bruce Herzberg, eds. *The Rhetorical Tradition: Readings from Classical Times to the Present.* 2nd ed. Boston: Bedford/St. Martin's, 2001.

Bordin, Ruth. *Frances Willard: A Biography.* Chapel Hill: U of North Carolina P, 1986.

Campbell, Karlyn Kohrs, ed. *Man annot Speak for Her.* 2 vols. Contributions in Women's Studies 101. New York: Greenwood Press, 1989.

Donawerth, Jane. "As Becomes a Rational Woman to Speak': Madeleine de Scudery's Rhetoric of Conversation." Wertheimer 305–19.

– –. "Conversation and the Boundaries of Public Discourse in Rhetorical Theory by Renaissance Women." *Rhetorica* 16.2 (Spring 1998): 181–99.

– –. "Nineteenth-Century United States Conduct Book Rhetoric by Women." *Rhetoric Review* 21.1 (2002): 5–21.

– –. "Poaching on Men's Philosophies of Rhetoric: Eighteenth- and Nineteenth-Century Rhetorical Theory *by* Women." *Philosophy and Rhetoric* 33.3 (2000): 155–62.

– –. "The Politics of Renaissance Rhetorical Theory *by* Women." Levin and Sullivan 256–72.

– –. *Rhetorical Theory by Women before 1900: An Anthology.* Lanham, MD: Rowman and Littlefield, 2002.

– –. "Textbooks for New Audiences: Women's Revisions of Rhetorical Theory at the Turn of the Century." Wertheimer 337–56.

Dow, Bonnie J. "The 'Womanhood' Rationale in the Woman Suffrage Rhetoric of Frances E. Willard." *Southern Communication Journal* 56.4 (Summer 1991): 298–307.

Ede, Lisa, and Andrea Lunsford. *Singular Texts/Plural Authors: Perspectives on Collaborative Writing.* Carbondale: Southern Illinois UP, 1990.

Fell, Margaret. "An Epistle to Convinced Friends" (1656). *A Brief Collection of Remarkable Passages and Occurrences ... With undry of Her Epistles.* London, 1710. 95–97.

– –. *A Loving Salutation to the Seed of Abraham among the Jewes.* London, 1656.

– –. "Women's Speaking Justified, Proved and Allowed of by the Scriptures (1600)." Donawerth, *Rhetorical Theory* 59–72.

Hobbs, Catherine, ed. *Nineteenth-Century Women Learn to Write.* Charlottesville: UP of Virginia, 1995.

Gifford, Carolyn DeSwarte. "Frances Willard and the Woman's Christian Temperance Union's Conversion to Woman Suffrage." *One Woman, One Vote: Rediscovering the Woman Suffrage Movement.* Ed. Marjorie Spruill Wheeler. Troutdale, OR: NewSage Press, 1995. 117–33.

Glenn, Cheryl. *Rhetoric Retold: Regendering the Tradition from Antiquity through the Renaissance.* Carbondale: Southern Illinois P, 1997.

Goldsmith, Elizabeth C. *"Exclusive Conversations": The Art of Interaction* in *Seventeenth-Century France*. Philadelphia: U of Pennsylvania P, 1988.

Hull, Suzanne W. *Chaste, Silent & Obedient: English Books for Women, 1475–1640*. San Marino, CA: Huntington Library, 1982.

Johnson. Nan. "Reigning in the Court of Silence: Women and Rhetorical Space in Postbellum America." *Philosophy and Rhetoric* 33.3 (2000): 221–43.

– –. *Gender and Rhetorical Space in American Life, 1866–1910*. Carbondale: Southern Illinois UP, 2002.

Jordan, Mary Augusta. *Correct Writing and Speaking*. The Woman's Home Library. New York: A. S. Barnes, 1904.

Kates, Susan. *Activist Rhetorics and American Higher Education, 1885–1937*. Carbondale: Southern Illinois UP, 2001. 27–52.

– –. "Subversive Feminism: The Politics of Correctness in Mary Augusta Jordan's *Correct Writing and Speaking* (1904)." *College Composition and Communication* 48.4 (December 1997): 501–17.

Kunze, Bonnelyn Young. *Margaret Fell and the Rise of Quakerism*. Stanford, CA: Stanford UP, 1994.

Leeman, Richard W., ed. *"Do Everything Reform": The Oratory of Frances E. Willard*. New York: Greenwood, 1992.

Levin, Carole, and Patricia A. Sullivan, eds. *Political Rhetoric, Power, and Renaissance Women*. Albany: SUNY Press, 1995.

Logan, Shirley. *"We Are Coming": The Persuasive Discourse of Nineteenth-Century Black Women*. Carbondale: Southern Illinois UP, 1999.

– –, ed. *With Pen and Voice: A Critical Anthology of Nineteenth-Century African-American Women*. Carbondale: Southern Illinois UP, 1995.

Lunsford, Andrea, ed. *Reclaiming Rhetorica: Women in the Rhetorical Tradition*. Pittsburgh: U of Pittsburgh P, 1995.

Mattingly, Carol. *Well-Tempered Women: Nineteenth-Century Temperance Rhetoric*. Carbondale: Southern Illinois UP, 1998.

Perkins, Kathleen. "Mary Augusta Jordan." *American National Biography*. Ed. John A. Garraty and Mark C. Carnes. New York: Oxford UP, 1999. Vol. 12: 274–75.

Peterson, Carla. *"Doers of the Word": African-American Women Speakers and Writers in the North (1830–1880)*. New York: Oxford UP, 1995.

Ritchie, Joy, and Kate Ronald, eds. *Available Means: An Anthology of Women's Rhetoric(s)*. Pittsburgh: U of Pittsburgh P, 2001.

Ross, Isabel. *Margaret Fell: Mother of Quakerism*. London: Longmans, Green, 1949.

Royster, Jacqueline Jones. *Traces of a Stream: Literacy and Social Change among African American Women*. Pittsburgh: U of Pittsburgh P, 2000.

Schultz, Lucille M. *The Young Composers: Composition's Beginnings in Nineteenth-Century Schools*. Carbondale: Southern Illinois UP, 1999.

Scudéry, Madeleine de. *Les Conversations sur Divers Sujets*. Amersterdam, 1686. Folger #171523. Volume I.

– –. *Conversations Nouvelles sur Divers Sujets, Dedie'es Au Roy*. La Haye, 1685. Folger #171523. Tome II.

– –. "On Conversation," "Speaking Too Much or Too Little, and How to Speak Well," and "On the Manner of Writing Letters." *Letters, Orations, and Dialogues of Madeleine de Scudéry*. Trans. Jane Donawerth and Julie Strongson. Chicago: U of Chicago P, 2004.

Solomon, Barbara Miller. *In the Company of Educated Women: A History of Women and Higher Education in America*. New Haven, CT: Yale UP, 1985.

Sutherland, Christine Mason, and Rebecca Sutcliffe, eds. *The Changing Tradition: Women in the History of Rhetoric*. Calgary: U of Calgary P, 1999.

Watson, Martha. *Lives of their Own: Rhetorical Dimensions in Autobiographies of Women Activists*. Columbia: U of South Carolina P, 1999.

Wertheimer, Molly Meijer, ed. *Listening to Their Voices: Essays on the Rhetorical Activities of Historical Women*. Columbia: U of South Carolina P, 1997.

Willard, Frances E. *Woman in the Pulpit*. Boston: D. Lothrop, 1888.

CONCLUSION

Comprehension Questions

1   Identify and briefly describe three primary tenets of Enlightenment thought.

2   Describe the racist and sexist elements in the Enlightenment writings of Locke, Rousseau, Hume, and Hegel.

3   What does Donawerth mean by "collaborative voice"?

4   According to Schott, why do contemporary feminists take issue with Enlightenment ideals?

Critical Thinking Questions

1   Elaborate on how social location (e.g., as a woman, a slave) shapes/affects how one understands the world and exercises public voice. Provide a specific example to illustrate your point.

2   What strategies did women and African Americans use to argue for the application of Enlightenment ideals to their communities?

3   Women and African Americans took issue with the uneven and/or selective ways Enlightenment ideals were applied during the 1600s to 1700s. Do you see parallels in contemporary society? How are present-day public speakers from marginalized groups advocating for rights to equality and freedom?

Unit Summary

"Unit 4" explored the period known as the Enlightenment (seventeenth and eighteenth centuries), homing in on the ideals espoused in the period's influential thinkers such as Kant, Locke, Rousseau, Hume, and Hegel. From the critical/cultural perspective advanced throughout this collection, we took note of the ways Enlightenment concepts such as freedom, education, and equality were selectively applied and privileged the epistemological positions of men of European descent. Still, we learned, women and African Americans spoke out and put pen to paper, giving us different ways to consider epistemological issues and concerns surrounding public participation.

In this anthology's final section, "Unit 5," we jump ahead two hundred fifty years to what is referred to as the contemporary era of rhetorical thought. "Unit 5" provides a broad overview of more recent scholarship on public communication that considers the dynamics of race, class, and gender power disparities.

UNIT 5

CONTEMPORARY EFFORTS TO RETHINK AND REVISE RHETORICAL THEORIES

Consider:

1. Identify a few key ways life in the twenty-first century differs from that of ancient Greece and Rome or the Enlightenment.

2. How might these economic/political/cultural differences influence how we speak in public?

3. How might these economic/political/cultural differences affect how we understand the nature of public communication and democratic struggle?

Clearly much has changed politically, culturally, and economically since the days when Aristotle taught at Plato's Academy, Cicero debated in the Roman Senate, medieval women shared their mystic visions, and Enlightenment philosophers pondered the relationship between knowledge and communication. Through democratic struggle and concerted public efforts on the part of oppressed groups and allies, slavery was abolished (1865 in the United States, 1833 in England); systemic racism has been/continues to be challenged; and around the world, women have obtained suffrage and attained positions of political and economic influence. The Enlightenment ideals of equality, opportunity, and freedom remain as centerpieces of United States political thought and continue to shape policy formation and public discourse. And, democratic struggles on the part of marginalized groups (e.g., Black Lives Matter, #MeToo movement, efforts to end mass incarceration) remain vocal about the ways these ideals are not applied evenly. Individually and in groups, people continue to exercise public speech to argue for inclusion within, or more fundamental alteration of political and economic structures. In the "Unit 5" introduction, our goal is to shed light on how this context has shaped our theories and understandings of rhetoric in the twenty-first century.

Reworking How We Conceptualize Rhetoric

Recall the definition of rhetoric elaborated in the "Unit 1" introduction:

- Rhetoric is public communication.
- Rhetoric is intentional and motivated.
- Rhetoric plays a role in how we acquire knowledge.
- Rhetoric relies on appeals to logic and ethics.

And recall that our goal in this book was to *deepen* our understanding of the assumptions underlying our theories and thus challenge those theories altogether—and to *broaden* our understanding of what counts as rhetoric.

At least since the 1960s, rhetorical theories have engaged in these efforts by complicating, challenging, or expanding the traditional understanding of rhetoric just noted. This scholarship—which will be touched upon only briefly in this final unit—takes a critical approach to the study of rhetoric, one that challenges traditional conceptualizations of the nature of rhetoric and how it functions in society. Scholars have sought to reveal how traditional concepts and theories do not adequately capture how rhetoric operates in a diverse contemporary society, and have elaborated on how traditional concepts have historically promoted a European, elite, male bias. Not unlike the debates between Plato and the Sophists, contemporary scholars continue to debate the relationship between rhetoric, truth, reality (Cherwitz and Hikins 1983; Farrell 1976; Scott 1967), particularly in light of the ways one's standpoint—or position as a marginalized "other"—shapes or influences how one views and comes to understand the world (Droogsma 2007; Hallstein 2000; Triece 2001, 2013; Wood 2005). And scholars continue to expand on what counts as rhetoric and to explore the challenges specific to marginalized groups who speak publically.

In the "Unit 5" introduction, we focus on two primary thrusts in contemporary scholarship. First, contemporary scholarship has *challenged* traditional concepts of rhetoric. Second, contemporary scholarship has *broadened* what counts as rhetoric, or what may be included in the canon.

Deepening Our Understanding of Rhetoric

Numerous contemporary theories have challenged how we understand public communication and its roles in society. Rhetorical scholarship of this nature takes a critical stance toward the nature of rhetoric and focuses on the relationship between public discourse and power. In contrast with traditional approaches to rhetorical theory that are grounded in ancient Greco-Roman views on public address, much contemporary rhetorical theory encourages us to rethink the function and purpose of public discourse in a democracy with an eye on uncovering how rhetoric justifies or legitimates power disparities and social hierarches, often in subtle ways (Black 1970; Cloud 1994; McGee 1980; McKerrow 1989; Shome 1996; Wander 1983). These studies have suggested new ways of examining public messages, speaker, and audience, and have explored rhetoric's role in legitimizing the power held by certain groups. This scholarship draws upon ideology and Marxist studies, and has been variously termed "critical rhetoric" (McKerrow 1989), critical theory (Pollock and Cox, 1991), or "materialist rhetoric" (Cloud 1994, 2006; Greene 1998).

The concept of the "second persona" (Black 1970) marks a departure from the traditional Aristotelian approach to rhetoric through its suggestion that we might benefit from looking at the audience implied—rather than actual audience—in a public message. This approach encourages us to explore the ideological dimensions of a speech—that is, the values, beliefs, and interests promoted—and render a moral judgment from such an analysis. An "ideological turn" (Wander 1983) in rhetorical studies similarly challenges traditional Greco-Roman understandings of rhetoric by suggesting that critics explore the ways speeches legitimize or mystify power disparities and promote the interests of society's political and economic elite. The term "critical rhetoric" (McKerrow 1989) has been applied to studies that explore both domination and freedom as they are exercised through discourses. Critical rhetoric also encourages us to examine the fragmented nature of contemporary public discourse or the ways messages come to us in bits and pieces through mass media, as opposed to complete and uninterrupted speeches. Similarly, critical theory—rooted in the studies of German philosophers of the Frankfurt School—sees its "primary function [as] critique—or ... the reappropriation of discourse to emancipatory interests" (Pollock and Cox 1991). Materialist rhetorical theories—although in disagreement about how to conceptualize the "material"—shed light on the relationship between public messages and an extra-discursive context in which they are situated, one characterized by capitalism and wealth disparities.

Feminist, critical race, and postcolonialist scholarship expand the critical approach to rhetoric by calling attention to the gendered, raced, and imperialist dimensions of power (Blair, Brown, and Baxter 1994; Biesecker 1992; Bowen and Wyatt 1993; Dow 2016; Shome 1996). Feminist rhetorical scholars have challenged traditional ways of theorizing what constitutes a public (Davis 1998; Flores 1996), suggested different ways to conceptualize speaker as citizen (Chávez 2015), and have debated the very nature of persuasion and civility. Foss and Griffin (1995) suggest that attempts to persuade are inherently patriarchal and domineering; in contrast, Lozano-Reich and Cloud (2009) maintain the importance of persuasion and suggest that appeals to civility are a "form of gender discipline." Among feminist scholars, women of color and lesbian/queer women continue to challenge the white, heterosexual bias of much feminist research (Carlacio 2016; Davis 1998; Gaines 2016; King 2016). "Racialized critical rhetorical theorizing" (Hasian and Delgado 1998) and "Latina/o Critical Race Theory (LatCrit)" (Anguiano and Castañeda 2014) focus attention on the ways institutionalized racism affects understandings of and messages about race. Postcolonialism "seeks to expose the Eurocentrism and imperialism of Western discourses" (Shome 1996, p. 41). In short, rhetorical theorists continue to debate the relationship between rhetoric and power, how power may be more evenly distributed, and what is the role of rhetoric in democratic struggles for equality and social justice.

Broadening What Counts

A second approach to the study of rhetoric attempts to expand the canon or body of messages deemed worthy of study. In this approach, scholars have broadened "what counts" and strived for inclusiveness and recognition of the voices of marginalized "others" who, since the writings of the ancient Greek and Roman scholars, have been ignored, silenced, or denigrated. In the 1960s, as movements for social justice (e.g., anti-war, gay liberation, women's rights, Black Power) were taking to the streets, rhetorical theorists recognized the importance of studying messages other than the speeches of the politically powerful. Social movement scholars theorized leadership and the role of speaker, how to motivate audiences who operate within deeply entrenched constraints, and many noted how traditional understandings of civility and persuasion do not apply in the same ways when studying movements (Cloud 2005; Haiman 1967; Scott and Smith 1969; Simons 1972; Triece 2001).

Feminist scholars have focused specifically on bringing to life the voices of women who over-came the barriers of their sex—and often race and class—to be heard (Campbell 1986, 1989; Foss, Foss, and Griffin 1999; Lunsford 1995; Spitzack and Carter 1987; Triece 2001, 2013). Efforts to expand the rhetorical canon have come under criticism for not challenging the basic precepts of the canon itself. From this perspective, women become tokens in what remains a male and mas-culinized domain (Biesecker 1992). Thus, key for much critical theorizing, feminist or otherwise, has been to avoid essentializing or generalizing about the experiences of marginalized groups, which leads to overlooking important differences among members of those groups. Additionally, scholars such as Raka Shome (1996) encourage a theoretical "self reflexivity" that calls on us to remain aware of how our theories may play out in the real world in ways that reinforce rather than challenge disparities. And scholars emphasize the importance of combining inclusivity with a critical examination of the "very value system on which the rhetorical canon and our scholarship is based" (Shome 1996, p. 49).

Preview of Unit Readings

The first reading in "Unit 5," Molefi Asante's "Rhetoric of Resistance," is a chapter from his book, *The Afrocentric Idea*. Asante's work deepens our understandings of rhetorical theory. He challenges traditional Greco-Roman conceptualizations of audience, and the canons of invention and word choice, and explores the rhetorical possibilities and constraints faced by African American protesters. As you read Asante's work, which was published thirty years ago, consider how his writing remains relevant today.

The second reading, "To Tell It Like It Is," explores the rhetorical strategies of Fannie Lou Hamer, an influential yet lesser known civil rights activist of the 1960s. Maegan Parker Brooks's analysis of Hamer's speeches, which were given in the late 1960s, *broadens* the traditional canon of great speeches by including the efforts of an African American woman who spoke out during a time of persistent institutionalized racism. As Brooks shows us, Hamer relied on traditional rhetorical appeals such as logos but used them in combination with more confrontational tactics. Consider how Hamer's position as an African American woman influenced her rhetorical options and constraints.

References

Anguiano, Claudia, and Castañeda, Mari. 2014. "Forging a Path: Past and Present Scope of Critical Race Theory and Latina/o Critical Race Theory in Communication Studies." *The Review of Communication, 14,* 107–124.

Biesecker, Barbara. 1992. "Coming to Terms with Recent Attempts to Write Women into the History of Rhetoric." *Philosophy and Rhetoric, 25,* 140–161.

Black, Edwin. 1972. "The Second Persona." *Quarterly Journal of Speech,* 56, 109–119.

Blair, Carole, Brown, Julie R., and Baxter, Leslie A. 1994. "Disciplining the Feminine." *Quarterly Journal of Speech, 84,* 383–409.

Bowen, Sheryl Perlmutter, and Wyatt, Nancy, eds. 1993. *Transforming Visions: Feminist Critiques in Communication Studies.* Cresskill, NJ: Hampton Press.

Campbell, Karlyn Kohrs. 1986. "Style and Content in the Rhetoric of Early Afro-American Feminists." *Quarterly Journal of Speech, 72,* 434–445.

––. 1986. *Man Cannot Speak for Her.* New York: Greenwood Press.

Carlacio, Jami L. 2016. "Aren't I a Woman(ist)? The Spiritual Epistemology of Sojourner Truth." *Journal of Communication & Religion, 39,* 5–25.

Chávez, Karma. 2015. "Beyond Inclusion: Rethinking Rhetoric's Historical Narrative." *Quarterly Journal of Speech, 101,* 162–172.

Cherwitz, Richard A., and Hikins, James W. 1983. "Rhetorical Perspectivism." *Quarterly Journal of Speech, 69,* 249–266.

Cloud, Dana L. 2004. "The Materiality of Discourse as Oxymoron: A Challenge to Critical Rhetoric." *Western Journal of Communication, 58,* 141–163.

––. 2006. "The Matrix and Critical Theory's Desertion of the Real." *Communication & Critical/Cultural Studies, 3,* 329–354.

––. 2005. "Fighting Words: Labor and the Limits of Communication at Staley, 1993–1996." *Management Communication Quarterly, 18,* 509–542.

Davis, Olga Idriss. 1998. "A Black Woman as Rhetorical Critic: Validating Self and Violating the Space of Otherness." *Women's Studies in Communication, 21,* 77–89.

Dow, Bonnie J. 2016. "Authority, Invention, and Context in Feminist Rhetorical Criticism." *Review of Communication, 16,* 60–76.

Droogsma, Rachel Anderson. 2007. "Redefining Hijab: American Muslim Women's Standpoints on Veiling." *Journal of Applied Communication Research, 35,* 294–319.

Farrell, Thomas. 1976. "Knowledge, Consensus, and Rhetorical Theory. *Quarterly Journal of Speech, 62,* 1–14.

Flores, Lisa A. 1996. "Creating Discursive Space Through a Rhetoric of Difference: Chicana Feminists Craft a Homeland." *Quarterly Journal of Speech, 82,* 162–172.

Foss, Karen A., Foss, Sonja A., and Griffin, Cindy L. 1999. *Feminist Rhetorical Theories.* Long Grove, IL: Waveland Press.

Foss, Sonja K., and Griffin, Cindy L. 1995. "Beyond Persuasion: A Proposal for an Invitational Rhetoric." *Communication Monographs, 62,* 2–18.

Gaines, Rondee. 2016. "Rhetoric and a Body Impolitic: Self-Definition and Mary Mcleod Bethune's Discursive Safe Space." *Howard Journal of Communications, 27,* 167–181.

Greene, Ronald Walter. 1998. "Another Materialist Rhetoric." *Critical Studies in Mass Communication, 15,* 21–41.

Hallstein, D. Lynn O'Brien. 2000. "Where Standpoint Stands Now: An Introduction and Commentary." *Women's Studies in Communication, 23,* 1–15.

Haiman, Franklyn S. 1967. "The Rhetoric of the Streets: Some Legal and Ethical Considerations." *Quarterly Journal of Speech, 53,* 99–114.

Hasian, Marouf, Jr., and Fernando Delgado. 1998. "The Trials and Tribulations of Racialized Critical Rhetorical Theory: Understanding the Rhetorical Ambiguities of Proposition 187." *Communication Theory, 8,* 245–270.

King, Claire Sisco. 2016. "American Queerer: Norman Rockwell and the Art of Queer Feminist Critique." *Women's Studies in Communication, 39,* 157–176.

Lozano-Reich, Nina M., and Cloud, Dana L. 2009. "The Uncivil Tongue: Invitational Rhetoric and the Problem of Inequality." *Western Journal of Communication, 73,* 220–226.

Lunsford, Andrea A., ed. 1995. *Reclaiming Rhetorica: Women in the Rhetorical Tradition.* Pittsburgh: University of Pittsburgh Press.

McGee, Michael Calvin. 1980. "The 'Ideograph': A Link Between Rhetoric and Ideology." *Quarterly Journal of Speech, 66,* 1–16.

McKerrow, Raymie E. 1989. "Critical Rhetoric: Theory and Praxis." *Communication Monographs, 56,* 91–111.

Pollock, Della, and Cox, J. Robert. 1991. "Historicizing 'Reason': Critical Theory, Practice, and Postmodernity." *Communication Monographs, 58,* 170–178.

Scott, Robert L. 1967. "On Viewing Rhetoric as Epistemic." *Central States Speech Journal, 18,* 9–16.

Scott, Robert L., and Smith, Donald K. 1969. "The Rhetoric of Confrontation." *Quarterly Journal of Speech, 55,* 1–8.

Shome, Raka. 1996. "Postcolonial Interventions in the Rhetorical Canon: An 'Other' View." *Communication Theory, 6,* 40–59.

Simons, Herbert W. 1972. "Persuasion in Social Conflicts: A Critique of Prevailing Conceptions and a Framework for Future Research." *Speech Monographs, 39,* 227–247.

Spitzack, Carole, and Carter, Kathryn. 1987. "Women in Communication Studies: A Typology for Revision." *Quarterly Journal of Speech, 73,* 401–423.

Triece, Mary E. 2001. *Protest and Popular Culture: Women in the U.S. Labor Movement, 1894–1917.* Boulder, CO: Westview Press.

——. 2013. *Tell It Like It Is: Women in the National Welfare Rights Movement.* Columbia, SC: University of South Carolina Press.

Wander, Philip. 1983. "The Ideological Turn in Modern Criticism." *Central States Speech Journal, 34,* 1–18.

Wood, Julia T. 2005. "Feminist Standpoint Theory and Muted Group Theory." *Women & Language, 28,* 61–64.

Rhetoric of Resistance

by Molefi Asante

W e invent out of the substance of our culture and from nothing else. If by acci-
dent we create something—say, a discourse—that is not based in our culture,
then it is not truly invented and not a matter of rhetoric. As a creation, my discourse
is new, derived from substances organized in a novel way. A protest speaker, therefore, originates the protest universe of discourse from the unique cultural conditions
accompanying the state of oppression or denial that gives birth to the protest in the
first place. Erwin Bettinghaus perceptively wrote that "when audiences of particular
ethnic characteristics are exposed to messages, their responses will be determined
in part by the characteristic experiences which they share with other members of the
group and for which they have developed particular frames of references."[1]

The African American protest speaker (or writer) is in the employ of a determinism
defined by the possibilities and complexities of social protest within a larger society,
and is further constricted by the peculiarity of the black experience. As a protest
speaker, he or she is met with the limitations placed upon all protest speakers, but
because he or she is black, a further constraint, based upon socio-historical factors,
exists. The rhetorical materials—in fact, the available materials—he or she chooses as
a rhetor are limited, and thus the real challenge the African American speaker faces
is having to make do or create with the strategies and alternatives prescribed by the
social conditions. Choosing materials, then, is fundamentally a question of rhetorical
invention, because it deals with the coming to be of the novel.

The example of the African American poet Aimé Césaire from Martinique, shows
that even in the West Indian response to cultural domination the black speaker or

writer must function similarly to the black in the United States. In his great poem "Return to My Native Country," Césaire's indignation over the Martinican condition finally explodes into open revolt and fierce determination to assert a new life.[2] This was a rebellion of language, of symbol, of his entire behavior toward domination. What Césaire chose from the available materials dictated the overthrow of the language that was imposed upon him. How he responded to the substance of his condition showed him to be one of the finest modern poets. The spiritual distress that settled over France after the first mass carnage of Europeans during the First World War, the racial discrimination practiced by the French in the Caribbean, and the economic crisis in Europe called into question the old values as well as the place of Africans in colonial territories. W.E.B. Du Bois and Sylvester Williams had begun pan-African conferences, Jean Price-Mars had founded the Haitian Indigenist Movement, Harlem had a renaissance, and in France, Léopold Senghor, Léon Damas, and Aimé Césaire had started with what they had available and created the Negritude Movement. This is the circumstance of Césaire's creativity.

Restraints and Rebellions

We expect that the frame of reference for the new, the innovative, will always come from African American lifestyles and interactive experiences. How are the available resources related to the proposed *invented thing?* While avoiding a detailed classificatory scheme (and, it is hoped, a fragmentation), we can speak of general bodies of materials that are indispensable to the speaker: *uses and usages of words, prevailing behaviors,* and *"hearerships."*

Theoretically, all of the words in the world are available for the speaker, who can choose among them as they are needed; in reality, however, no speaker has actual access to all the uses and usages of all the possible words. American speakers, black or white, will certainly choose to speak to American English audiences, unless there are special demands for the occasion; and even so, they might be limited by their knowledge of the language. Therefore, speakers will use words that are accessible to them and to the majority of their audiences.

In addition to language, protest speakers have access to the prevailing rhetor actions (physical and verbal) of their culture, which perhaps are even defined by the rhetoricians of that cultural era. Some gestures, mannerisms, and language usages are satisfactorily employed and are in vogue at one time and place and not at others. Mass media have made the prevailing behaviors culturally available to most rhetors and audiences. While all speakers have theoretical, if not actual, access to the prevailing behaviors of a culture, accessibility, theoretical or actual, does not mean acceptability for those who choose not to employ the prevailing behavior. By following the speech patterns of the media, any African American preacher or other speaker could use the "general" American speech behaviors. But in most cases, particularly in the large Protestant denominations, it would be professional suicide to do so. This is why Jesse Jackson attempts to use the discourse styles that are acceptable to African American audiences.

Another general category of resources is "hearerships," collections or gatherings of persons who maintain, if only for the duration of the speech occasion, a special relationship with each other, if only the hearing of the speaker. This is not the place to explore the advantages of this concept over that of audience; suffice it to say that the concept of hearership includes a horizontal as well as vertical relationship between hearer and speaker. Hearerships can be available materials for speakers, who can choose the audiences they will address. By addressing some at the expense of others, they may significantly alter the outcome of the speech. Thus, choosing an audience is as creative a task as choosing what to say; and in persuasive cases, the one is assisted by the other.

These categories are common to most speakers, inasmuch as the use of words, prevailing behaviors, and hearerships are available to all speakers. However, *how* speakers choose and *what* they choose are matters of *what* it is possible for them to choose. Consequently, some positions, tactics, and usages that are considered off-limits by a black protest speaker are not restricted for other speakers, black or white. For example, black campaigners for equal rights and justice cannot successfully use derogatory expressions against other groups or about their own culture.

The black protest speaker is also uniquely constrained by circumstances, audiences, and personal attributes. The distinctiveness of this restriction is the frame of black protest. It is clear that the speaker's conception of the mission and the materials available to accomplish that mission have a temporal and spatial orientation. In some sense, the black protest speaker's manifestation of this distinctiveness is dependent upon the choice or creation of audiences. This takes into account the fact that some audiences are found and others are created. When a black protest speaker addresses a white audience, the speaker is restricted by the audience's sophistication (e.g., what they know about black language) and personal attributes, and by the aims of the speech. This has nothing to do with the unavailability of words; they are available in theory but may be unknown to the speaker (not part of his or her personal knowledge), or, if known, incompatible with the aims of the speech and therefore, for all functional reasons, off-limits. Thus, the effect is the same, and the speaker remains confined to a limited context.

It should be emphasized that the choice of protest limits the number of usable words, arguments, and strategies. Many aspects of this contextual limitation are related only to white audiences; others are more generally true and observable. The protest speaker must make sure that all the "entrances" and "exits" are covered as he speaks to white audiences; there can be no reckless abandon in language or behavior that will allow misinterpretations or misunderstandings. The protest speaker holds his or her cards close to the flesh when faced with white audiences.

Robert Pirsig's comment that the "traditional scientific method can't tell you where you ought to go, unless where you ought to go is a continuation of where you were going in the past,"[3] is further complicated by the "rational" order of the established system that stands in the way of creativity and innovation. The black speaker seeks to create, to imagine a new world, to appeal to a new order, to break with the past. In fact, it is not so much the change of logic that is sought as the change of the established system. The traditional uses of language are invalidated by the insistent voices of the powerless who seek to *seize* the floor, to *take* a position, to *hold* forth in the arena of persuasion. Yet in all of this the African American speaker appeals to his or her audiences only on the basis of language that is accessible for the appropriate arguments.

Frantz Fanon knew that one could assume that the oppressed would resort to the language of the oppressor for liberation, yet he called for a new person with a different rhetoric. Always, the protester must use symbols, myths, and sounds that are different from those of the established order. Otherwise, the protest speaker will always be at a disadvantage, because the oppressed can never use the language of the established order with as much skill as the establishment. The oppressed must gain attention and control by introducing another language, another sound. Fanon's advice to the colonized, in *The Wretched of the Earth,* is to 'leave this Europe where they are never done talking of Man, yet murder them everywhere they find them."[4] In this way, black protesters equalize the power situation between themselves and the oppressor, even if only in the area of symbolic grounding. Beyond this, of course, is the fact that such an action places the oppressed on the path to Afrocentricity; it is a liberating act, the intellectual equivalent of a slave's wave of good-bye to the master from the north side of the Ohio River.

Speaking the same language as the oppressor does not lead to a positive result, but introducing new ground stretches the dimensions of the protest medium. In other words, one does not assume that the protester has available the words of the established order. This is not to say that the protester's language may not *seem* to have the character of the established order. If we look at the discourse of Martin Luther King, Jr., we see that his Judeo-Christian rhetoric was often expressed in the language of the black community. Thus, while his themes of justice, equality, and love were universal, he frequently often used logic, myth, and expressions that were derived from the culture of the oppressed. This rhetoric, in its uniqueness, attracted attention.

This behavior by the black speaker has helped to shape the myth of the inaccessibility of black communication to outsiders. The form of our communication, emerging from the confrontation of slaveowner and slave, of master and property, was never open. Suspicion, distrust, and conspiracy accompanied the interactions of Africans and Europeans from the earliest periods in American history. The African who wanted to break out of the cultural and economic bondage of the American society often found even more reasons to remain suspicious of whites. Victims of a social reality that makes the combination of freedom and speech dangerous, black protest speakers frequently modify their speeches when talking to white audiences.

Although theme is seldom changed in such situations, tone and lyricism are often modified. White audiences are not expected to know what you mean when you refer to "Shine," "bloods on the block," "Mr. Hawkins," "simple," "when the word is given," and other "in-house" expressions; but since white audiences do increasingly share in the symbols of the black community, it is becoming more imperative to use an Afrocentric analysis to create a context for intercultural understanding. The Afrocentric approach identifies ways in which the black protester resists discourse limitations and creates new rhetorical ground.

To this point, our discussion accounts for the situational limitations imposed on black protesters, but if we accept the fact that the number of words in the American language is limited, we can see that, within such a system, black protest speakers use only a portion of the word resources available to all to coin expressions, appeals to the environment for others, and create combinations as they move back and forth across code boundaries. Their rhetorical actions are determined by situations both within and beyond their control. They can alter some situations, but at times are helpless unless they choose to employ guerrilla rhetoric. By utilizing the extreme dimensions of the available media of words, tones, fables, myths, legends, and sounds, the black protest speaker expresses a sort of word subtlety intended to subvert the established order by guerrilla rhetoric tactics.

The protest speakers' sensitivity to powerlessness in the society frees them to utilize the improvisational mechanisms of African American culture in responding to unpleasant situations. In some respects, H. Rap Brown, Eldridge Cleaver, Stokely Carmichael, and Bobby Seale were "jazz artists" in the 1960s. They often chose not to employ the *prevailing behavior* of white culture in their verbal responses. The police were "pigs" to Bobby Seale, and Hubert Humphrey was a "buffoon" to Eldridge Cleaver. In reply to the charge that the Black Panthers used too much profanity, the votarists would often argue that the society was profane, that poverty was profane, that the government was profane, and that the American system was the biggest profanity of them all.

Confronted by a hostile legal system that emanated from the prevailing behaviors of white American culture, black protesters of the 1960s were frequently at odds with the system. What constituted jurisprudence and law to the white society was seen as arbitrary and violent by the protesters. Indeed, John Illo has written that "jurisprudence is the prudent justification of an absurd society of institutionalized inequity and internal contradiction. Law, and juridical logic, and grammar conspire to frustrate the original idea of a just and good society, in which all men may freely become the best that they may be."[5] The black protester, set upon the road to disalienation, seeks to return us to reformist, perhaps revolutionary, ideas.

Those fundamental ideas of liberty, fraternity, and equality—long obscured by imposed categories—are restored in the functional rhetoric of the black protester. The characteristic tonal quality of the black speaker, referred to as a lyricism by Henry Mitchell, is more often used in settings that are peculiarly black American, not white American.[6] What is at work in these situations is the sermonic style of the preacher, the archetype of the protest genre. To the extent that Jesse Jackson used this tone in his campaign for the Democratic nomination for president in 1984 and 1988, he was perceived by many whites as being "too black" and not a candidate for all of the people.

There is an overwhelming opposition to the black cultural style of speech by white audiences, who see politicians more as technicians and less as moral persuaders. Certainly, Martin Luther King, Jr.'s "Been to the Mountaintop" speech in a Memphis church could not have been the same as his intellectual discourse to the Harvard University Law School; the speeches were different in tone because the speaker invented them differently. Intonation and tonal styling are substantive parts of the black speaker's invention. Furthermore, to the extent black protest speakers employ these characteristic linguistic behaviors, they are comfortable with their audience. This is not to say that they cannot be at ease with "straight lectures" before white audiences, but that they are more likely to use nuances and idiosyncrasies that are mutually "comfortable" only with black audiences.

Therefore, black protest speakers, trying to persuade white audiences of the need for a social transformation, are simultaneously exhibiting a distrust of whites by refusing them access into the inner linguistic secrets. Even in the most intense debate over social change, black protest speakers do not share all of their characteristic tonal patterns with white audiences; in fact, their speech further suggests what is, of course, true: blacks and whites have different patterns of experiences. Black protest, then, is framed by characteristic rhetorical and linguistic practices that are products of a special experience, environment, and heritage.

An Organic Continuity of Protest

Among the more widespread manifestations of the idea that black protest speakers consult unique contexts are the arguments invented to assault segregation, discrimination, and injustice in American society. What blacks argued a hundred years ago is still argued today. In 1843, Henry Highland Garnet noticed that "the gross inconsistency of a people holding slaves, who had themselves 'ferried o'er the wave' for freedom's sake, was too apparent to be entirely overlooked."[7]

Frederick Douglass emphasized the same theme in his famous Fourth of July speech in 1852:

> I say it with a sad sense of the disparity between us. I am not included within the pale of this glorious anniversary! Your high independence only reveals the immeasurable distance between us. The blessings in which you this day rejoice, are not enjoyed in common. The rich inheritance of justice, liberty, prosperity, and independence, bequeathed by your fathers, is shared by you, not me. The sunlight that brought life and healing to you, has brought stripes and death to me. This Fourth of July is yours, not mine. You may rejoice, I must mourn.[8]

Douglass goes on to make his point emphatically by highlighting the hypocrisy of the occasion: "whether we turn to the declarations of the past, or to the professions of the present, the conduct of the nation seems equally hideous and revolting. America is false to the past, false to the present, and solemnly binds herself to be false to the future."[9] Such language is not foreign to contemporary arguments. In the 1960s, Malcolm X said there was no democracy, only hypocrisy.

While there may have been a proprioceptive change, as one aspect of the problem activated a new discussion, the intent and structure have remained constant. Attempts to provide rhetorical solutions to political problems have produced many duplications from one era to the next, and the operating space seems more confining than ever.

The black protest speaker can define only two fundamental alternatives, *integration* or *separation,* and every argument is ultimately made for one or the other of these ends. When a speaker has only two alternatives, speeches tend to exhibit pat formulas. The better speakers have imaginatively organized and structured speeches from the available materials with an eye toward either integration or separation.

In relation to the two historically political goals of black protest, one can suggest that the politics has alternated between *provincial* and *mass phenomena,* the tactics of protest from *verbal* to *activist,* and the ideology from *religious* to *political.* The speakers decide their direction, and that choice determines the restrictions upon their invention. Protest speakers are not always free to choose, but if they choose the provincial phenomenon, then certain limitations occur. For instance, if they choose provincial over mass political phenomena as a channel for their aims, the instruments of mass dissemination are not essential to the rhetorical effort. In addition, there are technical limitations on the speakers because of their choice. In a mass situation, they would need to make some general appeals in order to save the movement from collapsing because of a too narrow focus. On a specific neighborhood problem, speakers could concentrate on some narrow goals and make particular appeals.

Furthermore, black speakers choose between governing principles, such as, whether the protest will ultimately rest on religious or political bases. After a position is chosen, arguments that are compatible with one's rhetorical purpose are created or discovered. In the 1960s, H. Rap Brown could never use the language of Martin Luther King, Jr., or vice versa, yet each could use similar rhetorical strategies against segregation and discrimination. Their specific differences were inherent in their choices of governing principles, not in the nature of the problem.

All rhetorics have their strict syntax of language, with rules and laws consistent with the speaker's objectives, traditions, and abilities. This is not merely the case between H. Rap Brown and Martin Luther King, Jr., Malcolm X and Jesse Jackson, Louis Farrakhan and Andrew Young, or Khalid Mohammed and Cornel West, but also for the less famous orators of the street masses and the speakers in the campus rallies. The choice of syntax for discourse reflects the inviolable rules of the particular speaker's type of rhetoric. In deciding upon a governing principle, the speaker stands on the side of a certain social syntax. Houston Baker, Jr., writing of Richard Wright's understanding of the American problem, says "Wright knew that in any black life, in any white-dominated society, a life crisis of black identity—an event equivalent to such other life crises as birth, social puberty, and death—was an inevitable event."[10] Wright knew, of course, what Du Bois had said, in *The Souls of Black Folks,* about the condition of being black in a white America. Du Bois put it succinctly when he wrote in *The Souls of Black Folks* that patience would show the reader "the strange meaning of being black here at the dawning of the Twentieth Century. This meaning is not without interest to you, Gentle Reader; for the problem of the Twentieth Century is the problem of the colorline. "[11]

Even in 1903 Du Bois could sense a "peculiar sensation" that he called "double-consciousness" where the Africans looked at themselves through someone else's eyes. In this respect, Wright and Du Bois carried forth the theme of a recurring response to white domination.

Addressing both the response and the condition has produced outstanding oratorical genius; the speakers and writers have had to keep the faith and yet save the day. James Cone's position is that the African American used the spirituals and the blues to speak to the same crisis of identity to which the public speeches appealed. Since the whites who practiced slavery contradicted God, blacks affirmed their "somebodiness" in attacking the whites' godlessness. In James Cone's words, "The mountains may be high and the valleys low, but 'my Lord spoke' and 'out of his mouth came fire and smoke.'"[12] There has always been a feeling that deliverance was right around the corner; indeed, the rhetorics and lyrics of the best orators and musicians remain full of this vision.

In addition to this vision, however, was the continuing presence of the idea of blackness itself within the framework of black protest. Even the productive discourse that rose from the urban streets and the rural roads of the 1960s found some of its source material in the emotional idea of black solidarity. In doing this, the protest writers and speakers were calling upon the older traditions found in Nat Turner, Henry Highland Garnet, and even Du Bois. It should be noted that Du Bois never intended his ideas to lead to what Marcus Garvey saw as Black Nationalism.[13] Nevertheless, the framing of black protest can only be adequately examined by considering the peculiar experiences, creative and material, of African Americans. Certainly Du Bois's race idea is one of those emotional and cultural experiences that has been used as a motive force.

Anthony Appiah has correctly challenged Du Bois's conception of race. However, in his attempt to lay bare the kernel of truth in Du Bois's universe of discourse about race, he has crushed it unintentionally. In his critique, Appiah argues righteously that

> to put it more simply: sharing a common group history cannot be a criterion for being members of the same group, for we would have to be able to identify the group in order to identify *its* history. Someone in the fourteenth century could share a common history with me through our membership in a historically extended race only if something accounts both for his or her membership in the race of the fourteenth century and for mine in the twentieth. That something cannot, on pain of circularity, be the history of the race. Whatever holds Du Bois' races together conceptually cannot be a common history; it is only because they are bound together that members of a race at different times can share a history at all. If this is true, Du Bois' reference to a common history cannot be doing any work in his individuation of races. And once we have stripped away the sociohistorical elements from Du Bois' definition of race, we are left with the true criterion.[14]

This criterion Appiah sees as "common descent and the common impulses and strivings."[15] Of course, the real issue is not race in any scientific or quasiscientific sense, nor even in Du Bois's sociohistorical sense. What Du Bois intended, when one examines the perspective of his work, was to make a statement about culture, not about race. His reading of race into the picture is perhaps due in large part to the Germanic influences upon his education and the whole European enterprise of race.

Henry Louis Gates, Jr., establishes the presence of race as a notion in the minds of Europe's most important thinkers. Gates claims that Hume, Kant, and Hegel made race a factor in their discussions of history, intelligence, and reason.[16] Kant goes so far as to correlate being black with being stupid! Gates responds: "Without writing, no *repeatable* sign of the workings of reason, of mind, could exist. Without memory or mind, no history could exist. Without history, no humanity, as defined consistently from Vico to Hegel, could exist."[17]

Resistance to this profoundly racist discourse prompted Africans in the United States to respond with their own discourses. Gates correctly argues that "political and philosophical discourse were the predominant forms of writing." The reason for this state of affairs was simple. The African's intellectual ability was universally denied by Eurocentric writings, and since Europeans held the monopoly of information from the sixteenth to the nineteenth century, the only action of the oppressed was reaction. In this respect, the African often found himself cast upon the moving tides of a turbulent Eurocentric ocean. Yet, as Gates says,

> The recording of an authentic black voice—a voice of deliverance from the deafening discursive silence which an enlightened Europe cited to prove the absence of the African's humanity—was the millennial instrument of transformation through which the African would become the European, the slave become the ex-slave, brute animal become the human being. So central was this idea to the birth of the black literary tradition in the eighteenth century that five of the earliest slave narratives draw upon the figure of the voice in the text—of the talking book—as crucial "scenes of instruction" in the development of the slave on the road to freedom.[18]

Resistance pours forth from the autobiographical pens of Ottabah Cugoano and Olaudah Equiano, although their political observations perhaps lacked candor, because of their circumstances. The fact that they spoke, that they had a voice to accompany the many faces of Africans, was in itself an achievement of courage and genius.

I mention resistance in the autobiographical genre mainly because Appiah has used Du Bois's *Dusk of Dawn* as one of the sources for his analysis of Du Bois's concept of race. In the final analysis, what Appiah renders clear is Du Bois's ambivalence about race in its elusive and unfounded biological sense. What I read in Du Bois's *Dusk of Dawn* should not be "distressing" for Appiah, inasmuch as the idea of culture was taken as seriously by Du Bois as we take it today. A close reading of *The Souls of Black Folks* further supports Du Bois's culture idea.[19] Race is essentially a political concept in racist societies, but it serves no practical biological purpose for the scientist. On the other hand, the idea of culture is both significant within the structure of a resisting ideology and advantageous within an examination of the causes of human misunderstanding. I must quickly add that the economic idea is, of course, a central creation of the interplay of cultural and environmental factors, and therefore contributes also to our way of viewing reality.

This is no apologia for Du Bois's use of the term *race* in *Dusk of Dawn;* rather, it expounds his attempt at resistance in the language of his contemporaries. Du Bois, of course, was not an Afrocentricist; he was, preeminently, a Eurocentricist.[20] And since it is possible to resist within the context of a Eurocentric philosophy, although not effectively, Du Bois was a superior combatant in that arena. Using the weapons and the armor of his enemies, he achieved prominence through the quality of his struggle. Harvard and Berlin had trapped him not only in the ideology of race but in the total European outlook toward the world.

Therefore, Du Bois's rather Germanic concept of race as a unit of cultural advancement in world-historical development shows the influence of his Berlin education. Such an idea, as propagated by the German philosophers of race, is contrary to the view that culture, rather than race as a biological idea, shapes human advancement. Since race is an ambiguous term anyway, although understandably a central concept in Du Bois's training, scholarship must find some other way to speak of the motive force of a people's history.

Three concepts have been advanced to deal with the questions of blackness as a philosophical rather than a biological issue: *negritude, authenticity,* and *Afrocentricity.* None of them represents a strictly biological position, but all are centered in the sociocultural reality of a geographical region, namely Africa. *Negritude* is the very movement of the literary and artistic sensibilities of African intellectuals in the field of creative motifs and ethos. The originators set free the interpretative and inventive spirit that existed in African arts. Their aim was the expression of blackness as image in the world of literature and art; thus, the major practitioners were poets and writers. *Authenticity* finds its triumph in allowing people to realize themselves through their own history. Therefore, the man whose biological father was Obenga but who now calls himself Merleau, due to the interjection of an artificial history, must reclaim his historical name and, hopefully, even himself. *Afrocentricity* is the most complete philosophical totalization of the African being-at-the-center of his or her existence. It is not merely an artistic or literary movement, or an individual or collective quest for authenticity; it is above all the total use of method to effect psychological, political, social, cultural, and economic change. The Afrocentric idea reaches beyond decolonizing the mind.

Blackness is more than a biological fact; indeed, it is more than color: it functions as a commitment to a historical project that places the African person back on center, and, as such, it becomes an escape to sanity. Therefore, when the Kenyan writer Ngugi wa Thiong'o gives up writing in English to write in Gikuyu, he is on the path to Afrocentricity. He has chosen a difficult road, but ultimately all African writing must retrace the steps to home. This will be followed by other facets of life as we become truly conscious of ourselves. The writers who do not understand this stage in our history suffer from a deep Eurocentric consciousness. For them, it is important to show, as Du Bois could not, that the crisis of the black intellectual, as formulated later and projected by Harold Cruse, is essentially a cultural crisis.

While Du Bois never did overthrow Eurocentric icons, he remains the major pre-Afrocentric figure in the philosophical and intellectual history of African people. Appiah writes that "though he [Du Bois] saw the dawn coming he never faced the sun."[21] However, to reverse Appiah's metaphor on the title of Du Bois's book in line with the latter's anticipation of Afrocentricity, I would say he saw the dusk coming as an anticipation of an Afrocentric perspective, although he could not isolate it in the fading sun of his life.

One does not have to excuse Du Bois to say that he appealed to a given universe for his resistance and, consequently, his protest; his act of rebellion, however much it was constrained, was a noble work in which he sought to use the available context, with all of its Eurocentric overtones, for his combat. The African American protest speaker or writer confronts the reality of the possible verbal space with every sentence of rebellion, forced, as it were, to speak a strange tongue.

Notes

1 Erwin Bettinghaus, Persuasive Communication (New York: Holt, Rinehart & Winston, 1968), p. 37.

2 Aime Cesaire, The Collected Poetry (Berkeley: University of California Press, 1983).

3 Robert Pirsig, Zen and the Art of Motorcycle Maintenance (New York: Bantam Books, 1972), p. 275.

4 Frantz Fanon, The Wretched of the Earth (New York: Grove Press, 1968). In the end, Fanon sees the specter of a neocolonialism in which those who were oppressed and who resisted their oppression often become oppressors themselves. Only in the avoidance of this cycle does the "new human" break the European tradition of killing people while talking about the "new man."

5 Illo, "The Rhetoric of Malcolm X," p. 5.

6 Henry Mitchell, Black Preaching (New York: Lippincott, 1970).

7 Henry Highland Gamet, "An Address to the Slave," in Smith and Robb, Voice of Black Rhetoric, pp. 22–32.

8 Frederick Douglass, My Bondage and My Freedom (New York: Arno Press and New York Times, 1968), p. 441.

9 Ibid.

10 Houston Baker, Jr., Blues: Ideology and Afro-American Literature: A Vernacular Theory (Chicago: University of Chicago Press, 1984). Baker's illuminating work should also be read as a treatise on the significance of the folk motif in the creation of African American verbal art.

11 Du Bois, Souls of Black Folks, p. 16. The entire corpus of Du Bois's work deals with the idea of double consciousness, the fact that the African in the United States existed in two separate realities. This thesis has been critiqued, however, in terms of choice—that is, by the possibility that an individual may choose to have a single consciousness.

12 James Cone, Spirituals and the Blues (New York: Seabury Press, 1972), p. 16.

13 Yet Du Bois moved to Africa and died in Ghana in 1963. The government of Ghana, under Kwame Nkrumah, accorded him its highest citizen honor. In 1986 the government of Ghana, under Jerry Rawlings, dedicated a memorial center in honor of Du Bois.

14 Anthony Appiah, "The Uncompleted Argument: Du Bois and the Illusion of Race," Critical Inquiry (Autumn 1985), p. 27.

15 Ibid., p. 28.

16 Henry Louis Gates, Jr., "Writing, Race, and the Difference It Makes," Critical Inquiry (Autumn 1985), pp. to-II.

17 Ibid., p. 11.

18 Ibid., p. 12.

19 See Du Bois, The Souls of Black Folks.

20 See Molefi Kete Asante, Afrocentricity: The Theory of Social Change (Buffalo: Amulefi, 1980), pp. 20–21.

21 Appiah, "Uncompleted Argument," p. 36.

"To Tell It Like It Is," 1968–1972

by Maegan Parker Brooks

Hamer placed her white-lapelled blazer on the chair behind her and her purse on the table in front as she rose to speak at the Holmes County Courthouse in Lexington, Mississippi, on May 8, 1969. Her hair was pulled up and back into a beehive; the sleeveless white shell she wore underneath the blazer permitted her greater range of motion as she dove into her passionate address. As vice president of the MFDP, Hamer was in Lexington speaking on behalf of the candidates running for office in the May 13 election. Flanked by such notables as MFDP chair Lawrence Guyot, state NAACP president Aaron Henry, and state representative Robert Clark, Hamer offered words of encouragement to the MFDP candidates, even as she used the speech to address problems plaguing the nation. Hamer's Holmes County address, "To Tell It Like It Is" is emblematic of her fiery turn-of-the-decade oratorical style through which she transformed her prior ethos as a simple honest sharecropper and a warrior into the persona of an uncompromising truth teller. Her prophetic position as an outsider—excluded from mainstream political and educational institutions yet schooled in suffering through Mississippi's fiery furnace—was amended during this period. Hamer now argued that sick as the systems were, she was better off having been excluded from them; free from their taint, she now stood in a privileged position to "tell it like it is."[1]

The truth, according to Hamer, was bound to make her audiences "feel uncomfortable," but she proclaimed repeatedly, "I got to tell you where it's at."[2] In Hamer's assessment, "America is sick, and man is on the critical list."[3] The national ills she railed against in "To Tell It Like It Is" ranged from the specific problems facing black candidates in Mississippi—race-based "redistricting" and the "power structure" alleging that black candidates were "unqualified"—to problems targeting the poor blacks in her state, who were being "starved out" through agricultural policies that benefited the wealthy, and because whites feared blacks' growing political influence—and even to problems facing the nation, including the anger expressed by its youth, black and white alike. As Hamer's oration encircled these topics, she asserted her prophetic position as an outsider whose distance from the center provided a superior vantage point: "I can challenge any white man anywhere on the face of this earth because God knows he made a mistake when he put me behind. I watched him, now I know him; he doesn't know me. You know that, baby."[4] What she learned from this position is that "[t]hese people have been trying to trick us a long time. A few years ago, they were shooting at us" then "they redistricted us" and now "what they decided to do was starve us out of the state." Hamer interpreted white resistance to black assertion as she always had—"[t]his man is scared to death because of what *he* done done"; she explained: "They're frightened of what they think that we'll do back to them." But Hamer wasn't promoting retribution in Lexington or anywhere else during her turn-of-the-decade speaking engagements: "I wouldn't drag my moral and my dignity low enough to do all the things ... to *you* that you've done to us" she made clear.[5]

Instead, Hamer was fighting for a "people's Mississippi" not "fighting to seat an all-black government in the state" but "it certainly ain't going to be an all-white one either."[6] Hamer located the solution to her state's and the nation's ills in a familiar source: scripture, and more specifically, the scriptural assurances that undergird her Jeremiad. Informing the audience seated in the courthouse gallery before her that "I'm going to tell you what we have to do at this time ... We got to think about the Holy Bible."[7] She pulled through her rhetorical touchstones, including "Has made of one blood all nations," further emphasizing the interconnection of the races with aphorisms like Donne's "no man is an island to himself," and her more insistent proclamation, "I want you to know something black and white, especially to white America: you can't destroy me to save your life without destroying yourself" (Acts 17:26, NKJV).[8] She also utilized scripture, in much the same way as she had throughout her rhetorical career, to convince her audience that God was on the side of the oppressed. Urging those seated before her to "put on the whole armor of God that [they] may be able to stand against the wiles of the devil," Hamer reminded them, "'He said, 'Thy will be done on earth as it is in heaven.'"[9] And yet, she knew "some of the stuff that's going on down here. God don't want this stuff in heaven. That means, we're going to have to push these men and these women and put them in office." Promoting leadership among the oppressed as the solution to societal ills, Hamer encouraged the candidates: "baby, you're going to be beautiful."[10] And she allayed their insecurities: "Don't worry about what the world say about you, and don't worry about what the power structure going to say about you because right now, whatever you do, if it's anything, you going to beat what he's already done ... you go on up there trusting God."[11]

Hamer's Holmes County address did not just extend her biblically rooted Jeremiad in support of the MFDP candidates, however. "To Tell It Like It Is" also revealed that by the end of the 1960s she was reaching a breaking point in her struggle to work within American institutions as an avenue for social change. Within her Holmes County address, she championed activists who took a militant approach, promoted an unabashedly uncompromising stance, and even showed signs of passing the torch to a younger generation. Twice during this speech Hamer acknowledged the growing militancy among the nation's youth, suggesting at one point: "I can see why these young mens are angry because they're going to make democracy work, or we ain't going to have nothing. And I'm grateful to them for it" and at another: "Young black men and young white men throughout the country and Mississippi, too, is angry because they found out what's been in the books hadn't been functioning like it's supposed to. And they found out that somebody has been lying. And that's why they're angry."[12] Although very few radicals in the late 1960s would label themselves as such, Hamer began characterizing America's angry youth as God's chosen people whom Jesus was referring to "when Christ said he would raise up a nation that would obey him."[13] She carried forth the militant spirit of the times in statements proclaiming, "I'm not compromising, and ... we're not going to put up with it," as well as "I don't believe in compromising. Because if something supposed to be mine a hundred years ago, don't offer me a piece of it now. I want every bit of it yesterday."[14] Even as her tone grew more insistent, Hamer took a step aside. Commonly promoting the activism of black men, as in "To Tell It Like It Is," where she cast herself in a supporting role, "honey, I'm right there patting you on the shoulder saying, 'Go ahead, brother,' because a few years back these brothers couldn't do it." Now that women have paved the way, getting "it prepared," she urged black men to "come on and do your [thing]."[15]

Hamer's Holmes County address offers a glimpse into the ways in which her activist career transitioned and transformed from 1968 to 1972. Most notably, she began distancing herself from the National Democratic Party (NDP), and preferred to sit outside the official ranks of political organizations like second-wave feminist groups and the Poor People's Campaign. What's more, she no longer advocated piecemeal solutions to larger systemic problems. Instead, Hamer focused her activist efforts on Freedom Farm, a cooperative she spearheaded in Sunflower County that confronted the multifaceted causes of the Delta's endemic poverty. When raising funds for Freedom Farm, moreover, Hamer consistently combined the narrative of her life of exclusion and oppression with radical appeals to repair human dignity and American democracy. Her message was radical in the sense that she urged fundamental changes at the root of political structures and human relations. As she told her Holmes County audience, "this country ... is upset, and the only way we going to have a change throughout this country is [to] upset it some more."[16]

As her tone grew more confrontational and as she grew more radical in her advocacy of social change, Hamer became an increasingly sought-after speaker. She received speaking requests from sororities across the country that looked to Hamer as a strong woman who could "help" their members "realistically" grapple with "the crucial issues which America faces today."[17] With similar admiration, a "chair-lady" from the Memorial Baptist Church in New York wrote to Hamer seven months before their congregation's annual Women's Day Celebration to secure her as their featured speaker.[18] In addition, representatives from private colleges and public universities across the nation invited Hamer to come and share her perspective with their student body. She was able to meet many of these requests, speaking at Harvard in November 1968 and Duke University and Mississippi Valley State University in February 1969. In addition, she spoke to the students at

Tougaloo College in Mississippi, Carleton College in Minnesota, and Seattle University in March of that same year. In April 1969, Hamer participated in a three-week lecture series at Shaw University, teaching students at this historically black college in North Carolina about "The Black American in the 20th Century."[19] In 1970, she traveled to Indianola, Iowa, and was a featured speaker during a "one month in depth course on civil rights" at Simpson College. The following year, Hamer traveled to the East and Southeast, addressing the students of Wheelock College in Roxbury, Massachusetts, as well as those involved in the Black Student Educational and Cultural Center at Florida State University in Tallahassee. She also addressed several college organizations explicitly concerned with issues of hunger, speaking to Walk for Development groups in Madison and Milwaukee and to Walk Against Hunger participants from the University of North Carolina-Chapel Hill.[20] For her civil rights and educational endeavors, moreover, Hamer earned honorary degrees from several collegiate institutions including Tougaloo College, Shaw University, and Howard University.

Hamer's turn-of-the-decade rhetorical transition from discourse that represents injustice and fosters recognition of societal ills to rhetoric that deliberately sits outside the centers of power to preach redemption through radical social change can be most clearly discerned through analysis of her involvement in the increasingly racially integrated realm of electoral politics, the budding women's liberation movements, and poverty politics. This focus illuminates the various ways in which Hamer utilized her persona as an uncompromising truth teller to urge the type of introspection that exposes complacency and hypocrisy, all the while promoting an interracial coalition among the poor. Although Hamer confronted each political realm simultaneously in her own liberation struggle, this [reading] will proceed thematically, accruing greater analytical depth by considering, in turn, the arenas of electoral, feminist, and poverty politics.

Electoral Politics

The period between 1968 and 1972 was marked by an influx of radicalism in American politics. As Vietnam War protestors rallied in opposition to America's international policies, urban centers also became sites of opposition and evidence of the failure of domestic programs. Urban uprisings began as early as 1964, but grew in both frequency and intensity toward the end of the decade. The aftermath of the riots was devastating as, in all, they affected nearly three hundred US cities, took the lives of 250 people, left thousands of people seriously injured and homeless, and cost millions of dollars in property damage.[21] Upon investigation of the 1967 uprisings, the National Advisory Commission on Civil Disorders (the Kerner Commission) found the root cause to be white racism.[22] The social reformers who comprised the Kerner Commission advocated dramatic institutionalized change to bridge the gap between the nation's principles and its practices. While many black activists agreed with the commission's assessment concerning the cause of America's race problems, by the time the report was released in February 1968, few were persuaded to forge interracial collaborations with white liberals. Instead, a growing number of black activist groups such as CORE and the Black Panther Party (BPP) focused on black-led community empowerment.

For people like Hamer, who spoke out about the danger of hypocrisy and the importance of reconnecting with American values by matching principle with practice, the realm of institutionalized politics had never provided a comfortable home. While many black activists used this discomfort to ground their refusal to forge coalitions with whites and to abandon the pursuit of racial advancement through institutionalized avenues, Hamer never completely lost her faith in interracial coalitions or in the potential for American institutions to effect the change she desired. In 1969, she preached an assertive form of forgiveness before her Holmes County auditors, maintaining: "we going to forgive our white brother for what he done in the past, but I'll be doggoned if he going to do it to us again."[23] That same year, she reasoned before an audience of Vietnam protestors in Berkeley that although "a lot of people ... said: 'well, forget about politics,'" this was a piece of instruction she found impossible to heed because, "Baby, what we eat is politic. And I'm not going to forget no politic. Because in 1972, when I go to Washington as Senator Hamer from Mississippi ... it's going to be some changes made."[24] Although Hamer never made it to Washington as a senator, she did exemplify her faith in the American system of politics through her position as a delegate to the 1968 DNC and in her 1971 campaign for state senate.

In fact, Hamer's continued faith in the American political system is one of the few explanations for her participation in the 1968 DNC. Unlike the 1964 challenge waged by the MFDP, the 1968 challenge to the segregated delegation from Mississippi came from a coalition of rights groups who formed the Loyal Democrats of Mississippi, commonly known as the "Loyalists." Not long after the 1964 convention, an interracial coalition of Mississippi politicians including Charles Evers, Aaron Henry, Pat Derian, and Hodding Carter III came together to ensure that the 1968 convention challenge would not be "too radical to ... prevail."[25] One way to interpret these politicians' motivations would be to reason that they were integration-oriented Mississippians who saw themselves as the most fitting representatives to spearhead the 1968 challenge because they were well connected, experienced, and less extreme in their ideology than most members of the MFDP. As such, they sought to ensure that the Freedom Democrats' radical appeals did not undermine this historic opportunity for an integrated delegation from Mississippi to be seated at the DNC.

Hamer, however, provided another interpretation. She suggested that middle to upper-class Mississippi politicians—black and white alike—formed the Loyalist coalition because if the MFDP had succeeded in 1968 "it would be too much recognition for a bunch of niggers. So, why not step on the bandwagon and take it over?"[26] As Hamer saw it, the Loyal Democrats' action in 1968 was not unlike the way in which seasoned civil rights movement leaders sought to control the MFDP challenge in 1964 or the way in which upper-class blacks paired with the white establishment to commandeer poverty programs in Mississippi. Now, as then, Hamer objected to being pushed aside because of her lower-class status.

Incensed as they were by being supplanted, the Freedom Democrats did not fold into the Loyalist coalition without some fierce opposition. At issue was not just the displacement; there was also a fundamental clash of principles. Original members of the MFDP including Guyot, Hamer, and Unita Blackwell fought for more radical solutions to meet the needs of the rural poor as well as dramatic shifts in foreign policy, issues that they felt were being pushed aside in an effort to ensure the seating of the integrated delegation. "For political purposes," explains Guyot, "we needed to create a coalition with some people who had opposed our very existence and sought to destroy us." Nevertheless, Guyot remains "very proud of the fact that [he] was able to hammer out an agreement" with the Loyal Democrats' coalition, which encapsulated Mississippi branches of the NAACP, the American Federation of Labor-Congress of Industrial Organizations (AFL-CIO), the Young Democrats, the Black Prince Hall Masons, and the Black Mississippi Teachers Association. Members of the MFDP ultimately compromised aspects of their more radical platform, posits Guyot, because "somebody was going to be seated other than the Regulars," and the MFDP "wanted to be a part of that."[27]

Just as the MFDP eventually relied upon the broad base of support the Loyalist coalition held to guarantee that they too would be a part of this historic political victory, the Loyal Democrats benefited from the perceived authenticity that the Freedom Democrats' membership bestowed upon their challenge. Common membership, however, was a far cry from support on both sides. Hamer told an interviewer before she left to the Chicago convention that she really did not know what to think about the 1968 challenge, comprised as it was of "folks … that [she] knew would sell whoever is for sale." As a chosen delegate, she had made up her mind to go to the convention because she agreed "that we should have a challenge," but that did not mean that she would identify with the Loyalists wholeheartedly. "I definitely think that we as FDP people should keep our identity, to let the world know that we are still FDP … The basic principles that I believed in then, I believe in them now."[28] This statement was more than an affirmation of the consistency of her beliefs—it also functioned as a critique of those members of the original MFDP who had lost their ties to the organization. Dr. Aaron Henry was one such person whose principles Hamer questioned because of his support for the two-seat compromise that President Johnson offered the MFDP back in 1964, and because of his recent selection as a more moderate black leader of Mississippi poverty programs.[29]

Though the Loyalists acknowledged that Hamer was central to their legitimacy as a collective, they did not provide her the platform that SNCC and the MFDP had four years earlier. Her riveting 1964 testimony secured her position as "the member of the delegation whom others most wanted to meet."[30] Guyot recalls, furthermore, that he was slated "to escort Fannie Lou Hamer to the podium for the purpose of her nominating Ted Kennedy President of the United States." Though John Lewis stopped them on their way to the microphone, Guyot uses this example to illustrate Hamer's symbolic standing within the National Democratic Party.[31] With this notoriety came a high degree of influence, which made some members of the Loyalist coalition nervous. Dorsey casts this tense relationship in the context of Mississippi politics by describing the "socialization of place." Wealthier blacks became "threatened by the upstarts who sort of displace the middle class in terms of their negotiating ability with the white people who are really the power brokers," she explains.[32]

Earlier in the decade, SNCC had undermined the traditional hierarchy in the black community by empowering the poor and bypassing those middle-class black power brokers who were reluctant to become involved in the movement. Now that the most dangerous work of confronting the violently repressive system of white supremacy was over, many more middle-class blacks were becoming involved with Mississippi politics. The national attention Hamer garnered during the 1964 DNC gave her formidable political influence on a much larger stage, and the means by which she garnered that influence—principled straightforward speech—made her impossible for the more traditional leaders within the Mississippi black community to control. The concern shared both by power brokers in the Loyalist delegation and by "establishment politicians" running the DNC was "that she might transform an already volatile convention with an emotional speech."[33] As a result, several steps were taken to quell the power of Hamer's discourse, including the decision not to televise her address and to closely monitor her activity throughout the convention.[34]

The 1968 convention's volatility stemmed not so much from domestic racial politics as it did from the Vietnam protestors and the Chicago police officers' handling of their demonstrations. After three years of involvement in the Vietnam War, American military action abroad became increasingly unpopular at home. Newly formed student groups and well-established leaders alike virulently opposed the war's continuation. Members of the Youth International Party, in particular, drew attention toward their cause and away from the internal politics at the 1968 DNC through protests that led to rioting and police brutality. By the end of the convention, over 500 protestors were injured, 152 police officers were reportedly wounded, and nearly 100 civilians had been affected by the violence. Though Hamer was an early and ongoing opponent of the war, first speaking out against American involvement in Vietnam in 1965 and continually reiterating her position at rallies and in published statements throughout the decade, she did not join the protests outside the convention.[35] Hamer even warned others not to protest alongside the Vietnam demonstrators because she believed that the establishment "planned to kill a lot of us," so we "told our black brothers, said: 'Don't go out there, because they're planning to get us, man.'" "So they didn't go," she explained before the Vietnam War Moratorium rally in Berkeley the following year, "but they was so determined to do something, they beat you kids nearly to death."[36]

With this chaos in the streets, the three credentials committee hearings, initiated by civil rights activist groups in Georgia, Alabama, and Mississippi, received less national attention than had the Freedom Democrats' 1964 challenge. There was also less controversy surrounding the nature of the challenging groups' claims. The Loyal Democrats from Mississippi, for example, followed the NDP's rules for the formation of an integrated representative delegation whereas the Mississippi Regulars disregarded these provisions. The Regular Party did not have a single black delegate, not even from congressional districts where over 70 percent of the population was African American. The regular delegation's disregard for the NDP's pledge to never again seat a segregated delegation made the committee's verdict relatively easy: eighty-four members of the credentials committee voted to unseat the Regulars and ten voted against the measure. Similarly, eighty-five committee members voted to seat the Loyalists in place of the Regulars and only ten voted against this provision. When she took her hard-won seat as a delegate on the convention floor, with her official credentials badge strung across her chest, Hamer received a standing ovation.

Victory was not as swift for the integrated Alabama and Georgia delegations. The case was clearest in Mississippi because the NDP had been monitoring the segregated party there and also because the Loyalists were well organized and their allegations well researched. Led by the politically experienced Julian Bond, the Georgia challengers received half of their state's delegate seats for the convention. Alabama's delegation, however, needed all the help they could get when their case was brought to the convention floor. This challenge was brought by the National Democratic Party of Alabama (NDPA), which formed in 1967 and whom Jeffries characterizes as drawing "inspiration from the LCFO," but "more closely resembl[ing] the Freedom Democrats" given its interracial membership and support of the NDP's candidates.[37] On August 27, 1968, during the convention's second evening session, Hamer delivered a short speech on the NDPA's behalf. Though the speech is no more than four paragraphs in length, it goes a long way toward exemplifying the evolution of Hamer's persona from a simple honest sharecropper to an uncompromising truth teller.

Hamer's 1968 DNC speech on behalf of the Alabama delegation was much like the scripted 1965 testimony she delivered before the House Elections Subcommittee: convicting and incisive. She began the address by speaking about herself in the third person, thereby acknowledging her symbolic status. "In 1964," she reminded the convention participants who had recently risen to their feet in support of her, "Fannie Lou Hamer was on the outside trying to get in." Offering this exclusion as a source of experiential wisdom, she went on to recount the facts in support of seating the Alabama delegation, continuing to remind the audience of knowledge they shared in common. "We know the long pattern of discrimination not only in ... Mississippi, but also in the State of Alabama," she reasoned logically, using the similarities between these two cases to argue from a successful outcome to a contingent instance. Extending this *parallel case*[38] logic into an argument by *a fortiori*, Hamer implied that aspects of Alabama's racist climate are even worse than Mississippi's and, thus, Alabama should be assured a victorious outcome. Hamer reminded her audience: "We also know that Governor Wallace is running today for President of the United States, and he is only pledged as a Democrat in the State of Alabama." In light of this shared knowledge, Hamer called her audience to action, urging: "It is time for us to wake up." Significantly, Hamer used plural pronouns such as "we" and "our" to transition from the persona of an outsider—speaking in the third person and "trying to get in"—to one who shared knowledge with her audience, and, ultimately, to a well-respected participant in the NDP who was invested in bringing an end to its hypocrisy.

Hamer's support for the delegation led by Dr. John Cashin, a black dentist from Huntsville, Alabama, was rooted not just in representing injustice, or in encouraging America to "wake up" and recognize its ubiquity. Rather, Hamer supported the Alabama delegation because, as she explained it, their challenge to be seated was a fundamental challenge to the identity of the NDP. "I support

Dr. Cashin from Alabama," she informed the seated delegates, "because it's time for us to stop pretending that we are, but act in the manner that we are, and if we are the Democratic Party of this Country, we should stop tokenism." Here, Hamer echoed Bob Moses's opposition to the Atlantic City compromise; in 1964, Moses told reporters bluntly, "the people want to represent themselves. They don't want symbolic token votes. They want to vote themselves."[39] Instead of offering two seats here, or a half-seated delegation there, Hamer pushed the party to take a radical stance, in line with their fundamental duty to represent American citizens, and "seat the delegation … that represent all the people, not just a few, representing not only the whites, but the blacks as well."[40]

Although Hamer was intimately aware of how complicated the process of unseating a delegation could be, the crux of her plea rested on a profoundly simple form of definitional logic: The NDP believes in representation for all, Cashin's interracial delegation is the only truly representative delegation from Alabama, therefore the NDP should seat Cashin's delegation. Much like the three simple words Hamer used to capture the national imagination four years earlier—"Is this America?"—she now seemed to be asking: "Is this the Democratic Party?" More than raising a critical question here, however, the strength of her political persona enabled her to confront the national party's hypocrisy head-on.

Yet again, Hamer's appeal for justice from the Democratic Party was unsuccessful in bringing about the outcome she desired. The integrated Alabama delegation was not seated in Chicago. This disappointment, unfortunately, was one among many for Hamer and those who sought to bring radical change to the convention. She and members of the MFDP were not only concerned about securing seating for representative delegations, they also worked to infuse issues like comprehensive healthcare, free higher education, land grants, subsidies for co-ops, a guaranteed annual income, and foreign policy concerns such as the removal of troops from Vietnam and an arms embargo against South Africa into the party's platform. In Hamer's words, they went seeking "real change" and "true reform—for a true Democratic Party," but what they found when they arrived in Chicago was "the funeral of the Democratic Party."[41]

A little less than a year after the convention, Hamer told the Democratic Reform Committee that she felt "fenced in" and "left out" in Chicago, that the convention was "closed to the people," and that "grassroot people in Mississippi and nowhere else in this country—whether they're white, black, or polka-dot— hadn't been represented" there. Hamer referred to Nixon's election as a direct result of the Democratic Party's failure to live up to its principles. She expressed her hope that the disappointing loss of the election and the disturbing violence outside of the convention, which left the "party … naked for all to see," would help trigger the process of radical change. She implored: "now maybe … you will start talking about principles and not just how many votes that [Chicago] Mayor Daley or any man at the top can steal for the party."[42] Hamer's use of pronouns shifted yet again in this speech. Whereas she attached herself to the NDP before, urging its restoration in her 1968 DNC address, here she offered the Democratic Reform Committee suggestions as to how *they* ought to improve their party. Both the tenor of her message and the shift of her pronouns indicate a critical transition, signaling that though Hamer was willing to lend her perspective to the Democrats, she would pursue alternative avenues to effect the change she advocated.

In 1971, Hamer ran as an Independent candidate for one of the two Eleventh District seats to the Mississippi state senate. Her district covered the large northwestern stretch of the state between Bolivar and Sunflower Counties and so did her campaign. She enlisted the help of old SNCC allies, John Lewis and Julian Bond, as well as new feminist friends, Liz Carpenter and Betty Friedan. She also drew upon the local endorsement of Gussie Mae Love, the mother of Jo-Etha Collier, who had been gunned down on May 25, 1971, in front of a Drew, Mississippi, grocery store by three drunken white men. Collier was celebrating her high school graduation, which had taken place just hours earlier, when she was fatally shot in the back of the neck. The murder elicited statewide and even national attention to the racial injustice that persisted in the Delta; Hamer spoke out about the murder and helped raise money for the family. Collier's mother often traveled with Hamer to campaign stops. The family so supported Hamer's endeavors and was so thankful for the financial assistance she provided them that they gave her the original copy of the high school diploma that Collier was holding when she died.[43] With the support of these well-known local and national figures, Hamer traveled throughout her district in a rented Winnebago motor home, meeting and talking with people face to face. She bought airtime on radio and television stations to broadcast her message of hope for the Delta and for the country's salvation.

Hamer's increased national notoriety enabled her to pull out all of the stops for this campaign and the effort seemed well justified, considering that she had a much stronger chance of being elected in 1971, than she had in either of her 1964 or 1967 runs for public office. The voting registration figures had changed dramatically over the last seven years. The number of registered black voters in the state of Mississippi increased from 7 percent to 34 percent; this marked change was brought about by the incessant advocacy of suffrage by groups like the MFDP, as well as by the removal of discriminatory obstacles like the literacy test, and by the federal registrars that the 1965 VRA brought into the state. Similar to the aim of her 1964 campaign when she challenged Representative Whitten, Hamer now took on Robert Crook in an effort to give these newly registered voters a reason to cast their ballot, in this her final major campaign for public office.

Undergirded by the principles of representation, service, and equality, Hamer's platform consisted of practical solutions to the problems that plagued the Delta. Increased farm mechanization had left many sharecroppers and day laborers jobless. By the turn of the decade, chemical weed killers and mechanical cotton pickers performed 90 percent of the labor involved in cotton production; plantation owners now needed only a few skilled workers who could run the equipment. Because agricultural technology displaced thousands of workers whose families had chopped and picked cotton for generations, many blacks were forced to leave Sunflower County in search of employment. The Delta experienced a 25 percent dip in its population within a decade of the turn to mechanization. Of those who stayed in the region, over 70 percent battled poverty—their median family income amounting to less than $500 a year.[44]

To combat this grave reality, Hamer advocated bringing more industry to the Delta and making jobs equally available to all races. Welfare was also a key plank of Hamer's platform. Through her national travels and her work with the NCNW, Hamer learned that there were federally funded health initiatives, free lunch programs, and food subsidies available to the poor in her district. From her struggles to maintain federal funding for Head Start programs, however, she was mindful of the state and local roadblocks that impeded federal entitlements. So she ran on the promise of securing health and welfare for impoverished members of her district—knowing this would be no easy feat.[45]

One speech manuscript, "If the Name of the Game Is Survive, Survive," from Hamer's 1971 bid for the state senate remains in its entirety. This speech was likely penned by Charles McLaurin, who was running for the other post in the state's Eleventh District. As a close friend and campaign manager for previous elections, McLaurin would often work with Hamer to construct her address before speaking engagements, and she would then use their preparation as a launching pad to deliver more extemporaneous remarks. As such, the manuscript offers an indication of Hamer's and McLaurin's philosophies for social change and a representation of the arguments made during their 1971 bids for public office, even if the prepared remarks do not provide a precise record of what Hamer actually said before an audience gathered in Ruleville on September 27, 1971.[46]

"I expect a drastic change to occur in this country, particularly in the Deep South," the speech began. The desperate need for this change, Hamer elucidated, was readily observable in the violence and riots pervading the nation, the hypocrisy of politicians and religious institutions, and the widespread poverty. These dire problems threatened the nation's survival, leading Hamer to the contention that "the salvation of this nation ... rest in the hands of the Almighty God and the black striving politicians attempting to save his people and thus the free world."[47] Consistent with her Jeremiad, Hamer underscored the struggle of impoverished blacks claiming that "God has blessed the black man to endure more than three hundred years of suffering," and yet "today he stands at the crossroads of the greatest period in American history, not as a slave, but as a man claiming full rights to all privileges to which this nation has to offer." The oppressed black person's entitlement was born from "his contribution to every stage of development that this country has had" and also from the black person's "struggle to survive."[48] Declaring that her Christian principles formed the basis of her political action, Hamer maintained: "As a believer in God, I keep struggling with the belief that the situation in the South CAN and MUST be changed as more and more Blacks become registered voters."[49] As she explained it, political action was inextricably bound to economic empowerment: "Land ... is important in the '70s and beyond, as we move toward our ultimate goal of total freedom." This assertion, in turn, laid the groundwork for a statement regarding her own attentive and principled leadership experience: "Because of my belief in land reform, I have taken steps of acquiring land through cooperative ownership."[50]

After Hamer outlined the nature of the problem and the source of the remedy, she expounded upon the types of solutions needed to combat threats against America's well-being. "If this nation is to survive," she declared boldly, "we must return to the concept of local self-government with everyone participating to the maximum degree possible." In an era when politics was tainted by the "'white racist politicians'" who sought to "to control the minds of blacks and poor communities," and during a time when Black Power organizations promoted alternative channels for reform and revolution, Hamer prescribed greater participation in mainstream politics as the cure to political ills.[51] She built upon SNCC's early vision of a representative and responsive government brought about by an interracial coalition of grassroots activists, participating at the community, state, and national level. Phrases such as "communication and race relations" and "total commitment to a true Democratic Process" are underlined in the manuscript version of the campaign speech, indicating the centrality of these ideas to Hamer's and McLaurin's philosophy of social change.[52] Though her address dangled promises that "the South will be a much better place to live than any place in the North" before her audience's eyes, Hamer was careful to remind her audience that "until communication and race relations improve and the total community become united then we will not see a real change in the South."[53]

If there is not a real change in the South, reasoned Hamer, more violent confrontations will ensue. She positioned her belief that "the key to real progress and the survival of all men, not just the black man, must begin at the local, county, and state levels of governments" between the poles of what she labeled "the late Dr. Martin Luther King's 'nonviolent approach'" and a "more militant approach" to social change. Suggesting that while she agreed with King's approach "in some cases … in other cases, one has to take a more militant approach and I am not referring to turning the other cheek." Hamer recognized the power of militancy as a tool to prompt awareness, reasoning that the "new militancy on the part of blacks and many young whites have caused [people], not only in the Deep South but the North as well, to realize that racism is an unnecessary evil which must be dealt with by 'men and governments' or by 'men and guns.'" Paraphrasing Malcolm X's well-known ultimatum (the ballot or the bullet) Hamer underscored the urgency of the change she advocated. "If survival is the name of the game," she put it plainly, "then men and governments must not just move to postpone violent confrontations, but seek ways and means of channeling legitimate discontentment into creative and progressive action for change."[54]

As Hamer's 1971 stump speech suggests, she saw a dire need for change in the Delta and in the nation. Oppressed blacks were best positioned to lead this process of change because of the wisdom gleaned from their struggle to survive. Their exclusion from the political process and the racism that continued to dominate their lives had reached a boiling point. Either the system would need to expand to include them and allow them to use their experiential wisdom to bring about constructive social change, or they would move to destroy the system that oppressed them. The nation's survival, Hamer's turn-of-the-decade Jeremiadic appeal reasoned, depended upon recognizing this critical crossroads and choosing the path candidates like she and McLaurin charted.

Unfortunately, staunch segregationists met the increase in black voter registration with increasingly sophisticated modes of intimidation, voter fraud, and racial gerrymandering. In addition to the mandatory federal examiners sent to the state to enforce the VRA, several groups allied with the Concerned Citizens of Sunflower County to Elect Black Officials predicted the segregationists' retaliation and also came to observe the elections. A team of students from Madison, Wisconsin, who served as observers in counties across Mississippi, returned to their own Dane County with an arsenal of incriminating stories to tell. One student journalist, Jonathon Wolman, wrote about the ways in which white poll workers manipulated the votes of blind and illiterate black voters.[55] A reporter for Madison's *Capital Times* echoed Wolman's observations with accounts of white poll workers throwing out black votes, deeming them "damaged" or "invalid."[56] Moreover, a *New York Times* piece reported the physical violence and arrests with which northern poll watchers were met in small Mississippi counties.[57] When the ballots were tallied, the results were characteristically disappointing: Hamer had lost to Crook by a margin of 11,770 to 7,201 votes. Results like these were common across the state as only 50 out of 309 black candidates were victorious. "And so it came to pass," Wolman told his fellow students at the University of Wisconsin, "that no major black candidate won any elected position in a state in which 25 counties out of 82 have a black majority."[58]

While Hamer firmly believed that the election was stolen, and though these northern observers would certainly concur, other explanations for her defeat have been offered. Some people reason that Hamer was the object of envy within her local community, that her nationally renowned symbolic status fostered resentment throughout Sunflower and Bolivar Counties.[59] Others suggest that black voters held candidates from their own race to different standards than their white counterparts and, thus, they may have found Hamer's ideology too radical or her educational credentials lacking.[60] Still, there are those who contend it was never Hamer's election to win, that though the VRA eliminated vestiges of Jim Crow such as the poll tax, literacy tests, and the widespread practice of publishing the names of black registrants in the newspaper, race-based gerrymandering still occurred. Frank R. Parker, the director of the Voting Rights Project and author of *Black Votes Count: Political Empowerment in Mississippi after 1965*, posits that after 1965, "the focus of voting discrimination shifted from preventing blacks from registering to vote to preventing them from winning elections," and one of the most popular modes of prevention was diluting the black vote.[61]

Unita Blackwell concurs with Parker's explanation. Blackwell, a member of the MFDP and the first female African American mayor in the state of Mississippi, remembers that during the 1971 election: "The vote wasn't out there in the first place. We couldn't win it," but Hamer ran anyway "because it was right to run, and it was a political showing that we needed as black people" to prove that "[we] could run for office, whether [we] win or not."[62] Blackwell's explanation is consistent with Hamer's prior political attempts—Whitten defeated Hamer handily in 1964, and she was disqualified on the very election rule she sought to challenge through her candidacy in 1967. So, it is plausible that Hamer ran again as a rhetorically symbolic gesture to prove it could be done and to demystify the political process, but this time her candidacy succeeded in reaching well beyond an audience of black Mississippians.

Hamer's run for the Mississippi state senate helped to bring the national spotlight back to the South, even if it shone just briefly. Her defeat was a microscope focusing the attention of the country on a sample of the sickness that still plagued its democratic body. Her campaign, and the vast increase of campaigns by black Mississippians, did exemplify small improvements in the patient's condition. Though a mere fifty successful elections was no political landslide, it brought the total number of black elected officials in Mississippi to 145, thereby making Mississippi the state with the most black elected officials in the South. This was no small achievement, especially considering that when SNCC began its work in the state blacks in Mississippi held the least amount of political power nationwide, and Mississippi was deemed the most fiercely segregated of any southern state.

Although Hamer lost yet another election and though she never managed to hold public office, she was instrumental to political progress. The contribution her campaign made to an audience of black Mississippians who were inspired by her action and who saw themselves represented by her platform, not to mention the attention her defeat brought back to the problems that remained in the state, demonstrate that many of Hamer's political successes are best captured in rhetorical terms. Terms like *consciousness-raising*, *dramatization*, and *exposure* move outside the realm of tangible institutionalized gains, offering a variety of ways to understand Hamer's contributions to history.

Within the political structure of the National Democratic Party, Hamer's rhetoric was feared and thus restricted. The experience of marginalization that accompanies poverty, moreover, was not one that Hamer chose to distance herself from. It was reflected in the image she conveyed, in the words she spoke, and in the political ideology she adhered to. This experience of marginality informed her radical approach to social change, which, in turn, led the middle-class power brokers within the Mississippi Loyalist and National Democratic Parties to fear and constrain her political expression. In a similar manner, Hamer's lower-class status may have led members of her own community— even people who shared her economic station—to resent her success, fear her radical ideology, or question her credentials.[63] So, even as electoral politics in Mississippi became increasingly integrated, thanks in no small part to Hamer's own activism, her lower-class standing kept her from working inside the system of governance to effect the type of radical social change she envisioned. Fortunately, the realm of electoral politics was not the only avenue of activism available to Hamer. There was another powerful social movement afoot, and this collective actively sought Hamer's prophetic insight and promoted her radical discourse.

Feminist Politics

As the 1960s drew to a close, black and white women were both inspired and disenchanted by the movements for social change that surrounded them. Their experiences within civil rights, Black Power, and newly formed student organizations reinvigorated the centuries-long struggle for gender equality. Turn-of-the-decade calls for female empowerment, economic opportunity, protection against discrimination, and reproductive rights were far from monolithic, however. Though the inceptions of both black and white women's movements for social change have been traced to late

1967 or early 1968, and while many of the movements' initial leaders worked alongside one an-other in the earlier part of the struggle for black freedom, black and white women's particular life experiences informed their respective demands and belied an unconditional unity.[64] Nevertheless, the radical way in which women of all races sought to reconfigure relations between the sexes as the basis of a more egalitarian society significantly contributed to the larger climate of social change surrounding Hamer's activism.

Ask just about anyone who knew her well and the response is the same: "Fannie Lou Hamer was not a feminist."[65] Core aspects of the women's liberation movements in their varied instan-tiations—black, white, middle to upper class, revolutionary, reform oriented, young and old—did not sit well with Hamer. Flowing from the civil rights movement of the 1950s and 1960s, as the second wave did, Hamer's movement experience could have secured her a prominent position of leadership among the ranks of the 1970s feminists. To assume such a post, though, would have meant making ideological compromises to fit within the confines of popular belief systems that did not comport with Hamer's lived experience. Instead of seeking a central position, therefore, she remained on the periphery of women's liberation movements as well as the realm of electoral politics. She held fast to her principles and let them echo through her prophetic speech. Just as she reasoned regarding the realm of institutionalized politics that "We must not allow our eagerness to participate lead us to accept second-class citizenship," she refused anything less than principled political action from her participation in the network of second-wave feminist organizations.[66] The principled objections that Hamer had to central spokes of feminist ideologies fell into three general categories. Specifically, Hamer objected to feminists' oppressive view of relations between the sexes. She took issue with feminist stances on birth control and other aspects of reproductive rights. And, she argued that the banner of "sisterhood" glossed over centuries of significant racial and class differences between women.

As a closer look at Hamer's discourse from this era makes clear, she was not antifeminist, nor was she against coalition building between women. "Fannie Lou Hamer supported women's empowerment," reasons Guyot, "but Fannie Lou Hamer was not a feminist. Fannie Lou Hamer was a humanist ... she had a broader vision."[67] This broader vision, at times, came into conflict with the aims of the mainstream women's liberation movement. What Hamer fought especially hard against was an overeager and overly simplistic push for unity amid difference. To Hamer, difference had always mattered and now the differences she saw between herself and various strands of feminism functioned not as impediments to social change, but as necessary considerations for meaningful progress.

In 1971, Hamer underscored these differences through five speeches and one article that each broached the topic of feminism to greater and lesser degrees. During her speeches at the founding conference of the National Women's Political Caucus (NWPC) and the NAACP special meeting on the particular plight of black women, for instance, Hamer addressed feminism throughout, relat-ing even seemingly divergent topics back to this central focus. Throughout her speeches at the University of Wisconsin-Madison and Tougaloo College, though, feminism was not the guiding topic, but her commentary on this aspect of the political scene was a salient feature of the addresses. In an article she wrote for *Essence* magazine, furthermore, Hamer targeted a younger generation of primarily black women with her message of both criticism and hope. Though the venues for and guiding focus of each of these six texts[68] differ markedly, reading them as a mosaic of Hamer's views regarding feminism helps guard against reducing her critique to a matter of identity politics. Hamer did not object to white feminists, black revolutionary freedom fighters, northern feminists, or feminists from a younger generation. Rather, as the consistency of her message across these varied texts indicates, Hamer's discourse dug deeper to uncover the principles that were violated through racism, classism, regionalism, or ageism, and she highlighted the effects of this exclusion on the lives of both women and men.

Hamer fundamentally objected to the second-wave feminist focus on seeking liberation from men. "My liberation is different from yours," she argued, "because the same thing that kept me from being liberated kept my black man from being liberated."[69] In this regard, Hamer was not unlike scores of black feminists who resisted prioritizing any one aspect above another in their simultaneous struggle for gender, race, and class equity.[70] For many black women, in fact, family was one of the most empowering sources in their lives.[71] This was certainly true in Hamer's case, as she distanced herself from the center of the feminist movements and moved herself closer to male influences in her family and in her community. Before her NAACP audience, Hamer proclaimed: "I'm not hung up on ... liberating myself from the black man, I'm not going to try that thing." She informed them proudly, "I got a black husband, six feet three, two hundred and forty pounds, with a 14 shoe, that I don't *want* to be liberated from." Instead, she offered a counter-prescription: "we are here to work side by side with this black man in trying to bring liberation to all people."[72] It was counterintuitive for Hamer to seek distance from one of the most enabling forces in her life. While traveling in Wisconsin, Hamer told one reporter about how her husband cared for their home and their adopted daughters in her absence. "Without a husband like that," she reasoned, "I couldn't be around doing what I do."[73] Hamer routinely bestowed this type of recognition upon Perry "Pap" Hamer. McLemore recalls how supportive Pap was of her and that "she was so supportive of him. She gave him his props."

Not only did Hamer acknowledge Pap and appreciate his support, she also advanced a conservative view of gender relations between them, asserting that "he was the man of the house," McLemore remembers.[74] Wally Roberts, a Freedom Summer volunteer, shares a similar memory about enjoying a meal at the Hamer's home and then rising to wash the dishes as a demonstration of his gratitude. Witnessing this, Pap asked him "angrily, 'What you doin' women's work for?'" After Pap left the room, Mrs. Hamer told a confused Roberts not to worry about her husband's exclamation, reasoning: "Pap don't have many ways left of being a man." Roberts characterizes this brief encounter as an "epiphany," through which he realized both "the degradation that must be the inevitable consequence of racism" and also the way in which Fannie Lou Hamer "had triumphed over the anger and rage that surely had struggled to control her spirit and her life."[75]

In Pap, Roberts saw a man who had been prohibited from providing for his family by economic reprisals. A skilled tractor driver, Pap had difficulty finding employment because of his wife's civic engagement. This added economic woes to the racist emasculation he endured as a black man in the Mississippi Delta. In Fannie Lou's comment to Roberts during the summer of 1964, he also foresaw something of the woman who would later tell the NWPC:

> I'm not fighting to liberate myself from the black man in the South because, so help me, God, he's had as many and more, severer problems than I've had. Because not only has he been stripped of the right to be a politician but he has been stripped of the dignity and the heritage and all the things that any citizen of a country needs.[76]

Roberts characterized Hamer as a woman who recognized gender-based oppression, but more than this, he realized that she was able to replace frustration or offense with understanding. Accordingly, he interpreted her small expression as an indication of Hamer's nuanced comprehension of the interconnections between racism, classism, and sexism. She took no offense to Pap's remarks, reasons Roberts, because she knew the larger context in which they were given; she understood the many factors impinging upon his life over which he had no control.

Hamer's effort to understand Pap's behavior and her insistence on building him up was indicative of the profound respect she had for black men. "I really respect this black man," she told an audience of Tougaloo College students, "because we've been catching hell and he's caught more than we've caught."[77] Believing that racist oppression was worse for black men than black women, Hamer worked to "uplift male leadership in Sunflower County" and "to project male leadership [into the] struggle," recalls fellow activist Owen Brooks.[78] Hamer's effort to increase black male leadership was frequently conveyed in gender-conservative arguments that distinguish her from both black and white feminists of the era. "I am a woman, strong as any woman my age and size ... but I am no man," Hamer remarked. "I can carry the message but the burdens of the nation and the world must be shouldered by men." Outlining what she deemed as preferable relations between the sexes, Hamer continued: "Women can be strength for men, women can help with the decision-making, but men will ultimately take the action."[79] While she did propose collaboration between the sexes here, Hamer also unabashedly placed women in a subordinate position with regard to effecting social change. Not only did she suggest that the hierarchical configuration would be a preferable arrangement, but she implied that this is the natural order, a belief she made transparent in speaking with a young man from the Delta region. "The men are the leaders ... you are born leaders," she informed him; "if you were made on earth to lead then you have to lead me. But don't wait until you get seventy-five to do it," she warned.[80] Many who heard this type of declaration from Hamer were surprised, even the young man who had come to Hamer for advice on a cooperative project, snickered at the thought of him leading her.[81]

Her rural southern upbringing in the black Baptist church, in addition to her class standing, provide partial explanations for the relatively conservative thrust of her remarks. Given the staunchly patriarchal nature of the black Baptist church, Hamer doubtlessly grew up seeing men in leadership positions. Although women certainly wielded influence within the church, formal positions of authority were reserved for men, and thus Hamer likely naturalized this arrangement as the proper order of things.[82] Observing the geographical difference between herself and the strands of feminism growing out of northern urban centers, moreover, Hamer told *Essence's* primarily black female readership: "I see so many hang-ups in the North that I don't see in the South. In the South men don't expect their wives to be seen and not heard and not doing anything." More than just a regional divide, however, Hamer was expressing an economic difference that also crossed racial lines. She agreed with the feminist assertion that "it's ridiculous to say that a woman's place is in the house, not doing anything but just staying at home." That type of claim was nonsensical to Hamer not so much because of its oppressive tenor, but rather due to its infeasibility. She could not imagine what would happen "if my husband was making $15 a week" and "I didn't try to get out there and make another $15 ... so them kids could eat." For practical reasons alone, Hamer maintained: "There's nothing wrong with a mother raising her children and there's nothing wrong with her working if it's necessary."[83]

At the same time she was promoting black male advancement, therefore, Hamer was also championing the independence of and the advances made by black women. Beyond their contribution to the household, Hamer acknowledged black women's political efforts in the South, arguing: "it was women that made what little progress we have had. It was women in Mississippi that really started the ball rolling."[84] Hamer's view of the role each sex should play in household affairs and in the broader political arena was multifaceted; she suggested that women were capable and effective leaders in both realms, but that men should assume a more prominent position.

In addition to her regional, religious, and class background, her relatively conservative ideology regarding gender relations can also be explained by contextual factors such as the 1965 release of *The Negro Family: The Case for National Action,* known more commonly as The Moynihan Report. In this report, Senator Daniel Patrick Moynihan argued that the destruction of the black family was the primary impediment to the black race's progress in both the economic and political arenas. Furthermore, he reasoned that the matriarchal structure of the black nuclear family was at the core of black men's inability to function as leaders in their communities.[85] Although Hamer virulently contested Senator Moynihan's assertions, writing: "you know that Moynihan who wrote about Black matriarchal society, knows as much about a Black family as a horse knows about New Year's," she also acknowledged the dearth of male leadership in black communities, and she sought to rectify that deficiency through her insistent promotion of black men.[86] So, while Hamer disagreed with Moynihan's assessment of the cause of black male inaction, she shared his concern for its effects. In fact, she offered her own diagnosis for the cause, explaining in a 1965 oral history interview that "As much as Negro womens are precious, men could be in much more danger. If my husband had gone through or attempted one-third of what I've gone through he would have already been dead."[87] Since black women "got the ball rolling" earlier in the decade—clearing a safer path for black men's involvement—Hamer tailored her turn-of-the-decade addresses to urging black men's participation. She concluded her address to the students at Tougaloo College, for example, by suggesting that the "salvation of this nation lies in the hands of black men," imploring them: "this nation needs you, mothers need you." The desperation evident in Hamer's plea for black men to "stand up with pride and dignity" demonstrates that Hamer regarded feminist calls for liberation from men as a further threat to the already fragile state of black men's civic involvement.[88]

Hamer was also quite wary of white feminists' advocacy of abortion rights, and she was not alone in her opposition. Sociologist Benita Roth contends, "Black feminists assailed white women's failure to acknowledge class and racial aspects of the abortion issue." Many black feminists argued that white women's insistent advocacy of "[a]bortion on demand" was short-sighted, maintaining that it overlooked "other reproductive concerns that were tied to class power: involuntary steril-ization; life circumstances that compel poor women to abort; and the possibility that women on welfare would be forced by the state to have abortions."[89] The concerns were close to Hamer's heart, rooted as they were in her own lived experience. Having been involuntarily sterilized in 1961, Hamer had reason to fear this form of public policy. In the late 1960s, furthermore, the Mississippi legislature was debating two bills, one that proposed sterilization for "anybody convict-ed of a third felony, at the discretion of the Parchman Penitentiary Trustees," and the other would mandate the procedure for any "parent of a second illegitimate child." These measures were not even veiled attempts at racist repression, as state representative Ben Own was quoted in the *Delta Democratic Times* proclaiming: "'This is the only way I know of to stop this rising black tide that threatens to engulf us.'"[90] The sterilization of black women "was so common" in the state, notes historian Danielle L. McGuire, "that blacks often called it a Mississippi appendectomy."[91] Although voluntary abortion is quite different from forced sterilization, Hamer feared that championing one form of reproductive control might open the floodgates for abuse of the other.

In fact, Hamer objected to all forms of reproductive control and even criticized women who gave their children up for adoption. "The methods used to take human lives, such as abortion, the pill, the ring, etc. amounts to genocide," she declared before her Tougaloo audience. "I believe that legal abortion is legal murder and the use of pills and rings to prevent God's will is a great sin," she elaborated.[92] Although Hamer delivered this particular critique in 1971, two years before the Supreme Court decided *Roe v. Wade*, Norma L. McCorvey's (Jane Roe) initial case had already begun making its way through the courts and into the national headlines. Hamer was, thus, objecting to a national push, spearheaded by feminist organizations, to legalize abortion.

Hamer's objection was at once personal, principled, and political. On a personal plane, she informed her Wisconsin auditors that "if they had had [birth control] pills" in her mother's day then she "probably wouldn't be standing here today." Having made what she deemed "a narrow escape to be here," Hamer now took it upon herself to "fight for other kids too, to give them a chance."[93] According to her friend and confidante, Reverend Edwin King, Hamer's objection to abortion was also rooted in race-based political terms. King remembers Hamer tentatively broaching the subject of abortion with him, fairly confident that he shared her pro-life stance. In their discussions of the topic, he recalls, "she analyzed it in [race-based] civil rights terms"; she would say to King: "It's those Republicans. Those white Republicans ... it is a new repression." Fearful of institutionalized retaliation to civil rights advances, Hamer interpreted the Supreme Court's decision to legalize abortion as a means, not unlike the sterilization proposals working their way through the Mississippi legislature, to repress the growing black population and the political influence their larger numbers now afforded them.[94]

Hamer also opposed abortion and contraception on moral grounds. King remembers Hamer casting her objection in biblical terms, as in her public statements when Hamer celebrated the sanctity of life, while championing God's love for all human beings. Mindful of her principles, in addition to her efforts to repair the structure of the black family, it is not altogether surprising that Hamer took a strong stance against an issue so central to many feminists. In light of the popularity of contraception, and the growing advocacy of abortion rights, however, Hamer was engaged in an uphill battle. Acknowledging this, she wrote in *Essence:* "Some of the hang-ups that the younger black women have today are kind of frustrating. Too many seem to have lost all sense of morals and integrity." Speaking about black women more broadly, Hamer contrasted the older and the younger generations, "That's one of the things that helped us, the moral integrity that we had even though we were poor. We had that."[95]

The younger generation's moral degradation, according to Hamer, is evidenced by their use of contraceptives, their promotion of abortion rights, and even their decision to let other people adopt their biological children. "I think it's a disgrace for people to put their babies up for adoption. There is no need to put this kid up for adoption," she argued. Hamer's bold contention did not stem from the naivete for which some black activists critiqued middle- to upper-class white women.[96] Rather, Hamer reasoned from her own experience of living in poverty and still being able to care for children in her community: "As long as I can eat, them two grandbabies of mine are going to eat. I'm raising them because their mother's dead, but she loved them babies with all of her heart"[97] Having adopted Dorothy, Vergie, and Dorothy's two children, Hamer could not have been opposed to the practice itself, but she took issue with separating children from their community-based family. Essentially, she was a strong proponent of "othermothering," a community-oriented form of raising children that was prevalent in both urban northern and rural southern black communities.[98] At the same time, Hamer was a staunch opponent of preventing, aborting, or abandoning any form of life.

In every address Hamer delivered about or around the topic of feminism, she engaged the issue of experience in such a manner that highlighted difference and the importance of considering how different life experiences inform politics. Hamer's routine consideration of difference challenged the feminist tendency to emphasize the unifying experience of gendered oppression, ostensibly shared by women across the boundaries of race, class, sexuality, geography, religion, and age. Toward audiences of northern white women, Hamer contended: "baby, your liberation ain't never been like mine ... 'cause, number one, you ain't never had to suffer like I suffer ... what happened to you is the Man never told you what was going on, but we've been knowing he was a rat."[99] Here,

Hamer argued both that black women have experienced harsher forms of oppression than white women and that black women were more aware of the white male patriarchal system, which oppressed black men as well as black and white women.

Not only did Hamer's objection to similitude challenge interracial sisterhood, but it also positioned black women in an experientially superior position. In light of all the oppression they endured, black women's marginality provided them with a superior vantage point. This position of difference, in turn, guarded against a hasty coming-together before there had been a recognition of past injustice. Speaking before an interracial audience gathered by the NAACP, Hamer reminded both black and white women of their shared history of exploitation. "I really feel more sorrier for the white woman than I feel for ourselves," Hamer explained, "because she been caught up [in]... feeling very special." Her address then turned to confront white women, in particular. Hamer declared directly: "you worked my grandmother, you worked my mother, and then finally you got hold of me ... You thought you was more because you was a ... white woman." According to Hamer, white men had placed white women "on a pedestal," which made them feel superior to black women, and provided them with the license to use black women "over and over and over."[100]

The tables, in Hamer's account, were now turning precisely because black women were emboldened and simultaneously revitalized by the black freedom movement. Essentially, black women, in Hamer's words, "busted the [white women's] castle open and [were] whacking like hell for the pedestal." Assuming the more experienced and knowledgeable position, Hamer informed white women: "when you hit the ground, you're [going to] have to fight like hell, like we've been fighting all this time."[101] As the indicting narrative of oppression and liberation that Hamer recounted suggests, she was unwilling to bury hundreds of years of exploitative treatment between white and black women under a false banner of unity. Nor was she willing to let white women assume a leading position in the struggle for human liberation, considering that black women already had a wealth of experience with this battle.

Hamer's critique of the historical disunion between women extended beyond a race-based objection and even beyond an objection to the class differences that were parasitic upon this racial distinction. Hamer also reminded middle- to upper-class black women of how they had treated their lower-class sisters. At the same NAACP conference, Hamer raised the specter of intra-racial class tension. She began with a small dose of her derisive wit: "A few years ago throughout the country the middle-class black woman—I used to say not really black women, but the middle-class colored women, c-u-l-l-u-d," Hamer emphasized with an air of elitism, "didn't even respect the kinds of work that I was doing."[102] No doubt Hamer was referring to those blacks, with more formal education than she possessed, who took issue with her leadership in the movement and with the honorary degrees bestowed upon her.[103]

Continuing to temper her critique with humor, Hamer carried forth Ella Baker's assertion that she had never "been diploma conscious," reasoning similarly: "But you see now, baby, whether you have a Ph.D., a D.D., or no D, we're in this bag together. And whether you're from Morehouse or Nohouse, we're still in this bag together."[104] Considering the setting for this speech—an NAACP conference on the special plight of black women—Hamer's remarks can be read as more than a variation of her refrain that Americans from all walks of life need to band together to fight injustice. This statement touches on an issue even more germane to the black community. Specifically, Hamer confronted the type of racist oppression that lumps a diverse group of people together based upon the arbitrary factor of skin color. This is the type of racism that black club women at the turn of the nineteenth century organized to combat with their "lift as we climb" philosophy. And this is the type of racism, which breeds intra-racial classism.[105] By borrowing the same logic, middle- to upper-class black women have relied on for decades—that each member of the black race is only as strong as its weakest link—Hamer called this argument into question in such a manner that revealed its elitist underpinnings.

Through her discourse on feminism, Hamer distanced herself from young black women, from white women, and from middle- to upper-class black women. Her indicting words rejected the wide-ranging acceptance undergirding feminist calls for sisterhood. Yet, Hamer would commonly advocate unity on her own terms. The following quotation from the speech Hamer gave at the founding of the NWPC aptly conveys this balance: "[F]or so many [white women] it was a rude awakening a few years ago when they woke up and found out that not only were they not free but that they had a whole lot of problems not like mine but similar to mine. But somehow we're going to have to bridge this gap."[106] Although she was quick to assume a superior posture when it came to understanding the nation's history of oppression—remarking elsewhere in this speech, "honey, this hasn't just started"—and while she was careful to guard against conflating white and black women's experiences of oppression, Hamer also promoted unity. In fact, some of her statements reaffirming unity in the face of diversity were quite encouraging. "If you think about hooking up with all these women of all different colors and all the minority [groups] hooking on with the majority of women of voting strength in this country," Hamer prodded her audience, "we would become one hell of a majority." In other statements she espoused a similar faith in collaborative political action, declaring: "we're going to have to work together ... because when women team up together we can do a whole lot of things."[107] Through statements like these, it becomes clear that Hamer "supported the advancement of the rights of as many different people as possible," as Guyot put it.[108] She was not averse to coming together to work with women across experiential divides. She recognized the political advantages of unity. Her principled prophetic position, however, guarded against becoming so tempted by this potential power that she overlooked the truth of her own experience and accepted a "second-class position"—one of compromise and sacrifice—within feminist movements for social change.

So, Hamer remained on the relative margins of feminist politics as well. From this position as an outsider, however, Hamer crafted a prophetic uncompromising truth-telling platform informed by her superior vantage point. While it seems a bit odd that feminist organizations invited Hamer to deliver speeches in which she criticized their objectives and exposed their hypocrisy, members of these organizations likely discerned her benevolent objectives, even shrouded as they were within her confrontational speech. Hamer was popular within feminist circles because she was a strong woman. She was part of the civil rights stream out of which the second-wave feminist collectives flowed. Her values clashed with segments of this larger movement, but as a humanist she was still invested in the success of their push for liberation.

Poverty Politics

Although Hamer played symbolic roles in the increasingly integrated realm of electoral politics, and while she was a widely solicited speaker among feminist organizations, the bulk of her energy during the turn-of-the-decade portion of her activist career was expended in the ongoing fight against poverty. By the end of the 1960s, whether black activists urged communist or capitalist oriented solutions, the problem of economic inequality was central to programs for community development. King and the SCLC spearheaded a Poor People's Campaign (PPC) to demand an economic Bill of Rights. The actual demonstration, wherein an interracial coalition of the nation's dispossessed erected a tent city on the Washington Mall, occurred a month after King's assassination. Though Hamer did not participate in the encampment, she did express her personal disgust with federal policies for the poor in an address to marchers departing to the protest from Marks, Mississippi.[109]

A year later, former SNCC executive secretary James Forman issued a "Black Manifesto" to white religious organizations threatening violence and demanding $500 million dollars in reparations for the National Black Economic Development Conference (NBEDC).[110] Hamer, who attributed her political conversion in no small part to Forman's 1962 speech at her Ruleville church, was one of the initial signatories of Forman's "Black Manifesto." Her support for For-man's program was based on more than their friendship, however. Hamer not only signed the "Manifesto," she also served on the board of the NBEDC, and in her own speeches she actively encouraged churches to heed Forman's demand for the "seed money" that would foster black economic development.[111]

As the PPC emphasized, poverty was not only a problem for black Americans. The federal government acknowledged that poverty affected all races and it sought to bridge the nation's ev-er-widening economic gap through a variety of social welfare programs. Some of these programs were shortsighted and some long lasting, but all were met with unprecedented involvement. In fact, the "most dramatic increase" in families receiving public assistance occurred between 1968 and 1972, "when the welfare rolls grew [from 1.5] to three million."[112] While growing economic need in areas like the Mississippi Delta, where farm mechanization threatened to starve out unskilled sharecroppers, provides part of the explanation for this dramatic increase, historians also suggest that the black freedom movement succeeded in raising expectations among Americans. That is, the movement succeeded in making blacks more conscious of their rights and more assertive in their demands for basic entitlements like food, housing, education, and job opportunities.[113]

For Hamer, economic concerns had always been a central part of her struggle, which reached its culminating point with the formation of the Freedom Farm Cooperative in 1969. Freedom Farm was a response to Hamer's lifelong battle with poverty. It was an extension of the political career she had built over the last decade; and it was also a means to grapple with controversial poverty politics at the local, state, and national level. Efforts to combat poverty at the national level waxed and waned over the years, but in the mid-1960s the struggle became heartened when the OEO was formed to carry out the programs mandated by President Johnson's War on Poverty initiative. In 1966, Hamer attended an OEO conference in Madison, Wisconsin, to learn ways she could help people in her community benefit from these federal poverty programs. As the programs were instated at the local level, however, several debilitating problems arose.

The first problem was access. For most people living in the Mississippi Delta in the mid- to late 1960s, life was difficult by any measure. In 1968, when the federal government launched its emergency food and medical program, 39 of the 256 counties it targeted were in the state of Mississippi, with Sunflower County near the top of its priority list.[114] Although federal money was coming into the Delta to combat rampant malnutrition, in Hamer's assessment, it was not reaching its intended beneficiaries. She told one interviewer that "when this white man handle this [poverty] program, it is rotten to the core, because you wouldn't believe it, and my little girl … wouldn't believe … a man going to bring me out of poverty, he forced me to be in it."[115] When speaking before northern audiences, she supported this assertion with stories about food stamps being withheld from mothers of infants by local welfare workers, and children in their teens dying of malnutrition.[116]

Moreover, Hamer posited that withholding federal aid at the local level was just another in a long line of efforts by the white power structure to drive black people out of Mississippi. She explained that local officials "don't want poor people to have anything to eat, so that they will go away, up North, maybe, to the ghettos and slums of Detroit and Chicago and Newark and New York City."[117] Fellow Mississippian Edwin King's memories from this era support Hamer's contention, as he recalls signs posted in Mississippi welfare agencies advertising how much more money recipients could get if they moved, for example, to Detroit.[118] Dittmer also suggests that white leaders in the state "adopted policies whose impact was to accelerate the black migration—particularly in the heavily black Delta counties—that had been underway since the 1940s."[119] The federal money intended to combat malnutrition was being withheld from its beneficiaries for reasons Hamer and others interpreted as politically motivated and racially based.

Although poor blacks had trouble receiving the economic aid that the federal government designated for them, according to Hamer, plantation owners had no problem receiving their subsidies. Senator Eastland, for instance, owned 5,800 acres of rich Delta soil and Hamer loved to point out that people in Sunflower County called him "Big Jim" because "he's the biggest welfare recipient in the state."[120] Under the auspices of the 1965 federal farm bill, which Eastland helped push through the Senate, the government paid him not to plant. Receiving nearly $170,000 in federal payments in 1967, Eastland was perhaps the biggest, but he was not the only landowning "welfare recipient" in the state. Asch documents that "seventy-seven Sunflower County planters received more than $25,000 apiece in 1967" to let their land sit idle.[121] While this policy helped control agricultural prices and guarded against a surplus, Andrew Young pointed out that the governmental policy also made it so "the men had no jobs" in the Delta. So, while the landowners got subsidies, the farmworkers never saw this money.[122] To Hamer, who watched her own daughter grapple with the lifelong effects of malnutrition and who, herself, remembered being perpetually hungry as a child, this waste of fertile acreage was proof positive of America's sickness.

The corruption and counterintuitive practices signaled to her that solutions to the problems associated with poverty—hunger, powerlessness, poor education, sickness—would not come from the top down. Real change in the realm of poverty politics would need to be radical, beginning at the grassroots. "If what the politicians have done to the poverty program hasn't taught us anything else," she exclaimed, "it has taught us that we are not going to get much help from the politicians."[123] The reasons she gave for this fact were simple: "we are poor and we are black." An admittedly harsh reality, Hamer's experience in the realm of electoral politics, not to mention the battles waged over the control of Head Start money in the state, revealed to her the difficulties of working within racist and classist structures. Thus, the conclusion Hamer reached by 1968 "as hard as this may seem," was that "the time has come now when we are going to have to get what we need for ourselves. We may get a little bit of help, here and there, but in the main, we are going to have to do for ourselves."[124]

By the end of the 1960s, the civil rights organizations, volunteers, and ideologies that abounded throughout the Delta earlier in the decade were few and far between. But like her mother, who would use scraps of cloth and patches to dress her children, tie bags around their feet for shoes, and cut the tops off of beets to feed them, Fannie Lou Hamer was resourceful. So even in the absence of the organizational assistance on which she had relied earlier in her career, Hamer found new sources of experiential wisdom and financial backing. Her resolve to become self-reliant took the form of an interracial farming cooperative. Owen Brooks, of the Delta Ministry of the National Council of Churches—one of the few organizational strongholds that remained in the region— posits that the "cooperative ethic" was reinfused into the country's consciousness during and after the civil rights movement of the 1950s and 1960s. Cooperatives, explains Brooks, were "important to the struggle because [they] allowed ... grassroots people to become involved in raising and producing and developing an economic alternative for themselves."[125] Hamer certainly saw this potential in Freedom Farm, as she repeatedly cast the project in terms of political leverage. "'For the first time we are not beholdin' to the power structure,'" she told a student reporter in Madison, who reasoned, in turn, that "Hamer emphasizes ... the leverage of owning land and the fact that the land supports people [and has] given those people a wedge into the political machine—rich, white and racist—that has always run Mississippi."[126] To challenge the "rich, white and racist" members of the "political machine," Hamer encouraged poor black and white people to form their own power structure based on their majority status and enabled by the relative protection that the cooperative afforded them against retaliation.

Hamer was inspired not only by the cooperative ethic that the civil rights movement reignited, but also by the more specific model of the North Bolivar County Cooperative (NBCC) just northwest of Ruleville. Dorsey, an integral member of that farming cooperative, remembers how Hamer adopted their model and benefited from the NBCC's labor, equipment, and even the seeds her co-op donated for Freedom Farm's first crop. In a pamphlet promoting the NBCC, the founders explain the purpose and the function of such an organization while also promoting pride, strength, and unity among black people. The NBCC ran a store with books, records, and "other educational material about black people"; in this way, explained the pamphlet, the "co-op is helping us learn about our history." The founders also connected the cooperative effort to electoral politics within the state suggesting that the jobs the co-op provided gave its members strength, offering them freedom from the control of the white establishment: "When black people have a steady job, we don't need to worry about what the white folks are thinking. We can vote for whom we want without having to fear anybody." And, above all else, the cooperative fostered unity among black people so that they could "become a strong force," reasoning: "the co-op can help bring us together. We own it. We run it. We benefit from it and only we can make it grow."[127]

Hamer drew upon the NBCC's message of race pride, strength, and unity, but she also distinguished her cooperative from existing models. "She was one of the first people who really started" communicating a message to "poor *white* people." Dorsey recalls that Hamer wanted whites to envision Freedom Farm as "an opportunity ... to put aside the difference in our colors." Hamer encouraged poor whites to understand that "if you can't feed your children, if you can't protect your family, if you can't earn a living, then there's something wrong with that picture. And that you need to cast your lot with us and try to make it right."[128] Freedom Farm was, thus, fundamentally rhetorical in the sense that it functioned as a symbol of unity and possibility. Hamer's effort to reach out to poor whites also sent a message of forgiveness and understanding. Bridging the gap between the races and banding together, furthermore, communicated strength and security to the white landowners, constituting the farm cooperative as a "power structure" for poor people.[129]

Members of the NBCC not only lent Hamer their founding principles and helped her get the first crop planted; they also put Hamer in contact with charitable organizations, which enabled her to purchase the initial acreage for Freedom Farm. On their trip to Madison for the OEO conference in 1966, Dorsey introduced Hamer to a Madison man named Jeff Goldstein, who served as the treasurer for Measure for Measure. Founded by John Colson in 1963, Measure for Measure took its name from the Shakespeare play by the same title, which was itself derived from the New Testament instruction attributed to Jesus Christ: "Take heed what you hear. With the same measure you use, it will be measured to you; and to you who hear, more will be given" (Mark 4:24, NKJV).[130] This biblical instruction informed Measure for Measure's charitable philosophy. It was not complicated, according to Goldstein, "we would simply support self-help projects that were either part of or alongside the civil rights movement." Rather than take the lead on these projects, the Madison-based organization was responsive to the needs and ideas of those they assisted. "We were dependent on the people down South," he jokes: "Of course, we had the weird idea that they knew best what their community needed."[131] The symbiotic relationship Measure for Measure formed with Hamer "worked like a charm." Goldstein offers countless examples of how Measure for Measure was able to meet Hamer's requests. Perhaps the most serendipitous was also the first. Hamer asked the organization for $10,000 to put toward Freedom Farm's first forty-acre plot of land. While the request seemed out of the small organization's league initially, it was not long before two English professors from the University of Wisconsin approached Goldstein. The professors informed him that their aunt had bequeathed them $10,000, which they wanted to donate to Measure for Measure.

That $10,000, combined with money raised from Hamer's connections at Harvard University, donations from Washington, DC's American Freedom from Hunger foundation, and from Hamer's longtime friend and ardent movement supporter Harry Belafonte, gave Freedom Farm its start. In 1969, the fledgling organization drafted by-laws and created a board. On their first forty acres of land, the Freedom Farm Cooperative planted cash crops like soybeans and cotton to sell and pay the taxes, the administrative staff, and the few hired hands, who cultivated food crops such as cucumbers, corn, peas, beans, squash, okra, and collard greens. The cost for membership was set at $1 per month, though only thirty families could afford to pay dues, so the other 1,500 belonged in name. Regardless of one's membership status, any family who needed food could work the land for a few hours and take home a bushel of produce.

In addition to produce, Hamer also partnered with the NCNW and undertook a Pig Project. The NCNW had been active in the Delta region, and well acquainted with Mrs. Hamer, since the summer of 1964 when they began the interracial and interregional support program dubbed "Wednesdays in Mississippi."[132] The Pig Project, or "pig bank" as it was commonly known, began four years later as an effort to provide protein to the many people in the Delta who could not afford to buy meat. The NCNW donated forty pigs, thirty-five gilts, and five boars. Once a gilt became impregnated by a boar, she would be given to a needy family, contingent upon the family's willingness to return her and two of her offspring to the bank after she birthed a litter. The family also had to agree to pass on several pigs from the sow's large litter (typically eighteen to twenty piglets) to other needy families in the area. The program took off; by 1972, the original forty pigs had multiplied to nearly three thousand, providing families across the Delta with food and relative security.

More than this, the pig bank and the vegetables grown in the Freedom Farm functioned rhetorically in the sense that they constituted a new sense of selfhood for the impoverished inhabitants of the Delta. Hamer referred to the NCNW-sponsored pig bank as a "beautiful program," expressing her gratitude to a representative from the organization: "Honey, I wouldn't take nothing for our golden pigs." She underscored their utility with pride, "Child, we cured our meat this year and then Pap brought it home and I wanted some of it hanging up so I could paint it [with seasoning] and then we painted it and put it in the freezer." Elaborating on her praise for the program, Hamer contended further: "There's nothing no better than get up in the morning and have ... a huge slice of ham and a couple of biscuits and some butter." What's more, she bragged, "today, you know, we can have company anytime we get ready ... We can have ham and we can have biscuit and you got a good meal and it's a good project." She even joked about their newfound plenty, "at one time it looked like pigs was coming out of our pockets!"[133] These remarks aptly convey the importance of the pig bank for Hamer and other poor inhabitants of the Delta. Those who sustained and benefited from the pig program, much like the Freedom Farm cooperative, were quite proud of its effects. Though having pork in the freezer, ham for breakfast, or cured meat for company may not seem like a notable conversation piece, it was for Mrs. Hamer and others like her who had suffered without such resources their whole lives. Having them now, and being able to share them, gave the pig bank participants a new sense of pride and security. Hamer commonly cast Freedom Farm in these terms. "If you give them the food, they'll eat for a few days; if you give them the tools, they'll produce for themselves," she would say. "The land has given us hope, dignity and self respect."[134] Thus, even as the interracial nature of Freedom Farm communicated a message of unity toward poor whites, and sent a message of strength to powerful whites who had taken advantage of the Delta poor for centuries, Freedom Farm's produce gave its participants security and pride, enabling them to see themselves as controllers of their own destiny.

As this message of self-empowerment spread, Freedom Farm and the poverty programs associated with it grew exponentially. By 1970, Hamer raised enough money from her grant applications and national travels to foot the down payment for 600 more acres of land, increasing Freedom Farm to 640 acres total. In light of this expanding acreage, it is not surprising that Freedom Farm had the third-largest payroll in Sunflower County, close behind the Head Start program with which Hamer was affiliated, and the garment factory she supported. In fact, Goldstein remarked that the "best we ever did" for Mrs. Hamer was when he discovered that there was "a huge supply ... of treadle sewing machines" in Madison-area attics. So, he asked Hamer if she could use them and soon discovered that the sewing centers she was assisting had limited access to electricity, so the treadle machines were a highly desirable donation.[135]

Perhaps her longest-lasting triumph, though, was the money she raised for the construction of two hundred units of low-income houses, many of which still stand in Ruleville today. She helped her neighbors gain access to low-interest government loans, and Freedom Farm helped those who could not acquire these loans by purchasing their home and selling it back to them for a reasonable monthly payment. Though modest, these new homes were better insulated, more heartily constructed, and had indoor plumbing, all of which positively distinguished them from the "tar paper shacks" to which many of the Delta poor were previously consigned.[136] Through initiatives such as these, the poverty programs Hamer developed for Sunflower County met not only the physical needs of her impoverished neighbors, but the programs also accomplished a psychological transformation by offering a sense of self-reliance and human dignity.

Given the high cost of keeping alive these various projects—growing vegetables, breeding livestock, and securing decent homes, not to mention awarding scholarships to area youth—the cooperative constantly struggled financially. While its participants' dues and their labor, combined with help from the NCNW and some governmental assistance in the form of low-interest loans, accounted for a portion of the funds used to stay afloat, a great deal of the Freedom Farm programs were financed from money Hamer raised through her national travels. Never one to adequately care for herself, Hamer donated virtually all of the honoraria she received from her speaking engagements. But even this money, which ranged on average from $200 to $500 per event, would not have been enough to sustain her ambitious Freedom Farm.[137]

To accomplish this, Hamer undertook a series of fundraising tours speaking on television programs like the *David Frost Show,* to solicit funds for the farm. Her appearance on that particular program elicited a flood of responses to the station, many of which included financial donations. One such letter read: "Dear David, This is only a dollar but please give it to Mrs. Fannie Lou Hamer to buy land for our people and the cause she spoke so eloquently about on today's program." Another came from a viewer in New York who was similarly inspired by Hamer's "eloquent and moving description of" her poverty programs in Mississippi. This viewer admitted that "it is hard to believe that conditions such as you describe still exist in the United States," but that Hamer's "sincerity convinced" him that she was "telling the truth." The viewer went on to praise Hamer's "courage and devotion," likening her to Washington, Jefferson, "and other great American patriots."[138]

Hamer's fundraising speaking tours on behalf of Freedom Farm also brought her back to places like Seattle, Madison, and the Boston area, where she had previously fostered connections. The archived collection of her papers contain two boxes filled with at least one thousand donation envelopes sent from audience members to the NCNW's Freedom Farm Fund after hearing Hamer speak about the cooperative. The donations commonly range from ten to fifteen dollars and the envelopes bear return addresses from places as far reaching as Anchorage, Alaska, Sugarland, Texas, and Issaquah, Washington.[139] Through either Hamer's live or mediated speeches reaching into these various locales, Hamer solicited direct donations from individuals and she also tapped into larger networks of student projects aimed at raising funds for self-help organizations.

These projects commonly took the form of sponsored walks, hikes, or runs wherein the participants collected pledges from donors in their community. The Young World Development group orchestrated both "Hunger Hikes" and "Walks for Development" through which they raised nearly $200,000 for Freedom Farm in a four-year period.[140] Hamer had always been fond of young people, but in response to the contributions made by students across the country, she began touting them as the indisputable saviors of this sick nation. This sentiment was only further solidified as groups of students began not only donating money, but coming to Ruleville to watch the polls during the 1971 election and bringing books, clothing, water tanks, and even driving farming equipment down from Wisconsin to Mississippi.

Young people reciprocated the admiration and praise Hamer lavished upon them. After a speech Hamer delivered on the University of Wisconsin-Madison campus, for instance, the student newspaper ran an article about her that demonstrated the close attention youth still paid to Hamer's struggle. It read, in part, "The dignity of the people, reinforced by the Sunflower Farm Co-op is the strongest basis yet for viable political struggle ... an example from which student radicals likely have a lot to learn."[141] Closer analysis of Hamer's national travels to raise money for Freedom Farm's many operations suggest that her speeches sought to do much more than fundraise. In fact, these speeches suggest that Freedom Farm, as a symbol, not only sent a message of unity toward poor whites, a message of strength to landowners, and messages of security, dignity, and pride to its participants, but that Freedom Farm also sent a message of interconnection to northern audiences. Hamer's speeches featured Freedom Farm as a symbol to demonstrate that northern audiences could help Deltans help themselves while also revealing their commitment to the maxim: "nobody's free until everybody's free."

Hamer's connection with activists in Madison, Wisconsin, was perhaps the strongest she fostered with any northern community. She referred to the charitable organizations in Madison as her "radical caucus," and Hamer achieved nothing short of iconic status through her frequent travels there. The *Washington Post* even took notice of this impenetrable bond, informing their national readership: "In Madison, Mrs. Hamer became something of a celebrity. One university student, who had met her in Mississippi, drove around the state capitol square with a sign on his car, announcing her arrival." On the same trip, Measure for Measure threw a sherry reception for her and raised over $4,000 for poverty programs in the Delta.[142] Each of the Measure for Measure veterans with whom I spoke had fond memories of Hamer's relationship to their city. For instance, Martha Fager remembered Hamer as "a much beloved member of the community" and Jeff Goldstein insisted that she got "barrels of love in Madison."[143] Like many relationships in Hamer's life, the "warmth and love" of this union was constituted, in large part, through her speech.[144] Yet, like most of Hamer's speeches from this era, the addresses she delivered in Madison were highly confrontational and utterly judgmental.

While newspaper articles, archival sources, and members of the Madison community all indicate that Hamer spoke in Madison quite often during the last ten years of her life, the recordings of four speeches—two delivered in 1971 and two in 1976—are the only complete accounts of Hamer's Madison addresses that have been recovered to date. Through an analysis of Hamer's two speeches delivered in January 1971, one at the Great Hall on the University of Wisconsin-Madison campus and the other at a local church, a clear pattern of address emerges. In each speech, Hamer combined her representation of impoverished Mississippians' plight with a critique of northern individuals and national institutions. This combination was oriented toward inducing critical self-reflection that would yield responsive giving.

Attention to the finer aspects of the rhetorical pattern featured in her Madison addresses, moreover, reveals the larger program for radical social change Hamer was crafting. She began both of these addresses in her characteristic fashion, by recounting her story of growing up poor and black in the Mississippi Delta. This aspect of her address resonated with many Madison auditors, who—decades later—still recalled that Hamer's speeches "told us what it was like to live in Mississippi."[145] After describing a life of sharecropping, white supremacist retaliation to her attempts at civic engagement, and the current plight of Mississippians who are still "living in run-down dilapidated shacks," Hamer would target a specific source of institutionalized oppression.[146] She brought her audience into the speech by matching the oppression she targeted with the venue of her address.

Toward her university audience, for instance, Hamer lamented the miserable state of the country as evidenced by the college shootings at Kent State and Jackson State colleges. Altering her familiar refrain, she reasoned: "America is sick and man is on the critical list ... when people can be shot down at a college ... there's something very wrong." As she was wont to do, Hamer tempered her revulsion with resolve by probing at the root of the nation's problems. "We have to work to make this a better place and we have to deal with the politics and the history of this country that's not in the books," she instructed her college-educated audience. Providing examples such as the fact that "it was a black doctor that learned to give blood transfusions," and "the first man to die in the revolution was Christopher Attuck [Crispus Attucks] another black man," Hamer then indicted them, "you never taught us that, white America ... you never taught that in the institution." Contrasting lessons like "Columbus discovered America" with the fact that her own congressional challenge was not taught, Hamer further proved that "[t]he education has got to be changed in these institutions."[147]

Similarly, in the speech she delivered at a Madison-area church, Hamer criticized institutionalized religion. "The church is really lagging," she maintained. Speaking to the hypocrites, whom Hamer described as those parishioners who go to church on Sunday and "then leave until next Sunday," Hamer informed them that their apathetic practices are "not serving God." And she reminded them, "We are our brother's keeper."[148] Hamer's criticism of both the hallowed institutions at which she spoke also persisted in the memories of her audience, as Goldstein recalled bluntly: "She told you what the shit was and told you how to get rid of it."[149] In a similar vein, other Measure for Measure members contend that she "opened people's eyes" and that Hamer's speeches "grabbed the audience to tell them what was right."[150]

Once she had essentially weeded the garden by tugging at the flaws of the broader American systems of oppression, Hamer planted the seeds for change. Consistent with her prophetic style of discourse, she showed the audience their hearts by inducing self-reflection. "Must I be carried to the sky on flowery beds of ease," she challenged both audiences to ask themselves, "while others fight to win the prize and sail through bloody seas?"[151] Using the words of an Isaac Watts hymn, Hamer conveyed the interconnection of the human struggle and she attached it to Measure for Measure's driving ideology: be compassionate toward those who seek assistance, for by the same standard you will also be treated. Through this oratorical pattern, furthermore, Hamer sought to provoke critical reflection among her audience in such a manner that would compel them to "search their hearts *and* their pocketbooks."[152]

Finally, Hamer paired the self-reflection she urged with a model for social change. The exemplar was the same in both the university and the church speech: Hamer championed the actions of America's youth. "The church is behind the young people" in terms of moral development "because the young people throughout the country is proven to us that they really care." In stark contrast to "people my age or older and a little younger than I am," she argued that, with young people's actions you "don't see all of the kind of hypocrisy and all of the kind of put on." In her estimation, the youth of this country "are the nation that I believe is going to obey God," she proclaimed in a Madison church.[153] Her message was consistent on the University of Wisconsin campus as well, identifying people her age as "hopeless cases" and praising instead young people's ability to "bridge the gap between the races." Like the marginalized person who gains a superior perspective by sitting outside the center of power, "the children know what's going on and you [are] not going to be able to fool them any longer," Hamer told her contemporaries. To the contrary, the youth should be leading the nation; "fighting" as they are "for justice for all human beings," they represent "the chosen people that's going to lead this country out if it's not too late."[154]

Considering Hamer's fervent praise for student activists, it is not difficult to see why they listened to and revered her prophetic style of speaking. In light of her critique of the hypocritical, ignorant, and apathetic ways of her contemporaries, however, Hamer's popularity among the older generation of audience members in Madison is not as easy to explain. Firsthand accounts from those who sat in packed venues to hear her speak do suggest that she was just as beloved among audience members in her age group as she was among the youth. Hamer's popularity was explained by one Measure for Measure couple as resulting from the fact that she was "preaching to the choir," telling white liberals what they already knew about the problems of this country.[155] While this explanation is partially illuminating, tapping into a shared recognition of the nation's malaise is not the same as compelling people to not only recognize their interconnected fate, but also to act in a specific manner to redirect it. Recall that Hamer did not just secure passive agreement from audiences on her fundraising tours; her speeches resulted in myriad forms of direct action. Adult members of the Madison community donated money, food, clothing, books, sewing machines, and farm equipment. In addition, Madisonians took trips to Ruleville to help with her projects and to see for themselves the pangs of poverty they had heard Hamer describe. Thus, these liberal people who might have already been prone to give, gave responsively, in line with the program for social change Hamer advocated and thereby according her a large measure of respect. So, while this symbiosis between Hamer and the Madison-area liberals can be explained, in part, by a previous state of ideological alignment, Hamer's choice to expend her activist energy cultivating a relationship there, and the Madison folks' willingness to follow Hamer's lead, are also testaments to her rhetorical acumen.

What Hamer advocated through her Madison speeches and in her poverty programs, more generally, was radical social change that went to the root of the problem, quite literally. She took a step back from the increasingly integrated realm of state and national politics and returned wholeheartedly to the land and the community that sustained her. Her shift in focus was not a 360-degree movement, however, because she assumed a community-based focus armed with national notoriety. Hamer utilized her talent as a speaker to raise much-needed money for the Delta. She used these funds to change the self-perceptions of both its impoverished inhabitants and of her northern audiences. Her poverty projects, thus, "spoke to" multiple audiences, offering an invitation of unity to poor whites, communicating the presence of strength to the oppressive white power structure, constituting a self-image of security, dignity, and pride for poor blacks, and even challenging northerners' relative life of ease in the midst of southerners' suffering. Hamer's poverty programs showed Americans their own hearts and called them back to principled solutions that would effect radical social change. Positioning America's youth as the model for activism, she advocated an interracial grassroots movement concerned with the fate of all people—a collective oriented toward promoting human dignity by maintaining people's well-being. Hamer reasoned plainly, "it's no way on earth that we can gain any kind of political power unless we have some kind of economic power."[156]

Conclusion

The period between 1968–1972 in Hamer's activist career was her most widely acclaimed. Although she was an incredibly humble person, being named the "First Lady of Civil Rights" by the League of Black Women, receiving the Noble Example of Womanhood and the Mary Church Terrell Awards, in addition to numerous honorary doctorate degrees, must have been validating experiences. Perhaps Hamer's most remarkable commendation came from a rather unlikely source. Charles M. Dorrough Sr., the mayor of Ruleville, had long opposed Mrs. Hamer's efforts to alter the segregated social fabric of the city he led. However, in 1970, in honor of Ruleville's first-ever "Fannie Lou Hamer Day," Dorrough sent Hamer a letter of praise. In this letter, he acknowledged not only that Hamer had "put up a valiant fight for those things [she] truly believed in," but that in the process she had been "exposed to the real dangers and wrath of the enemy." Beyond this, he surmised, "If more Americans gave of themselves as you have for the things they believe in, ours would be a better nation." Dorrough concluded his missive with a statement that reflected a surprisingly clear understanding of Hamer's battle: "The history books of tomorrow will record your efforts," he predicted, "but I am sure you are more interested in tangible things around your own community that speak of a better, more comfortable way of life for those you love."[157]

Just as Hamer finally succeeded in securing such a life, however, the Herculean effort she exerted to achieve it caught up with her. Nervous exhaustion, for which she had been hospitalized several months prior, kept her from delivering an address at the 1972 Democratic National Convention. Even without her renowned speaking ability, Hamer left a mark on the gathering held in Miami Beach, Florida. David Lopez, a delegate from Texas, read her short seconding speech for Frances "Sissy" Farenthold's vice presidential nomination. After Lopez read her statement, a sickly Hamer rose to momentarily address the crowd: "Madam Chairman, fellow Democrats, and sister Democrats, I am not here to make a speech," she made clear from the outset, I am "just giving support and seconding the nomination of Sissy Farenthold for Vice President. If she was good enough for Shirley Chisolm," Hamer reasoned, "she is good enough for Fannie Lou Hamer."[158] This brief statement in which Hamer refers to herself in the third person, coupled with Hamer's greater effort to fulfill her duty as an elected delegate, indicate Hamer's recognition of her own political influence as well as her strong desire to remain involved with national politics, in some capacity.

Over the next four years, [...] the many needs surrounding Hamer persisted. She continued to struggle with the tension between her compelling desire to provide for the Delta poor and the increasingly poor state of her own health. In a vain attempt to keep Freedom Farm financially solvent, Hamer would undertake a few more national trips, but after 1972, her poor health did not permit much travel. Thus, the period in Hamer's activist career between 1968 and 1972 is significant not only because of the wide acclaim she garnered, and the uncompromising truth-teller persona she assumed throughout the variety of battles she waged, but this period is also significant because these battles were among her last.

Notes

1 Fannie Lou Hamer, "To Tell It Like It Is," Speech Delivered at the Holmes County, Mississippi, Freedom Democratic Party Municipal Elections Rally in Lexington, Mississippi, May 8, 1969, in *The Speeches of Fannie Lou Hamer: To Tell It Like It Is*, ed. Maegan Parker Brooks and Davis W. Houck (Jackson: University Press of Mississippi, 2011), 87. The visual account of Hamer's address was made possible by photographs comprising Sue (Lorenzi) Sojourner's *Mrs. Hamer Speaks* photography exhibit within the touring show: "THE SOME PEOPLE OF THAT PLACE—1960, Holmes, Co.: The People and Their Movement," for more information see: www.crmvet.org/vet/ sojourne.htm.

2 Hamer, "To Tell It Like It Is," 88.

3 Hamer, "To Tell It Like It Is," 90.

4 Hamer, "To Tell It Like It Is," 88.

5 Hamer, "To Tell It Like It Is," 89.

6 Hamer, "To Tell It Like It Is," 89.

7 Hamer, "To Tell It Like It Is," 87.

8 Hamer, "To Tell It Like It Is," 87–93.

9 Ephesians 6:11–12 and Matthew 6:10, respectively quoted in Hamer, "To Tell It Like It Is," 92.

10 Hamer, "To Tell It Like It Is," 92.

11 Hamer, "To Tell It Like It Is," 93.

12 Hamer, "To Tell It Like It Is," 88 and 90, respectively.

13 Hamer, "To Tell It Like It Is," 87.

14 Hamer, "To Tell It Like It Is," 93 and 91, respectively.

15 Hamer, "To Tell It Like It Is," 93.

16 Hamer, "To Tell It Like It Is," 88.

17 Ruby S. Couche, Letter to "Soror" from the National Sorority of Phi Delta Kappa, October 18, 1968, in Fannie Lou Hamer Papers: Speaking Engagements File (1968–1977). Accessed via microfilm at the Wisconsin Historical Society, Madison, Wisconsin (WHS).

18 Betty Neal, Letter to Mrs. Hamer from the Memorial Baptist Church, October 22, 1968, in Fannie Lou Hamer Papers (WHS).

19 Phaon Goldman, Letter to "Dr. Fannie Lou" from Shaw University, February 25, 1969, in Fannie Lou Hamer Papers (WHS).

20 Speaking Engagements File (1968–1977), Fannie Lou Hamer Papers (WHS).

21 See Vincent Harding, Robin D. G. Kelley, and Earl Lewis, "We Changed the World 1945–1970," in *To Make Our World Anew*, ed. Robin D. G. Kelley and Earl Lewis (Oxford: Oxford University Press, 2000), 245.

22 Given the nature of the cause, the commission reasoned that "Only a greatly enlarged commitment to national action, compassionate, massive and sustained, backed by the will and resources of the most powerful and the richest nation on this earth, can shape a future that is compatible with the historical ideals of American society." Kerner Commission Report as cited in Harding et al., "We Changed the World," 252.

23 Hamer, "To Tell It Like It Is," 93.

24 Fannie Lou Hamer, "To Make Democracy a Reality," Speech Delivered at the Vietnam War Moratorium Rally, Berkeley, California, October 15, 1969, in *The Speeches of Fannie Lou Hamer*, 101.

25 Kay Mills, *This Little Light of Mine: The Life of Fannie Lou Hamer* (New York: Plume, 1993), 223.

26 Interview with Fannie Lou Hamer by Dr. Neil McMillen, April 14, 1972, Ruleville, Mississippi, in *The Speeches of Fannie Lou Hamer*, 166.

27 Interview with Lawrence Guyot by Maegan Parker Brooks, September 20, 2012 (phone).

28 Interview with Fannie Lou Hamer by Robert Wright, August 6, 1968, Oral History Collection, Civil Rights Documentation Project, Moorland-Springarn Research Center, Howard University.

29 Hamer describes this tension in the interview with Fannie Lou Hamer by Anne Romaine, 1966, Social Action Collection (WHS). See also Dittmer's discussion of Henry's role in the poverty program politics; see John Dittmer, *Local People: The Struggle for Civil Rights in Mississippi* (Urbana: University of Illinois Press, 1995), 377–378.

30 Mills, *This Little Light of Mine*, 217.

31 Interview with Guyot by author.

32 Interview with Dr. L. C. Dorsey by Maegan Parker Brooks, June 10, 2007, Jackson, Mississippi.

33 Mills, *This Little Light of Mine*, 217.

34 In "To Make Democracy a Reality," for instance, Hamer describes being trailed throughout the convention by a federal agent and also having her bags searched, with items from within confiscated. See Hamer, "To Make Democracy a Reality," in *The Speeches of Fannie Lou Hamer*, 102–103.

35 See Doug Archer, "'Send Troops to Mississippi, Not Vietnam,' Says Mrs. Hamer," *Worker*, July 13, 1965, and "We Support Oct. 15—Display Ad 12," *New York Times*, October 8, 1969, 12; See, for example, Hamer, "What Have We to Hail"; "To Make Democracy a Reality"; "America Is a Sick Place and Man Is on the Critical List," 119; "Until I Am Free, You Are Not Free Either," 129; and "Is It Too Late?," 133, all in *The Speeches of Fannie Lou Hamer*.

36 Hamer, "To Make Democracy a Reality," 103.

37 Hasan Kwame Jeffries, *Bloody Lowndes: Civil Rights and Black Power in Alabama's Black Belt* (New York: New York University Press, 2009), 217–218.

38 Parallel case arguments rely upon a comparative logic in which two instances from the same general class are likened to each other. Oftentimes, advocates will use the successful outcome in one case to argue for the adoption of a particular policy with an unknown outcome. If the comparative logic holds, then the success in one case should lead to success in the other. See James Jasinski, "Parallel Case," *Sourcebook on Rhetoric: Key Concepts in Contemporary Rhetorical Studies* (Thousand Oaks, CA: Sage, 2001). See pp. 32–34 for further explanation of the concept and references for additional reading.

39 Bob Moses quoted in Dittmer, *Local People*, 299.

40 Fannie Lou Hamer, "Speech on Behalf of the Alabama Delegation at the 1968 Democratic National Convention, Chicago, Illinois," August 27, 1968, in *The Speeches of Fannie Lou Hamer*, 85.

41 Fannie Lou Hamer, "Testimony Before the Democratic Reform Committee," Jackson, Mississippi, May 22, 1969, in *The Speeches of Fannie Lou Hamer*, 95–97.

42 Hamer, "Testimony Before the Democratic Reform Committee," 95–97.

43 Jo-Etha Collier's original diploma is filed within Fannie Lou Hamer's papers at the Amistad Research Center, Tulane University, New Orleans, Louisiana (FLH Papers).

44 Chris Myers Asch, *The Senator and the Sharecropper: The Freedom Struggles of James O. Eastland and Fannie Lou Hamer* (Chapel Hill: University of North Carolina Press, 2008), 256; See also J. Todd Moye, *Let the People Decide: Black Freedom and White Resistance Movements in Sunflower County, Mississippi, 1945–1986* (Chapel Hill: University of North Carolina Press, 2004), 157.

45 Fannie Lou Hamer, "Platform," 1967 State Senate Race Materials in Party Platform and Materials, Reel 3, Folders 16 and 17 in Fannie Lou Hamer Papers (WHS); "Elect Mrs. Fannie Lou Hamer," 1971 Campaign Card, courtesy of Jeff and Sarah Goldstein.

46 The original manuscript of the speech, which can be found in the Special Collections Section at Tougaloo, College, TO12, Box 1, Folder 6:1, Mississippi Department of Archives and History, Jackson, Mississippi (MDAH), bears Mrs. Hamer's signature. Upon discussing the speech with Charles McLaurin,

he claims to have written it for her. Her signature, however, indicates her approval of the text. Furthermore, the content within the speech is remarkably similar to commentary Hamer was making throughout this period in her activist career. One of the few aspects of the address that seems to distinguish it from others she delivered is the consistent use of male pronouns throughout the speech and the use of "man" to represent all humankind. While Hamer would use male pronouns universally on occasion, her pronoun use and her representation of humankind typically varied to more explicitly include women within her speeches. E-mail correspondence between Davis W. Houck and Charles McLaurin, January 13, 2010.

47 Emphasis in original. See Fannie Lou Hamer, "If the Name of the Game Is Survive, Survive," campaign speech delivered in Ruleville, Mississippi, on September 27, 1971 (MDAH).

48 Fannie Lou Hamer, "If the Name of the Game Is Survive, Survive," Speech Delivered in Ruleville, Mississippi, September 27, 1971, in *The Speeches of Fannie Lou Hamer*, 144.

49 Emphasis in original. Hamer, "If the Name of the Game Is Survive, Survive," 1971 (MDAH).

50 Hamer, "If the Name of the Game Is Survive, Survive," 142.

51 Hamer, "If the Name of the Game Is Survive, Survive," 143.

52 Emphasis in original. Hamer, "If the Name of the Game Is Survive, Survive," 1971 (MDAH).

53 Hamer, "If the Name of the Game Is Survive, Survive," 144.

54 Hamer, "If the Name of the Game Is Survive, Survive," 142.

55 Jonathon Wolman, "Mississippi Elections: By Hook or Crook," *Daily Cardinal*, November 5, 1971, 1.

56 Tom Hibbard, "Local Students Tell Why Blacks Didn't Get Vote," *Capital Times*, November 12, 1971, 9.

57 Thomas A. Johnson, "Mississippi Poll Watchers Say Harassment Barred Fair Tally," *New York Times*, November 6, 1971.

58 Jon Wolman, "Mississippi Elections: Facing an Old Political Reality," *Daily Cardinal*, November 11, 1971.

59 Jason Berry posited: "In a land where no one has great power ... a person who suddenly obtains some of it, no matter how little, becomes the object of envy." Kay Mills extrapolated upon this resentment thesis, maintaining simply: "people are reluctant to vote for those they envy." See Mills, *This Little Light of Mine*, 289.

60 Related to the idea that local people resented Hamer's celebrity status was the explanation that Hamer's 1965 dispute with a group of Sunflower County women over Head Start programs in their area led to lingering resentments and may have cost her the 1971 election. In this case, it was also power, influence, and resources that were at the core of the dispute, which was only exacerbated by the paucity of all three. See Mills, *This Little Light of Mine*, 203–215, for more in-depth coverage of the Head Start dispute.

61 Frank R. Parker, *Black Votes Count: Political Empowerment in Mississippi after 1965* (Chapel Hill: University of North Carolina Press, 1990), 3.

62 Blackwell cited in Mills, *This Little Light of Mine*, 289.

63 Reverend Edwin King remembers: "there were people who were appalled that this person didn't have education and why should she be a leader?" Interview with Reverend Edwin King by Maegan Parker Brooks, June 15, 2007, Jackson, Mississippi.

64 See Roth's book chapter for the relationship between the beginnings of both. Benita Roth, "The Making of the Vanguard Center: Black Feminist Emergence in the 1960s and 1970s," in *Still Lifting, Still Climbing: African American Women's Contemporary Activism*, ed. Kimberly Springer (New York: New York University Press, 1999), 72–73.

65 Quotation is from Interview with Guyot by author; similar sentiments were expressed by nearly everyone I asked about Hamer's relationship to feminism.

66 Hamer, "Is It Too Late?," 133.

67 Interview with Guyot by author.

68 The six texts analyzed are Fannie Lou Hamer, "Speech to Tougaloo Students," January 11, 1971, Special Collections, Audio-Visual Records, MP 80.01 Newsfilm Collection, Reel D-0321, Item 1102, Stennis/Hamer/Legislature/Police (MDAH); Hamer, "Until I Am Free, You Are Not Free Either," Speech Delivered at the University of Wisconsin, Madison, January 1971; Hamer "Is It Too Late?," Speech Delivered at Tougaloo College, Tougaloo, Mississippi, Summer 1971; Hamer, "Nobody's Free Until Everybody's Free," Speech Delivered at the Founding of the National Women's Political Caucus, Washington, DC, July 10, 1971; Hamer, "It's in Your Hands," in *Black Women in White America*, ed. Gerda Lerner (New York: Vintage, 1972), 609–614; "Fannie Lou Hamer Speaks Out," *Essence* 1, no. 6 (1971): 75.

69 Hamer, "Speech to Tougaloo Students" (MDAH).

70 For more on poor black women's insistence that they should not have to prioritize one particular aspect of their struggle at a time, see Roth, "The Making of the Vanguard Center," 83.

71 Roth explains in her chapter exploring the emergence and influence of black feminism that "family was the least oppressive institution in [black women's] lives and constituted a refuge from white domination." Roth, "The Making of the Vanguard Center," 77.

72 Hamer, "It's in Your Hands," 612.

73 Gay Leslie, "Rights Matriarch Pleads for Action Now," *Wisconsin State Journal*, July 19, 1969.

74 Interview with Dr. Leslie McLemore by Maegan Parker Brooks, June 13, 2007, Jackson, Mississippi.

75 As remembered by Wally Roberts, "Fannie Lou Hamer 1917–1977," *Veterans of the Civil Rights Movement*. Available online, accessed February 8, 2007, http://www.crm vet.org/mem/hamer.htm.

76 Hamer, "Nobody's Free Until Everybody's Free," 136.

77 Hamer, "Speech to Tougaloo Students" (MDAH).

78 Interview with Owen Brooks by Maegan Parker Brooks, June 14, 2007, Jackson, Mississippi.

79 Hamer, "Is It Too Late?" McLaurin claims to have penned this speech for Hamer as well. Like "If the Name of the Game Is Survive, Survive," the manuscript of this speech also bears Mrs. Hamer's signature. And it also is consistent with her turn-of-the-decade ideology, when compared to other recordings of speeches, statements, and writings from this period.

80 National Council of Negro Women Records, MAMC_001 Series 15 Sub-series 6, Folder 1, Fannie Lou Hamer, n.d. 1973. Mary McCleod Bethune Archives, Washington, DC (NCNW).

81 This laughter was recorded on a NCNW archive tape along with the young man's statement "you've been fumbling around pretty good for quite sometime," made in response to Hamer's modest declaration that she was fumbling around until men could come and take the lead (NCNW).

82 For more on sexism within the black Baptist church and its effect on rhetorical leadership, see "Introduction," *Women and the Civil Rights Movement, 1954–1965*, ed. Davis W. Houck and David E. Dixon (Jackson: University Press of Mississippi, 2009.

83 "Fannie Lou Hamer Speaks Out," 75.

84 Hamer, "Nobody's Free Until Everybody's Free," 138.

85 Daniel Patrick Moynihan, *The Negro Family: The Case for National Action* (Washington, DC: US Department of Labor, 1965).

86 "Fannie Lou Hamer Speaks Out," 75.

87 Interview with Fannie Lou Hamer by Project South, 1965, MFDP Chapter 55, Box 6, Folder 160, Department of Special Collections, Stanford University Libraries, Stanford, California.

88 Hamer, "Is It Too Late?," 133.

89 Roth, "The Making of the Vanguard Center," 77.

90 Ben Own quoted in Franklyn Peterson, "Sunflowers Don't Grow in Sunflower County," *Sepia* 19 (1970): 17.

91 Danielle L. McGuire, *At the Dark End of the Street: Black Women, Rape, and Resistance—a New History of the Civil Rights Movement from Rosa Parks to the Rise of Black Power* (New York: Vintage, 2010), 192.

92 Hamer, "Is It Too Late?" 133.

93 Hamer, "Until I Am Free, You Are Not Free Either," 122.

94 Interview with King by author.

95 "Fannie Lou Hamer Speaks Out," 75.

96 See, for example, Toni Morrison's discussion of the difficulty black women have respecting white women as a result of their historical relationship with one another in "What the Black Woman Thinks About Women's Lib," *New York Times*, August 22, 1971, SM14.

97 "Fannie Lou Hamer Speaks Out," 76.

98 For more on "othermothering," see Roth, "The Making of the Vanguard Center," 78.

99 During her speech to students at Tougaloo College, Hamer paraphrased earlier comments she made to a group of white women in New York City. See Hamer, "Speech to Tougaloo Students" (MDAH).

100 Hamer, "It's in Your Hands," 610.

101 Hamer, "It's in Your Hands," 610.

102 Hamer, "It's in Your Hands," 613.

103 Edwin King, Lawrence Guyot, and L. C. Dorsey all acknowledge the intra-racial class tension that arose as Hamer became better known and widely celebrated. For instance, King recalled that when Hamer received her honorary doctorate from Tougaloo College, alumni objected to the accolade because she was unlettered. Interviews with King, Guyot, and Dorsey by author.

104 Ella Baker quoted in Barbara Ransby, *Ella Baker and the Black Freedom Movement: A Radical Democratic Vision* (Chapel Hill: University of North Carolina Press, 2003), 363; and Hamer, "It's in Your Hands," 613, respectively.

105 For more on the "lift as we climb" ideology, see Deborah Gray White, *Too Heavy a Load: Black Women in Defense of Themselves, 1894–1994* (New York: W. W. Norton & Company, 1999).

106 Hamer, "Nobody's Free Until Everybody's Free," 136.

107 Hamer, "Nobody's Free Until Everybody's Free," 135–139.

108 Interview with Guyot by author.

109 Mills, *This Little Light of Mine*, 211.

110 For an in-depth analysis of Forman's appeal, see Maegan Parker, "Ironic Openings: The Interpretive Challenge of the 'Black Manifesto,'" *Quarterly Journal of Speech* 94, no. 3 (August 2008): 320–342.

111 See, for example, Hamer, "If the Name of the Game Is Survive, Survive," 143, and Dan L. Thrapp, "Forman Supplanted as Manifesto Spokesman," *Los Angeles Times*, August 17, 1969, 8—Hamer is listed as an NBEDC board member within this piece.

112 Harding et al., "We Changed the World," 246.

113 Harding et al. explain the phenomenon of "rights consciousness" and "rising expectations" in "We Changed the World," 246.

114 Office of Economic Opportunity,"Federal Government Launches Emergency Food and Medical Program," March 23, 1968, Press Release in Fannie Lou Hamer Papers, Reel 15,"Collected Newsletters and Articles" (WHS).

115 Interview with Hamer by Wright.

116 Hamer, "Until I Am Free, You're Not Free Either"; Fannie Lou Hamer, "Speech in Madison-area Church," Madison, Wisconsin, 1971. Transcribed by Maegan Parker Brooks from audio recording, courtesy of Jean Sweet.

117 Fannie Lou Hamer, draft of "Sick and Tired of Being Sick and Tired," in n.d. (1968) Box 5, FLH Folder, *Katallagete!*/James Y. Holloway Collection, 1945–1992, in Civil Rights and Race Relations Collection at the University of Mississippi Archives and Special Collections, Oxford, Mississippi.

118 Interview with King by author.

119 Dittmer, *Local People*, 388.

120 Megan Landauer and Jonathan Wolman, "Fannie Lou Hamer '... Forcing a New Political Reality,'" *Daily Cardinal*, October 8, 1971.

121 Asch, *The Senator and the Sharecropper*, 227.

122 Interview with Ambassador Andrew Young by Maegan Parker Brooks, June 25, 2007, Atlanta, Georgia.

123 In the draft of this article, there is a typographical error, which I have corrected in the text of the [reading]. The draft actually reads: "If what the politicians have done to the proverty program ..." See Hamer, draft of "Sick and Tired of Being Sick and Tired," in *Katallagete!*/James Y. Holloway Collection.

124 Hamer, draft of "Sick and Tired of Being Sick and Tired," in *Katallagete!*/James Y. Holloway Collection.

125 Interview with Brooks by author.

126 Landauer and Wolman, "Fannie Lou Hamer '... Forcing a New Political Reality,'" *Daily Cardinal*, 1971.

127 "North Bolivar County Cooperative Membership Booklet," in Box 11, Fannie Lou Hamer Papers at the Amistad Research Center, Tulane University, New Orleans, Louisiana (FLH Papers).

128 Interview with Dorsey by author.

129 Landauer and Wolman, "Fannie Lou Hamer '... Forcing a New Political Reality,'" *Daily Cardinal*, 1971.

130 Martha Fager, a founding member of the organization, remembers Alicia Cathwell suggesting the name. Interview with Martha Fager by Maegan Parker Brooks, July 6, 2007 (phone).

131 Interview with Jeff and Sarah Goldstein by Maegan Parker Brooks, July 2, 2007, Madison, Wisconsin.

132 For more information about the NCNW's Wednesdays in Mississippi program, see http://wimsfilmproj-ect.com/.

133   National Council of Negro Women Records, MAMC_001 Series 15, Sub-series 6, Folder 1, Fannie Lou Hamer, n.d. 1973 (NCNW).

134   Landauer and Wolman, "Fannie Lou Hamer '... Forcing a New Political Reality,'" *Daily Cardinal*, 1971.

135   Interview with Goldsteins by author.

136   Jeff Goldstein's son briefly commented on his experience in Mississippi traveling with his parents as a child, and he remembers the distended bellies of the children and the "tar paper shacks" they lived in. Interview with Goldsteins by author.

137   Correspondence regarding requests for Hamer to speak indicate the range of her honoraria, which typically included the cost of travel and an additional $200–$300. See Fannie Lou Hamer Papers: Speaking Engagements File (1968–1977) (WHS).

138   Letters from Marion Loundsbury, October 1, 1969, and David Elliot January 14, 1968, respectively, Boxes 24 and 25 (FLH).

139   Boxes 24 and 25 (FLH).

140   Interview with Goldsteins by author.

141   Landauer and Wolman, "Fannie Lou Hamer '... Forcing a New Political Reality,'" *Daily Cardinal*, 1971.

142   Marian McBride, "Fannie Lou Hamer: Nobody Knows the Trouble She's Seen," *Washington Post*, July 14, 1968, H12.

143   Phone interview with Fager by author; interview with Goldsteins by author.

144   Interview with Goldsteins by author.

145   Sarah Goldstein offered this particular statement.

146   Hamer, "Madison-area Church," 1971.

147   Hamer, "Until I Am Free, You Are Not Free Either," 129.

148   Hamer, "Madison-area Church," 1971.

149   Interview with Goldsteins by author.

150   Interview with Fager by author; Interview with Greg Bell by Maegan Parker Brooks, May 7, 2007 (phone).

151   Hamer, "Madison-area Church," 1971; Hamer, "Until I Am Free, You Are Not Free Either," 130.

152   This particular statement was captured in the recording of her question-and-answer period following the more formal address she delivered: Hamer, "Madison-area Church," 1971.

153   Hamer, "Madison-area Church," 1971.

154   Hamer, "Until I Am Free, You Are Not Free Either," 130.

155 Interview with Jean and Charlie Sweet by Maegan Parker Brooks, April 24, 2007, Madison, Wisconsin.

156 Hamer, "Until I Am Free, You Are Not Free Either," 127.

157 I corrected a spelling error made in the original letter—changing "rath" to "wrath" in my representation of Dorrough's remarks. Letter from Ruleville mayor C. M. Dorrough Sr. to Mrs. Fannie Lou Hamer, March 26, 1970, in Correspondence-Tougaloo, 1976–1977, Box 1, Folder 1, FLH Files, Coleman Library, Tougaloo College, Jackson, Mississippi.

158 Fannie Lou Hamer, "Seconding Speech for the Nomination of Frances Farenthold," Delivered at the 1972 Democratic National Convention, Miami Beach, Florida, July 13, 1972, in *The Speeches of Fannie Lou Hamer*, 146.

CONCLUSION

Comprehension Questions

1 Since the 1960s, theories of rhetoric have engaged in two primary efforts. Identify and describe these efforts.

2 According to Molefi Asante, what are some of the unique constraints or issues that African American protest speakers must consider when addressing white audiences?

3 According to the reading by Maegan Parker Brooks, what similarities can be identified between the rhetorical efforts of Fannie Lou Hamer and those of women who spoke centuries before her (such as women of the medieval era or the Enlightenment)?

Critical Thinking Questions

1 The readings in "Unit 5" encourage us to consider the public-speaking constraints faced by individuals from marginalized groups who speak out. Drawing upon current movements for social change, explain barriers to public speaking these groups face. For instance, consider issues pertaining to cultural values/beliefs, access to media, ethos and perceptions of the speaker.

2 What were some of the unique issues Fannie Lou Hamer faced as an African American and a woman? How does the intersection of race and sex influence the efforts and strategies of contemporary advocates for social change?

Unit Summary

"Unit 5" explored how scholars of the late twentieth to early twenty-first century have challenged traditional rhetorical concepts such as message, audience, speaker, and public. Additionally, these scholars have continued the ongoing debate dating back to Plato and the Sophists regarding the relationship between rhetoric, knowledge, and reality. Contemporary rhetorical theorists have also endeavored to bring to life and incorporate the voices of persons ignored or silenced by the traditional canon of "great men and great speeches." Toward this end, scholars have examined the efforts of African American women and Latinas, LGBTQ advocates, working-class people, and colonized "others" who often take different approaches to public speaking.

CONCLUSION

Theories of Rhetoric: An Anthology has provided us with new ways to consider an ancient discipline. Traditional approaches to rhetorical theory often lack a recognition or deeper discussion of the assumptions underlying the theories at hand. This anthology introduced a new way to examine rhetoric—a critical/cultural approach—that invites us to explore the ways theories are shaped by the prevailing political and historical context of the time period. A critical/cultural approach calls attention to the often-hidden assumptions underlying theoretical development. Notably, this collection has called to light the ways traditional understandings of rhetoric have often precluded the experiences and voices of marginalized persons.

"Unit 2" explored the classical era and pointed out that, contrary to common understandings of the Greco-Roman origins of the discipline, the study of rhetoric dates back to the writings of Ptah-Hotep, around 3100 BCE. "Unit 2" also introduced us to the lives of women and slaves in ancient Greece and Rome with readings that shed light on how we may better understand their rhetorical efforts. "Unit 3" surveyed the medieval era, including the wide-reaching influence of Christianity, and explored how women stepped outside of their traditionally prescribed roles to express themselves through visionary writing and letters. In "Unit 4," we advanced three hundred years to explore the Enlightenment, a time marked by advances in science, philosophy, and political thought. This unit highlighted the ideals of Enlightenment thinkers and exposed the racism and sexism in much of their writings. We also learned about the efforts of women and slaves who spoke publically, often risking their lives, to challenge the power disparities of their day. And finally, "Unit 5" brought us to the twenty-first century with an overview of the primary efforts of more recent scholars who have adopted theoretical approaches that recognize the connections between rhetoric and power.